PUBLISHING
IN
CHINA
An Essential Guide

PUBLISHING
IN
CHINA
An Essential Guide

Xin Guangwei

Translated by:

Zhao Wei
Li Hong
Peter F. Bloxham

THOMSON

Australia • Canada • Mexico • Singapore • Spain • United Kingdom • United States

Publishing in China: An Essential Guide
by Xin Guangwei
(Translated by Zhao Wei, Li Hong and Peter F. Bloxham)

For more information, please contact:
Thomson Learning
(a division of Thomson Asia Pte Ltd)
5 Shenton Way
#01-01 UIC Building
Singapore 068808

Or visit our Internet site at *http://www.thomsonlearningasia.com*

Thomson Learning offices in Asia: Bangkok, Beijing, Hong Kong, Kuala Lumpur, Manila, Mumbai, Seoul, Singapore, Taipei, Tokyo.

Printed in Singapore
2 3 4 5 6 7 8 9 10 SLP 08 07 06 05 04

ISBN 981-254-360-0

All maps are provided by China Geological Publishing House

Contents

Appendices

Preface

The parable, The Blind Men and the Elephant, tells the story of five blind men trying to get a sense of what an elephant was like by touching it. The first man touched the elephant's leg, and thought that the elephant must be a pole. The next man touched the elephant's side, and assumed that he was touching a wall. Another touched the animal's tail, and said he had hold of a rope. The next one touched its ear, and thought that the elephant must be a dustpan. Finally, the last man touched its tusk, and concluded that the elephant was in fact a bamboo shoot.

People with different cultures and languages are sometimes like these blind men as they struggle to understand elements of foreign cultures. In fact, we are sometimes no better than these blind men when we try to understand our own people, our own nation, and the events surrounding us.

There are generally two ways to avoid such misapprehension. One is to take the time to conduct a broad and extensive investigation until a comprehensive understanding of the subject is reached. The other is to listen to experts and professionals, those who have the greatest available knowledge.

As both Wei Zheng (Tang Dynasty minister), and Halliburton observed: Hear one side and you will be in the dark; hear both and all will be clear.

Publishing in China is the first book to examine the Chinese publishing industry in detail. It was originally intended for publication in Chinese, and its target audience would have been restricted to Mandarin speaking publishers. Halfway through writing the book, I was approached by Mr. Paul K. H. Tan, Director, Publishing and North Asia, of Thomson Learning (a division of Thomson Asia Pte. Ltd.), Ms. Christy Yuan, and Ms. Caroline Ma of its Beijing Representative Office. They expressed their interest in publishing an English version of the book, believing that many publishers from North America and Europe would also be very interested in the Chinese publishing market. Inspired by their proposal and their enthusiasm, I incorporated this new direction and audience in my writing.

Publishing in China hopes to provide as complete a picture of the Chinese publishing industry as possible, and to appeal to readers from the East and from the West. China needs to understand the world. And the world needs to understand China.

Xin Guangwei

Acknowledgements

This book was completed with the help and assistance of many of my friends. My heartfelt thanks to each of them.

Firstly, I want to thank the book's three translators: Ms. Zhao Wei, a former senior staff member of Random House Inc. in New York; Dr. Li Hong, who has just returned to China after completing her History program in the U.S.; and Professor Peter F. Bloxham, the external liaison officer of Harper Adams University College in the U.K. Without their help, this book would not have been published in English in such a short period of time. My old friend, Mr. Tang Hongzhao, translated the Preface and two other important appendices. Mr. Gabriel L. Levine, formerly with Random House in New York, contributed to the translations of many chapters of this book. My thanks to both of them.

Secondly, I want to thank two of my research assistants in publishing, Ms. Zhao Chunxia and Ms. Han Wenjing. They produced and translated many of the figures and illustrations, and provided data support. Also, I want to thank Ms. Hsu Kai-chen, a senior correspondent and publishing researcher from Min Sheng Daily in Taipei; Mr. Zeng Xietai, Vice President of Sino United Publishing (H.K.) Ltd.; Ms. Anita W. L. Wan, Assistant to the Managing Director of The Commercial Press (H.K.) Ltd.; and two publishers from Macau, Mr. Chan Su Weng and Ms. Christine Lee Po Wa. They all provided assistance and help for chapters related to publishing in Taiwan, Hong Kong, and Macau.

I also want to thank Mr. Liu Bolin, Mr. Zhu Chaoxu, Mr. Shen Changwen, Ms. Ma Zheng, Ms. Sun Wei, Mr. Wei Hongxue, Ms. Zhang Xianshu, Ms. Zhang Zeqing in Beijing, and Ms. Sun Hsiang-Yun, Ms. Chiang Huei-Hsien, and Ms. Lee Yuh-hwa in Taipei. They provided materials and pictures, answered my queries, and provided assistance in innumerable ways during the book's development.

I also want to express my appreciation to Thomson Learning's Mr. Tan Tat Chu and Mr. Paul K. H. Tan in Singapore, Ms. Christy Yuan and Ms. Caroline Ma in Beijing, and Ms. Pauline Lim and Ms. Joan Ho in Singapore. They not only helped speed up the production of the book but also provided plenty of editorial assistance.

Xin Guangwei

Overview

When Patrick J. McGovern, Founder and Chairman of the International Data Group (IDG) visited Beijing for the first time in 1978, he was greatly impressed by the sight of people crowding into bookstores. In 2002, when German book dealer Reinhard Neumann visited bookstores in Beijing, he also saw crowds of people buying books.

Twenty-five years ago, the annual book output in the Chinese mainland was less than 15,000 titles and the per-capita GDP was only about US$130. By 2002, the annual book output had increased to 170,000 titles, and the GDP per capita reached about US$963, eleven and seven times higher respectively. Meanwhile, the bookstores have remained full of people buying books.

The crowds of people in bookstores reveal an undeniable truth: the publishing industry in the Chinese mainland is very large, and will continue to expand moving forward.

The market potential is even more encouraging. In 2003, the GDP per-capita in the Chinese mainland reached US$1,090 compared to US$35,401 (2001) in the United States of America. In 2002, book sales were about US$5.3 billion, i.e. more than US$4 per person, compared to the U.S., where book sales were US$26.8 billion, i.e. more than US$90 per person. The U.S. figures are about 5 and 20 times higher respectively, and the German statistics are 1.7 and 27 times higher respectively.

The significantly large difference indicates that the country has lagged behind but it also shows that the publishing market will have vast potential with continued rapid economic development. One can make an estimate: if expenditure on books increases by US$0.10 per person, the Chinese mainland book market would grow by US$130 million. In fact, in recent years, the average increase in book sales has grown to US$300 million per year.

More importantly, this market is now opening up to the rest of the world. Nowadays, you can see hundreds of thousands of Chinese publishers at the Frankfurt Book Fair. So far, more than 70 foreign publishing companies have established subsidiaries or offices in the Chinese mainland. IDG, which arrived 25 years ago, now owns about 80 various companies around the country, and its 36 publications have reached revenues of US$80 million and operating profits of US$28 million a year, growing at 28% per year. Mr. McGovern said during a speech at the Taipei International Magazine Conference, "We [IDG] are No. 1 in the market share of the technical publications in China." (November 16, 2004.)

The total population in the Chinese mainland, Taiwan, Hong Kong, and Macau is about 1.315 billion, living in a total area of 9.6 million square kilometers. In terms of social forms, China is one country with four regions and two systems. The four regions refer to the Chinese mainland, Hong Kong, Macau, and Taiwan, and the two systems refer to the socialist system in the Chinese mainland and capitalist system in the other three areas. There are four different currencies, Ren Min Bi, Hong Kong Dollar, Macau Pataca, and Taiwan Dollar.

The Chinese mainland, Taiwan, and Hong Kong are the three major bases of Chinese language publishing in the world. Combined, the industry as a whole has more than 9,000 book publishing houses, more than 17,560 magazine titles and more than 2,820 newspapers titles, with an annual book output of over 216,000 titles (including 133,000 new titles per year) and total annual sales of about US$7.5 billion. In recent years, these three markets have become increasingly integrated, moving toward becoming one large open market. The largest of the three—the Chinese mainland—has attracted the most attention due to its large size and rapid growth.

Figure 1.1
World Market Share of Chinese Books

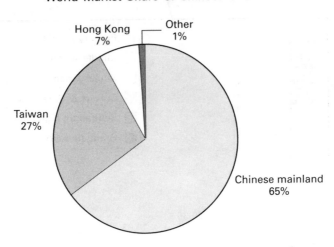

A. Overview of the Publishing Industry in the Chinese Mainland

1. The Basics of the Chinese Mainland

It is necessary to have some knowledge of the country's structure in order to fully understand its publishing industry.

In 2002, the population in the Chinese mainland was 1.284 billion, of which 484 million lived in cities and towns and about 800 million in rural areas. More than 900 million were aged between 15 and 64 years old.

There are about 1.17 million educational institutions with over 318 million students, of which about 0.5 million are graduate students, 14.63 million undergraduate students, 95.96 million middle school students, 122 million primary school students, 20.36 million kindergarten (including pre-school) students, and 374,500 in-school disabled children. In addition, there were about 12.68 million self-taught students who registered for the national higher education examination. (See Figure 1.2.)

Figure 1.2
Student Numbers at Different Levels in the Chinese Mainland

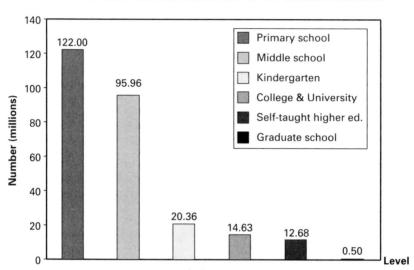

Source: *China Education and Research Network*

Administrative divisions are based on a loose three-tier system, dividing the country into provinces, counties and townships; with provinces being the equivalent of states in the United States. In fact, between most province and county tiers, there are municipal cities. Generally, people are inclined to consider provinces, municipalities, and counties as the three administrative tiers with townships having little bearing.

The provincial tier includes provinces, autonomous regions, and municipalities directly under the central government, such as Guangdong Province, Liaoning Province, the Tibet Autonomous Region, Guangxi Zhuangzu Autonomous Region, Beijing municipality, and Chongqing municipality. In total, there are 34 administrative divisions at the provincial level including 23 provinces, five autonomous regions, four municipalities directly under the central government, and two Special Administrative Regions. (Refer to Figure 1.3 for Map of China.)

There are 660 cities in China, of which 25 have a population of more than 2 million (including 8 with more than 4 million), 141 between 1 and 2 million, 279 between 0.5 and 1 million, and 217 less than 500,000 (including 37 with less than 200,000 people).

Figure 1.3
Map of China

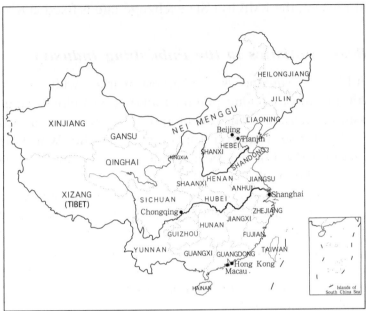

In 2002, the average net income in the rural areas was about US$298 per capita, and in the cities and towns the figure was approximately US$928, three times higher. In 2003, the national GDP reached about US$1.4 trillion, and the income per capita reached about US$1,090—for the first time surpassing the US$1,000 mark. However in Shanghai, the average income was even higher at approximately US$1,791 per capita.

There are 2,698 public libraries in the Chinese mainland. The National Library of China in Beijing is the largest in Asia, and the Shanghai Library is the largest among the provincial libraries.

In 2002, the basic import duty was about 12%, but in 2005 it is expected to decrease to a level below the average level of other developing countries, and the average duty for imported industrial products is expected to drop to about 10%. By 2002, more than 400 of the 500 top companies in the world had invested in the country and it is ranked sixth in the world in terms of international trade volume. Its top trade partners are Japan, America, the European Union, the Association of

Southeast Asian Nations (ASEAN), South Korea, Australia, Russia, and Canada.

At present, the RMB to USD exchange rate is fixed at 8.3 to 1.

2. *Basic Statistics in the Publishing Industry*

The Chinese mainland is the largest market with the fastest growth and most exciting potential among all Chinese language publishing markets. The acceleration of reforms in China, especially those required for entry into the World Trade Organization (WTO), has been gradually increasing the overall capacity of the publishing industry.

According to statistics from the General Administration of Press and Publication (GAPP), in 2002 the Chinese mainland published 171,000 titles, of which 100,700 were new. The total output volume reached 6.87 billion copies with a total marked price of RMB53.51 billion (approximately US$6.45 billion), and total sales came to RMB43.5 billion (about US$5.24 billion) with 7.027 billion copies sold.

In 2002, the Chinese mainland printed 2.951 billion magazines, 36.783 billion newspapers, and produced 226 million audio items with 12,300 titles, and 218 million video products with some 13,600 titles. The total title output of electronic publications amounted to 4,700, with a total production of 96.81 million items. There were in total 568 book publishing companies, 9,029 magazine titles, and 2,137 newspaper titles, in addition to 292 audio-video publishing companies, and 102 electronic publishers. The number of authorized book and magazine printing companies reached 1,155 and 78 companies produced and duplicated CD-ROMs.

At present, there are about 80 various publishing groups, of which nearly 20 are book publishing groups, more than 40 newspaper groups, and more than 10 magazine groups.

Of the three sectors of the industry, content editing (publishing), printing, and distribution, the first sector is the most profitable, accounting for 66% of the total profit, followed by distribution, accounting for 26%, and printing, accounting for 8%.

In 2002, the average expenditure on publications per capita was RMB33 (about US$3.98), or about 5.5 books, 2.3 magazines, and 28.63 newspapers per year. A survey of citizens' reading habits provided by the China Publishing Science Institute showed that more than 60% of people read books at least once a month, while nearly 40% do not read at all.

There is a substantial imbalance in publishing capacity among the different regions in the Chinese mainland due to differences in economic development and population density. Generally speaking, the east coast is well developed, while the central part of China is less well developed and the Western regions lag far behind. The most developed places are Beijing, Shanghai, Jiangsu, Guangdong, Zhejiang, Shandong, Liaoning, Hunan, Hubei, and Sichuan. In short, Beijing, the Pearl River Delta, and the Yangtze River Delta are the leading regions of the publishing industry.

3. The Structure and Organization of the Publishing Industry

Compared with many other industries, the publishing industry is still firmly in state control. However the 16th National Congress of the Communist Party of China in 2002 accelerated reforms.

With the *Regulations on Management of Publications* promulgated by the State Council, government permission must first be obtained before starting a publishing business. The government formulates an overall plan for the total number, structure and deployment of all publishing establishments and it imposes general control and adjustment.

The industry is divided into three major sectors: content editing (publishing), printing, and distribution. Of the three, the government exerts the strictest control over the first, especially over the formation of publishing units, leaving the other two sectors relatively unrestricted. Presently, all publishing houses are state-owned, and there has been no major difference in the total number of publishers. For instance, in 1992 there were 519 book publishing houses, and in 2002 the number was 568, showing only marginal growth.

A current principle guiding the formation of publishing establishments is based on trade and industrial systems (*tiao*, vertical line) and administrative regions (*kuai*, block), and thus it is called the "*tiao-kuai*" arrangement principle. The arrangement based on *tiao* means that the central government considers each ministry, the ruling party and its major subdivisions, each of the other political parties, every major industrial system, and a large mass organization as a *tiao* (they all have vertical organizational layers and thus from the top to the bottom there is a vertical connection and delegation of responsibility and accountability from the top down to the bottom) and approves the establishment of one or more books, newspaper, magazine, audio-video, and electronic publishing units within each *tiao*. For instance, the Ministry of Commerce owns one publishing house, China Commerce Publishing House, one magazine (*China Commerce*), and one newspaper (*China Business Herald*). It is similar for other ministries.

By similar arrangements, subdivisions of the Communist Party of China such as the Department of Publicity of the Central Committee of CPC and the United Front Work Department, democratic parties such as China Zhi Gong Party (Public Interest Party) and China Democratic League, and mass organizations such as the All-China Women's Federation, can all have one publishing house, one newspaper, and one magazine. For instance, the China Democratic League has Qiushi Publishing House and publishes the *Qunyan* magazine, and the All-China Women's Federation owns the China Women's Publishing House, the *China Women's News* newspaper, and the *Women of China* magazine.

In addition, major industrial systems and government organizations directly under the State Council (with an administrative status of sub-ministerial level) also have set up publishing units using the same structure. For instance, the electric power industry has China Electric Power Publishing House, the *China Electric Power* magazine, and the *China Electric Power* newspaper. The publishing house, magazine and newspaper belonging to the Chinese Academy of Sciences are the Science Press, *China Science*, and *Science Times.*

Most of the publishing units set up by the ministries and major industrial systems are located in Beijing and are national publishers, also known as central level publishing units. Their names generally are composed of two parts, the name of the ministry or industry plus publishing house or press, such as China Commerce and Trade Press, China Zhi Gong Publishing House (belonging to China Zhi Gong Party), China WaterPower Press (belonging to the Ministry of Water Resources), and China Seismology Publishing House (belonging to the National Seismological Bureau), and China Three Gorges Publishing House (belonging to the China Three Gorges Project Development Corporation). From their names, people can tell to which ministry or industrial system they belong and what their respective publications specialize in.

The *Kuai* (block) arrangement is mainly based on provincial-level divisions including provinces, autonomous regions and municipalities under direct control of the central government. The government grants approval for each division to set up a similar number of books, newspapers, magazines, audio-video, and electronic publishing houses. For instance, Jiangsu Province has formed one publishing house in each of the following subjects: politics, law, education, literature, science and technology, ancient classics, and fine arts. It also has one provincial newspaper (*Xinhua Daily News*), several magazines, and some audio-video and electronic publishing houses.

The publishing houses set up at the provincial level are regional publishers, generally known as provincial-level publishers corresponding to the central-level publishers, and their names are also similarly composed, i.e. name of the provincial division plus coverage of publishing subject(s) plus publishing house or press. For instance, in Jiangsu Province, there are the Jiangsu People's Publishing House, Jiangsu Education Publishing House, Jiangsu Literature and Art Publishing House, Jiangsu Science and Technology Publishing House, Jiangsu Children's

Publishing House, Jiangsu Ancient Classics Publishing House, and Jiangsu Fine Arts Publishing House. When the word "People's" is placed in the name of a publishing house, it means that the focus is on politics and law. The other provinces have similarly organized publishing industries.

Publishing companies at the provincial level, including the book, magazine, audio-video and electronic units, are generally located in the capital city of the province. As for the publishers mentioned above, most are located in Nanjing, the capital city of Jiangsu Province. With the exception of newspapers, generally no publishing units are allowed in an administrative area below the provincial level. Every city or prefecture within the province has its own newspaper. For instance, in Jiangsu Province, the cities of Nanjing, Suzhou, and Yangzhou, have the *Nanjing Daily*, *Suzhou Daily*, and *Yangzhou Daily*. The other provinces have similar arrangements. In addition, a few counties issue their own newspapers.

Other than the provincial capitals, some large cities such as Dalian (Liaoning Province), Shenzhen (Guangdong Province), and Xiamen (Fujian Province), also have one book publishing unit and one audio-video publishing unit each. In Dalian, there is the Dalian Publishing House and the Dalian Audio-Video Publishing House. In addition, some special administrative regions also have set up their own book and audio-video publishing units, such as the Zhuhai Publishing House and Shantou Ocean Audio-Video Publishing House in the cities of Zhuhai and Shantou.

There are more than 55 ethnic minority groups in China and in order to promote the development of the press and publishing in these minority regions, the central government approves the formation of publishing units in the autonomous prefectures in addition to their establishment at the provincial level. For instance, in Yanbian Korean Autonomous Prefecture of Jilin Province there are the Yanbian People's Publishing House and Yanbian Education Publishing House. In Yili of Xinjiang Uyghur Autonomous Region, there is the Yili People's Publishing

House. An important mission of these publishers is to publish books in the minorities' native languages.

Currently, the government continues to restrict the topics covered and limit the publication types among publishers. When the appropriate government body in charge of publishing approves the formation of a publishing unit, it is made clear what topics and publication types the publisher can engage in. The publisher must operate within the approved limits. For instance, a book publisher is not allowed to issue magazines or produce audio-video publications, and vice versa. If a book publisher wants to issue magazines, audio-video, or electronic publications it must apply for another permit. In addition, according to the *Regulations on Management of Publications*, the publisher is required to have a government organization act as a sponsor and supervisor for the would-be publisher when permission is applied for.

Nevertheless, changes are taking place. The reforms in publishing, which started in the mid-1990s, have moved into a significant stage. For example, the government no longer imposes strict restrictions over the publishers on their publication coverage, and the publishers are claiming more autonomy.

Unlike the publishing sector, printing and distribution face few governmental restrictions. Both sectors allow for the participation of private business and have been open to foreign investment (see Chapter 10), and now there are more private companies than state-owned enterprises engaged in printing and distribution. Especially in printing, there are so few restrictions that both domestic and foreign companies have enough room to operate as they wish, with a management environment not much different from that of many other industries. For distribution, restrictions are focused on chain bookstores and wholesale rights but, as a whole, market forces have taken over. Private companies account for half of the entire distribution capacity in the Chinese mainland.

4. Laws, Administrative Management, and Awards

The supreme legislative body in the Chinese mainland (the National People's Congress) has not established laws specifically governing publishing. Currently, the most important publishing law is the *Regulations on Management of Publications*, promulgated by the Chinese central government (the State Council). In addition, the State Council and GAPP under the State Council have issued some other related regulations and laws which constitute the basic framework of publishing laws.

In addition to the *Regulations on Management of Publications*, other important laws and regulations governing publishing in the Chinese mainland include the *Regulations on Management of Audio-Video Publications* and the *Regulations on Management of the Printing Industry* both promulgated by the State Council, and the *Provisional Rules on Management of Internet Publications*, the *Regulations on Management of the Publication Market,* and the *Preparatory Measures on Choosing Important Topics of Books, Periodicals, Audio-Video Products, and Electronic Publications*, all promulgated by GAPP. For foreign investment, GAPP and the Ministry of Commerce co-issued *Administrative Measures on Foreign Investment for Distributing Books, Newspapers and Periodicals.*

On copyright protection, so closely related to publishing, the National People's Congress issued *The Copyright Law of the People's Republic of China*, and the State Council promulgated *The Rules on Implementation of Copyright Law* and *The Rules on Protection of Computer Software.*

The above laws and regulations constitute the major legal documents governing the publishing industry in the Chinese mainland.

The *Regulations on Management of Publications* stipulates that government publication administrative bodies have responsibility to govern all publishing activities in the Chinese mainland (if the publisher is in dispute with the government, the court steps in to solve the issue). The government oversight is divided into three levels: the state council, the provincial bureaus, and city or prefecture offices. The GAPP is the highest authority governing publishing, and there are press and publication bureaus at the provincial level as well as some at the under-provincial city or prefecture level.

The major functions of GAPP include: designing the development plan for the national press and publishing industry; imposing macroscopic adjustment to the industry and policies, and providing advice on their implementation, formulating regulations on publications and copyright management, and supervising the implementation of these regulations; accepting applications for the formation of new publishing, distribution, joint-venture establishments; managing and coordinating import and export of various publications; and leading the work on collecting and publishing ancient books. By a decision from the State Council, the National Copyright Administration of China (NCAC) is responsible for copyright issues.

The NCAC and GAPP are actually one government apparatus with two different names, and the director of GAPP also serves as the director of the NCAC. The Copyright Administration Department of GAPP is especially designated to take charge of copyright-related work.

There are many departments within GAPP, such as the Books and Publications Administration Department; the Newspaper and Periodicals Publication Administration Department; the Audio-visual, Electronic and Network Publications Administration Department; the Publication Issuance Administration Department; and the Printing and Reproduction Administration Department. (See Figure 1.4.)

Regional press and publication bureaus adopt a similar organizational structure as GAPP, and the regional administrative departments responsible for copyright enforcement also share a similar arrangement as the NCAC.

However, exceptions exist in the audio-video publishing industry. According to a division of work mandated by the State Council, two bodies co-govern the publishing, copying, and distribution of audio-video products. The Press and Publication

Figure 1.4
Organizational Structure of the GAPP

Source: *GAPP*

Administration governs the publication and reproduction, and the Cultural Administration is responsible for the management of the audio-video market and imports of licensed audio-video products.

Publications can be divided into two types: formal publications and internal publications. All formal publications must be issued by authorized publishers, and internal publications must abide by *The Rules on Management of Internal Material Publications*.

Professionals in the publishing industry should meet certain qualifications. Under *The Provisional Rules on Management of the Qualifications for Publication Professionals*, all personnel engaging in editing, publishing, proofreading of books, magazines, audio-video and electronic publications, must participate in examinations and obtain the Certificate of Professional Publishers of the People's Republic of China.

In order to encourage the publication of scientific and technological books and promote innovation, some government organizations, science research institutes, and industrial associations have established publication foundations. Prominent examples include the Publication Foundation for National Academic Works, Publication Foundation for Excellent National Minorities Books, Publication Foundation for Works on Electronic Information and Technology, Publication Foundation for Works on Oceanic Technology, Publication Foundation for Works on Surveying and Mapping Technology, and the Beijing Publication Foundation for Theoretical Works of the Social Sciences.

There are many publication awards established mainly by the government and industrial associations. The most prestigious awards are granted by GAPP, including the National Book Award, the National Periodical Award, the National Audio-Video Publication Award, and the National Electronic Publication Award. Leading awards sponsored by professional associations are the China Book Awards, the China Taofen Publication Awards, and the China Taofen News Awards. In addition, the highest propaganda organ—the Department of Publicity of the Central Committee of CPC offers the "Five-One Project Awards" which includes a book award.

5. Major Features of the Publishing Industry

At the start of the new century, the publishing industry of the Chinese mainland presents the world with the following:

i. The effort to build a legal system in the publishing industry has achieved preliminary results and has created an environment advantageous to law-abiding business operations. The previous situation in which no formal rules regulated the publishing industry started to change in the 1990s, and the emergence of regulations such as *The Copyright Law* and the *Regulations on Management of Publications* marked an important step in the construction of the legal infrastructure in the publishing industry. The enactment of the leading *"One Law and Four Regulations"* has built a basic legal framework for the publishing industry. Moreover, the implementation of *The Administrative Re-discussion Law* and *The Administrative Permission Law*, which regulate government functions in law enforcement, has further paved the way for increased legalization of the publishing industry.

ii. Profound reform has begun. Despite the fact that among various industries publishing lags behind in reform and is less market-oriented than many, changes have taken place and deep-rooted reforms are afoot. The 16th National Congress of the Communist Party of China made it clear that key attributes of culture, including publishing, contain industrial business in need of an organizational framework. Now, the publishing industry has been geared towards market competition, and publishing houses are moving towards becoming company-like in organizational structure, like large conglomerates in operational scope, and market-oriented in management practices. All publishing houses need to redefine their identities (mostly choosing between state-owned organization and quasi-private industrial/business enterprises), and many have chosen to be identified as industrial enterprises. Those keeping state-owned organization status are also forced to operate within the market rules and compete with others. Many publishing houses are emerging and developing rapidly. All these changes lead to not only the repartition of publishing resources and market share but also a fundamental transformation in the publishing industry.

iii. Building distribution channels and exploring the market potential of small and medium cities remain an imperative task. There are insufficient highly effective distribution channels in such a vast land, and this has greatly impeded the rapid development of the publishing industry. One obvious example is that many books with sales potential of millions are well short of such an achievement because of a lack of distribution channels. There are over a dozen huge bookstores with an area of over 100,000 square meters, but they are concentrated in a few big cities. Such a concentration, from a different perspective, reveals problems in the structure of bookstores. Chain bookstores have just opened in the Chinese mainland and there is in urgent need of big chain bookstores such as America's Barnes & Nobles and the Borders Group to increase distribution. Also, modern distribution systems are just at an early stage and thus far no such system has been able to prove its effectiveness. In addition, sellers of professional books and books with a small target audience should adopt better data management and make more use of electronic technology.

Presently, publications sell mainly in the big cities with populations of more than two to three million. Small and medium cities with a population of less than two million possess only limited sales networks, and these networks are not technologically updated and it is hard to distribute new books and magazines in a timely manner. Also, it is inconvenient to buy books through mail order in these cities. In total, there are about 450 cities each with 200,000 to 1 million people and a total population of 290 million. Therefore, there is great market potential in these small and medium cities that is waiting to be harnessed.

iv. The problems of regional monopolies and rampant piracy still await effective solutions. The planned economy determined that Chinese publications were generally distributed based on provincial divisions, and currently only a few publishers are able to distribute their publications nationwide. Meanwhile, some provincial governments try to protect local interests and thus create many barriers for book distributors that already suffer from a serious lack of distribution channels. In addition, piracy is rampant in many regions. The Chinese government has made considerable progress in reducing piracy (for instance, more than 100 illegal CD-ROM production lines have been destroyed, and the government rewards informers with RMB300,000, about US$36,145), but piracy still casts long shadows on today's publishing industry and stronger and tougher measures are needed.

v. The market is growing rapidly. As the largest developing country, the Chinese mainland possesses a fast growing publication market. Take as an example the 10-year development of the book market between 1992 and 2002. In 1992 more than 90,000 book titles were issued, with a total printing volume of 6.338 billion copies (sheets), using 665,700 tons of paper, and having a total list price of RMB11.08 billion (about US$1.33 billion). By 2002, the total book titles were 170,000, with a printing volume of 6.87 billion copies (sheets), using 1.074 million tons of paper, and having a total list price of RMB53.51 billion (about US$6.47 billion), showing increases of 90%, 8.4%, 61.4% and 383.2%, respectively.

In terms of market sales, book sales in 1992 were worth RMB4.2 billion (approximately US$506 million), and in 2002 they reached RMB43.5 billion (about US$5.24 billion), increasing over ten-fold in 10 years. In recent years, book sales increased by US$300 million each year with annual growth of 7%. If this trend continues, by 2010, book sales could amount to nearly US$8 billion, i.e. in the coming seven to eight years, the book market in the Chinese mainland has potential growth of US$2.5 billion.

vi. This market is opening to the world. Printing in the Chinese mainland had been largely opened before its entry into the WTO, and after entry, its distribution market will be further liberalized. Foreign investment in various forms has entered into different sectors of the Chinese publishing industry. (See Chapter 10.) Some preliminary estimates show that currently more than 70 foreign publishers have established subsidiaries or offices in China. The foreign investment shares in the growth of the market, and it also sharpens the competitive edge of Chinese enterprises and facilitates the local publishing industry to transition to a market-based economy. It is a win-win situation.

B. Overview of the Publishing Industries of Taiwan, Hong Kong, and Macau

Taiwan, Hong Kong, and Macau have populations of 23 million, 6.82 million, and 440,000 respectively.

In terms of output, Taiwan and Hong Kong rank second and third as Chinese publishing bases, but in terms of competitive capacity, Taiwan and Hong Kong are the most developed regions of the Chinese publishing industry.

These two regions share similarities in many respects such as their social systems, economic strength, and legal framework. Both of their publishing industries are completely market-oriented and corporate registration is a main requirement for entering the publishing business. Private companies dominate all sectors, be it in terms of production capacity or in total number of companies. Also, they both have high volumes of publication imports and exports. Average incomes in both regions amount to more than US$10,000 and people living in the two regions have similar modes and levels of consumption.

But differences exist between them, especially with regard to their cultural backgrounds, population size, and land area. Chinese culture dominates Taiwan and the Chinese language is dominant. British rule of over 150 years brought Western culture into Hong Kong and as a result, it was subject to a combined influence of Western and Chinese culture with use of both Chinese and English, with English being slightly preferred. Taiwan has three times the population of Hong Kong, and the people in Taiwan are educated in a Chinese cultural environment, hence Taiwan is much stronger than Hong Kong in terms of publishing capacity. Hong Kong, with a total area of 1,098 square kilometers, and Taiwan, with a total area 30 times larger than that of Hong Kong, have developed their publishing industry in different territorial environments, one based on a city and the other based in a larger area. Due to these factors, the publishing industries in these two regions have evolved their own unique characteristics.

1. *Taiwan*

The publishing industry in Taiwan displays five major characteristics:

i.   The market is saturated and competition is extremely intense. With a population of 23 million, Taiwan supports about 8,000 book-publishing houses and almost the same number of magazine publishers, with an annual book output of over 36,000 titles, and these figures continue to rise. As many new companies enter the market, many publishers and bookstores are squeezed out of business. In recent years, tough competition in the Taiwan publication market has been clearly reflected in the collapse and bankruptcies of some large publishing groups and companies such as Chin Show Cultural Enterprise, Kwang Fu Book Enterprises Co., Ltd, and the Senseio Bookstore.

ii. Taiwan is densely covered with bookstores serviced by distribution channels that appear sound and mature. Publications are well served by various highly developed distribution channels, including wholesale, sales through publishers' own distribution networks, direct, and online sales. Effective distribution channels facilitate publication sales since it is very convenient for people in Taiwan to make purchases.

iii. The market is readily open to world trade and imports a large number of publications. With few restrictions on foreign investment in Taiwan, foreign capital can enter into every sector of the publishing industry, and foreign companies are engaged in book and magazine publishing as well as audio-video production. In the copyright trade, Taiwan has brought in a large number of publications with foreign copyrights. The acquired foreign titles now account for 40% of the annual new title output in Taiwan, and for children's publications, foreign titles acquired from overseas represent half of the entire output.

iv. More shareholding companies and conglomerates are emerging. In order to enhance competitiveness in the hostile market, publishers are inclined to restructure themselves into these forms. Many publishing companies once owned by a sole owner or several partners began to distribute shares to employees to encourage their contribution and loyalty to the company. Now most publishing companies in Taiwan are limited companies. Forming conglomerates shows another way to compete with the tough competition. In recent years, more and more publishing groups and strategic conglomerates have been formed through mergers and share acquisitions.

Publishers are aggressive in promoting their businesses outside the island and exploring new opportunities. The market saturation in Taiwan has forced local publishers to turn their eyes elsewhere. Major areas they are exploring are Singapore, Malaysia and some other Southeast Asian countries with Chinese-speaking populations, as well as the Chinese mainland and Hong Kong. The Chinese mainland, the biggest market in the Chinese publishing industry, is undergoing marketization, which has generated a lot of business opportunities, and therefore Taiwan publishers have established various branches there. At present, the market is still in the process of opening up, otherwise, the number of Taiwan companies would have doubled.

2. Hong Kong

The publishing industry in Hong Kong, though based in a city, operates similarly to its counterpart in Taiwan due to their many common features such as a saturated market, intense competition, sound distribution system, and the tendency to form shareholding companies and conglomerates. Nevertheless, it has its own unique characteristics.

i. The Hong Kong market is highly internationalized, with both the Chinese and English languages in use. As a freely trading port, Hong Kong is known for its open investment environment, freedom from trade barriers, easy and free capital circulation, sound legal system, and clearly defined and low taxes. Now it is the tenth largest trader in the world, the seventh largest foreign exchange market, the twelfth largest banking center, and one of the four major gold commodity markets. For many years running, traditional American foundations have listed Hong Kong as the most economically free region. Meanwhile, since both Chinese and English languages are official languages there, Hong Kong has a bilingual market, differing from many other markets. All of these factors have laid a solid foundation for the further development of the publishing industry in Hong Kong.

ii. Hong Kong publishing professionals have an outstanding ability to explore and design new projects and are strongly competitive in the international market. The small population and very limited territorial environment where a free economy dominates has nurtured many Hong Kong publishers with strong business acumen and professional skills. In some publishing companies, only one or two people are responsible for the editing, printing, and distribution, yet the companies still operate smoothly and successfully. Moreover, the existence of many international companies enhances the competitive capacity of the local enterprises, and the small internal market and high degree of internationalization also help many publishers develop business practices and abilities well suited for competing internationally. Some publishers have directed their business towards overseas markets even from the very beginning. Southeast Asia, North America, the Chinese mainland, Taiwan, and Macau have all been long-time targets.

iii. Hong Kong remains a gateway for Chinese publications and also as an important import and export hub. Its advantages as an open market enables Hong Kong to have the greatest number of Chinese publications. Beyond being a consumer and producer, Hong Kong is also a transfer station for publications. In 2002, of all the imported books in the Chinese mainland, 23% came from Hong Kong, the largest supplier of imported publications. Many of these imported publications are produced by branches or subsidiaries of foreign companies in Hong Kong. Since there is no direct trade relationship between Taiwan and the Chinese mainland, both are heavily reliant on Hong Kong to trade with the other.

iv. Hong Kong has one of the best printing industries in the world and produces excellent publication design. Printing in Hong Kong is known for its high standards, superior quality, and excellent service. With about 5,000 printing companies, and easily accessible support from two printing bases—Shenzhen and Dongguan of the Chinese mainland, the printing industry in Hong Kong is strongly competitive and occupies an important position among its different manufacturing industries. In 2002, the total value of the books, magazines and other printing products produced in Hong Kong and later exported was worth US$500 million. Refined printing encourages high levels of publication design. Hong Kong publications have received many international prizes. The strong printing sector also propels and facilitates the development of other sectors of the industry such as publishing and editing.

Macau and Hong Kong are similar in many ways such as their social systems, laws, history, and market management. However, due to the much lower population (5% of Hong Kong population) and very limited area (2.5% of the area of Hong Kong), and a different cultural background, Macau has not developed a strong Chinese publishing industry. However, since Macau's return to China in 1999, considerable progress has been made.

C. Chinese Publishing Outside China

Chinese publishing is not limited to the Chinese mainland, Taiwan, Hong Kong, and Macau. In some countries and regions outside China, Chinese language publishing exists. In order to provide an overall image of Chinese publishing in the world, it is necessary to briefly touch on these other markets.

Preliminary estimates show that about 500 Chinese newspapers and magazines exist in the world besides those in the Chinese mainland, Taiwan, Hong Kong, and Macau, and annually about 1,000 Chinese titles are widely published outside China. In addition to the existence of about 50 Chinese websites in these other regions, there are also some Chinese radio and TV stations. The readers of these publications live in many places in the world. The total sales of the Chinese books and magazines outside China exceed US$100 million, and the market mainly consists of four blocks: North America accounts for about

50% of total sales, Europe accounts for about 10%, and Northeast Asia (e.g. Japan) and Southeast Asia (e.g. Singapore and Malaysia) together represent the remaining 40%. (See Figure 1.5.)

Outside China, North- and Southeast Asia, and North America are the two regions where Chinese publishing is the most active.

1. Malaysia, Singapore and Other Asian Countries

Outside China, Chinese publishing is most active in Malaysia and Singapore, and to some degree with their large production scale, the two countries are possibly becoming the fourth Chinese publishing base after the Chinese mainland, Taiwan, and Hong Kong.

At present, the annual Chinese book output in these two countries comes to about 600 titles with sales of US$25 million (according to Poh Seng Titt). Prominent publishing companies include SNP Panpac Pte. Ltd., Shinglee Publishers Pte. Ltd., Federal Educational Publishers, World Scientific Publishing Co., The Shanghai Book (CNPIEC) Co., (Pte) Ltd., Mentor Bookstore, The Commercial Press Bookstore, The Commercial Press (Malaysia) Ltd, and Xuelin Publishing. Popular Holdings Ltd. in

Figure 1.5
Market Share of Chinese Books Outside China

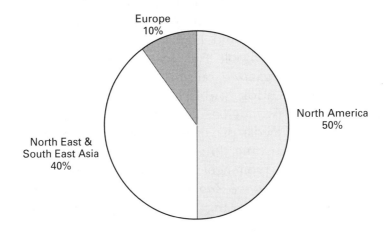

Europe 10%

North America 50%

North East & South East Asia 40%

Figure 1.6
Centers of Chinese Publishing in Southeast Asia

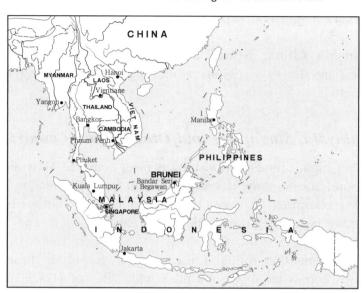

Singapore owns a bookstore chain with nearly 100 outlets and also engages in publishing books in Singapore, Malaysia, Canada, Hong Kong and Taiwan. SNP Panpac and Federal Educational Publishers also operate in other overseas markets.

Altogether, there are about 150 Chinese bookstores, of which about 100 are located in Malaysia. Singapore has a famous book center at the Bras Basah Complex. Both countries host annual international book fairs where Chinese books occupy an important position. The World Book Fair in Singapore showcases both Chinese and English books, while the Kuala Lumpur International Book Fair in Malaysia is the biggest Chinese book fair organized outside China.

Compared to book publishing, Chinese newspaper publishing in these two regions is even more developed. *Lianhe Zaobao* is a major media player and Singapore Press Holdings Ltd., Malaysia's Nanyang Press Holdings Berhad, and the Sinchew Group are prominent press groups. Singapore Press Holdings Ltd. owns *Lianhe Zaobao*, *Lianhe Wanbao*, and *Shin Min Daily News*, and Nanyang Press Holdings Berhad controls

Nanyang Siang Pau, China Press, 12 magazines, and one publishing company. In addition, some Chinese websites are operated out of both countries.

Southeast Asia and some other countries also have Chinese newspapers and a few Chinese bookstores, but not on a large scale. *World Journal* in Thailand, with a circulation of over 30,000, should be considered an important Chinese newspaper in that region. Every year, Japan imports the greatest number of Chinese books.

2. North America and Other Regions

Chinese publishing in the Americas is concentrated in North America, and the publishers are mainly from the Chinese mainland, Taiwan, and Hong Kong. These publishers and the local publishing houses together have launched a young yet well-organized Chinese publishing network.

Chinese publishing establishments in the United States (U.S.) are concentrated in the east and west in cities such as New York, Los Angeles and San Francisco, while in Canada they are mainly in Vancouver and Toronto. The China National Publications Import & Export (Group) Corporation (CNPIEC), China International Book Trade Corporation, China National Publications International Trade Corporation, Science Press, and Tianjin Press and Publishing Bureau all have branches or bookstores in these American cities, and the Liaoning Publishing Group has a bookstore in Toronto. The Sino United Publishing (Holdings) Ltd., the most influential Hong Kong publisher in North America, has opened bookstores in Vancouver, Toronto, Los Angeles, New York and San Francisco, and among its subsidiaries, Oriental Culture Enterprises Co., Inc. and Eastwind Books & Arts, Inc. are both doing very well in the U.S.

Taiwan has the strongest publishing and distribution networks in North America. The *World Journal,* sponsored by the United Daily News Group, is the most influential Chinese newspaper in North America. The company owns more than 20 chain bookstores and has distribution networks based in New

Figure 1.7
Centers of Chinese Publishing in North America

York and Los Angeles. Some other Taiwanese companies also have established branches in the U.S., for example, Li Ming Cultural Enterprise Co., Ltd. set up Li Ming Culture and Art Company.

There are independent Chinese publishing companies and bookstores in North America, and most of them are established by Chinese immigrants and operate on a small scale, such as Evergreen Publishing & Stationery, Oriental Culture Books, King Stone Bookstore, and Jieli Inc., of which both the Evergreen and Oriental Culture Books are among the few prominent Chinese bookstores in America.

Other than the *World Journal*, there are nearly a hundred other Chinese newspapers published in North America, and the influential ones include The *China Press* (America edition), *Sing Tao Daily* (America and Canada editions), *Ming Pao Daily* (America edition) and *Liberty Times*. Many Chinese newspapers are issued as weeklies.

In spite of sharing many similarities with North America, Chinese publishing in Europe exists on a smaller scale, and most of the publishing entities are set up by publishers of the Chinese mainland, Taiwan, and Hong Kong. The CNPIEC has subsidiaries or offices in Britain, Germany, and Russia, of which the Germany subsidiary is the largest publishing entity established by Chinese mainland publishers in Europe. Taiwan's Cheng Chung Book Co., Ltd. and Li Ming Cultural Enterprise Co., Ltd. have bookstores in London and Paris, while Hong Kong's Sino United Publishing has a branch in London. In addition, there are some independent Chinese bookstores, of which the most prominent ones are You-feng Bookstore and Phoenix Bookstore in France, opened by M. Kim Hun, a Chinese immigrant from Cambodia, and a Frenchman, Philippe Meyer, respectively. You-feng Bookstore even engages in publishing. Of Chinese newspapers in Europe, the *Europe Daily*, published by the United Daily News group of Taiwan, is most influential.

While a majority of Chinese newspapers and magazines in North America and Europe are published and distributed locally, other types of publications such as books and electronic books mainly come from the three main publishing regions of China. In recent years, the number of Chinese websites in North America have increased rapidly. So far, dozens of various Chinese Internet companies have been established. Many Chinese newspapers there also operate their own Chinese websites, providing various online information and services.

Australia and South America also have some Chinese publishing activities. In Australia, Chinese publishing is growing as Chinese is becoming a more important language.

D. Copyright Protection in China

China's first copyright law, *The Copyright Law of the Great Qing,* was promulgated in 1910, and in 1915, the Beijing government issued the second copyright law in Chinese history. The third copyright law was enacted in 1928 by the Nationalist government, which was in force in the Chinese mainland until October 1949.

With the founding of the People's Republic of China on October 1, 1949, all laws promulgated by the former government were abolished in the Chinese mainland including the copyright laws, which are still used in Taiwan to this day. In Hong Kong, British copyright law was used between 1949 and 1997.

In September 1990, 40 years after the previous copyright law, a new copyright law, *The Copyright Law of the People's Republic of China,* was drawn up in the Chinese mainland and came into effect on June 1, 1991. Some other related regulations were also issued, including the *Rules on Implementation of the Copyright Law*, the *Rules on Protection of Computer Software*, and the *Rules on Custom Protection of Intellectual Property*. In October 2001, the copyright law and its related regulations were first amended.

China joined the World Intellectual Property Organization in 1980 and became a member of the Berne Convention for the Protection of Literary and Artistic Works and the Universal Copyright Convention on October 15 and 30, 1992, respectively. On March 27, 1993, the Chinese mainland became a signatory of the Convention for the Protection of Producers of Phonograms against Unauthorized Duplication of their Phonograms, and with entry into the WTO on December 11, 2001, the *Agreements on Trade-Related Aspects of Intellectual Property Rights* began to be implemented.

Copyrights in the Chinese mainland are protected by both legal and administrative measures.

According to the copyright law, Chinese citizens, legal entities, and other organizations enjoy copyright protection for their works, whether published or not. The copyrights of foreigners and stateless persons are protected by Chinese law according to bilaterial agreements concluded between China and the country to which they belong or in which they reside, or according to international treaties to which both countries are signatories. Also, foreigners and stateless persons whose country or residing country has not concluded any agreement treaty with China or is not a party to any international treaty to which China is a party can also enjoy the protection of Chinese law if their work is first published in a member country of an international treaty to which China is a signatory, or simultaneously published in a member country of the treaty and in a non-member country.

The copyright law stipulates that acts of infringement, such as publishing a work without permission of the copyright owner, publishing a work of joint authorship as a work created solely by an individual without the permission of the co-author(s), or having one's name mentioned in another person's work in which the one has not contributed to the creation, will bear civil liabilities including ceasing the infringement, eliminating the bad effects of the action, making an apology, and paying compensation for damages.

For serious acts of infringement such as reproducing, distributing, performing, presenting, broadcasting, disseminating through information networks, and publishing works of others without the permission of the copyright owner, besides bearing civil liabilities, the infringer shall also submit to the disciplinary actions taken by the administrative department for copyright enforcement such as confiscating unlawful gains, confiscating and destroying copies of the material, and confiscating tools and equipment used to produce copies of infringement.

Under *The Criminal Law of the People's Republic of China*, for serious acts of infringement aiming for unlawful gains and having made a large sum from such gains, or involving other serious acts of infringement, criminal liabilities shall be investigated, and the infringer is subject to a punishment of under seven years in prison and liability to pay fines.

The Copyright Law also indicates that the Chinese government takes partial responsibility in the implementation of the copyright law. The NCAC is responsible for the administration of copyright protection nationwide, and the administrative departments for copyright under the governments of provinces, autonomous regions, and municipalities directly under the central government are responsible for the administration of copyright protection in their respective administrative regions. (See Chapter 1-A-4 for the structure of the copyright protection apparatus.) If a dispute occurs over administrative enforcement and penalties, the involved party may take legal action in a People's Court.

Different copyright laws have been applied in Taiwan, Hong Kong and Macau, and since their return to China, Hong Kong and Macau have adopted a new copyright law. The copyright laws in these three regions are similar to that of the Chinese mainland; yet, if dispute over copyright or infringement occurs, there is only one legal path to settle the dispute.

In the past 10 years, China has made some substantial changes in copyright protection. The current situation is neither as good as some people claim nor as bad as others may say. The reality is that piracy still exists and is a serious problem in some regions, but in the meantime, violators are punishable by law and the Chinese government has been taking strong measures against piracy. Otherwise, there would not have been more than 10,000 titles licensed from overseas annually, representing 10% of all new book titles. Without such strong measures, Harry Potter books, whose retail price is twice the norm would not have sold more than five million copies in the Chinese mainland.

In short, there has already been much done to fight piracy and great efforts are continuing.

The Book Publishing Industry in the Chinese Mainland

A. Publishing Houses and Sectors: A Broad Overview

1. Book Publishers

There are 568 publishing houses (including 36 imprints) in the Chinese mainland. Of these, 219 are national publishers mostly concentrated in Beijing, while the remaining 349 are spread evenly throughout the other provinces. Beijing, considered the center of publishing with 219 publishing companies, accounts for about 40% of the country's total number of publishing houses while Shanghai takes a distant second place with only 40 publishing houses. After these two cities, each of the other provinces has less than 20 publishing houses. In general, every government agency at the ministry level has one affiliated publishing unit which is called a national publisher. There are a few exceptions to this. For example, major government organizations such as the Ministry of Education and the Chinese Academy of Social Sciences have several publishing units under their respective umbrellas.

In terms of revenue, the majority of Chinese publishing houses operate on a medium scale. Among the 560 publishing houses, 70 achieve annual sales of RMB100 million, another 70 publishers have sales in the range of RMB50–100 million, 280 publishers have sales in the range of RMB10–50 million, and the remaining 140 publishers have annual sales of less than RMB10 million. The largest publishing house employs around 1,000 workers, while a small press might have about 20 employees (See Figure 2.1.)

Chinese book publishing underwent the fastest growth it has ever experienced over the last five to 10 years. During that time, a group of prominent publishers emerged from the various publishing sectors.

About 20 publishing groups have been formed, of which 13 are pilot groups approved by the General Administration of Press and Publication (GAPP). These pilot groups are: the Shanghai Century Publishing Group, Guangdong Publishing Group, Liaoning Publishing Group, Beijing Publishing Group, China Sciences Publishing Group, Shandong General Publishing House, China Publishing Group, Jiangsu Publishing Group, Zhejiang Publishing Group, Sichuan Publishing Group, Henan Publishing Group, Hebei Publishing Group, and Jilin Publishing Group.

The China Publishing Group, formed in March 2002, is the largest publishing group affiliated with the Department of Publicity of the Central Committee of CPC (See Figure 2.2 on page 36.) The group consists of a number of the most prominent publishers and distribution companies in the country. Its members include The Commercial Press, Zhonghua Book Company, SDX Joint Publishing Co., Ltd. People's Literature Publishing Group, People's Publishing Group, Encyclopedia of China Publishing House, People's Fine Arts Publishing House (all seven were formerly affiliated with the GAPP), Zhong Xin Lian CD Company, Xinhua Bookstore General Group, and China National Publications Import & Export (Group) Corporation. The group has assets valued at RMB5 billion (approximately US$603 million), annual sales of RMB2.5 billion, and 6,000 employees. It publishes a total of 6,000 titles of printed books, electronic publications, and audio and visual books annually, and owns 46 periodicals and 3 newspapers. Its annual copyright trading volume is 600 titles. The group also imports and exports 6,000 audio and video publications and hundreds of thousands of books and periodicals.

Figure 2.1

Top 50 Publishers in 2002

Rank	Publisher	Sales*
1	People's Education Press	1,159
2	Higher Education Press	621
3	Gansu People's Publishing House	376
4	Liaohai Publishing House	359
5	Foreign Language Teaching and Research Press	355
6	Jiangsu Education Publishing House	351
7	China Cartographic Publishing House	285
8	Science Press	284
9	Tsinghua University Press	280
10	Yunnan People's Publishing House	275
11	China Light Industry Press	252
12	Chongqing Publishing House	247
13	People's Medical Publishing House	245
14	Zhejiang Education Publishing House	239
15	Shanghai Foreign Language Education Press	232
16	Beijing Normal University Press	231
17	China Machine Press	211
18	Guangdong Education Publishing Press	206
19	Shanxi People's Publishing Press	203
20	Shandong Education Publishing Press	202
21	Beijing Publishing House	199
22	Shanghai Educational Publishing House	191
23	The Commercial Press	184
24	Anhui Education Publishing House	179
25	World Publishing Corporation	175
26	China Financial & Economic Publishing House	166
27	Planet Cartographic Publishing House	164
28	Hubei Education Press	162
29	Publishing House of Electronics Industry	157
30	China Renmin University Press	157
31	Central Radio and TV University Press	154
32	Hebei Education Press	152
33	Shanghai Literature & Art General Publishing House	148
34	Guangxi Normal University Press	148
35	Peking University Press	148
36	Inner Mongolia Education Press	146
37	Shanghai Fine Arts Publishers	140
38	Shaanxi People's Publishing House	139
39	Xinjiang Education Publishing Press	138
40	China Architecture & Building Press	132
41	Hunan Education Publishing House	132
42	Hainan Publishing House	130
43	Shanghai Scientific & Technical Publishers	123
44	Future Publishing House	122
45	China Labour Social Security Publishing House	121
46	China Financial Publishing House	120
47	Elephant Publishing House	119
48	Educational Science Publishing House	116
49	Shaanxi Normal University Press	116
50	Fujian Education Press	116

millions of RMB

Figure 2.2

Organizational Structure of China Publishing Group

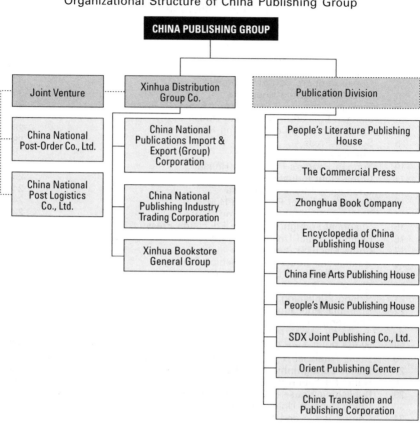

Top performers among the 20 publishing groups are the Liaoning Publishing Group and the Shanghai Century Publishing Group. The Liaoning Group consists of 12 businesses including book publishers, audio and video presses, and electronic publishing houses and is the largest publishing corporation in Northeast China. The Shanghai Group, the result of a merger of 12 publishers, is the largest publishing company in East China. In addition to the above-mentioned pilot groups, there are also self-formed publishing groups such as the Hunan Publishing Group, China Children Press & Publication Group, and China International Publishing Group. More publishing groups are now being formed. (See Figure 2.3.)

Figure 2.3

Publishing Groups in the Chinese Mainland

Name	Headquarter	Total Assets*	Annual Revenues*	Number of Employees
Beijing Publishing Group	Beijing	430	220	497
China Children's Press & Publishing Group	Beijing	600	300	500
China Publishing Group	Beijing	5,140	2,920	5,225
China Science Publishing Group	Beijing	460	520	780
Chinese Writers Publishing Group	Beijing	100	300	500
Guangdong Publishing Group	Guangzhou	1,590	1,200	921
Guangxi General Publishing House	Nanning	1,740	2,230	1,629
Hebei Publishing Group	Shijiazhuang	4,100	4,000	11,000
Henan Publishing Group	Zhengzhou	4,630	5,600	N/A
Hunan Publishing Group	Changsha	4,000	3,700	N/A
Jiangsu Publishing Group	Nanjing	6,500	7,070	9,495
Jilin Publishing Group	Changchun	1,700	960	5,600
Liaoning Publishing Group	Shenyang	2,500	2,210	4,799
Shandong General Publishing House	Jinan	5,450	6,120	19,171
Shanghai Century Publishing Group	Shanghai	1,090	830	2,842
Sichuan Publishing Group	Chengdu	1,200	890	2,956
Zhejiang Publishing Group	Hangzhou	3,590	3,750	9,418

millions of RMB

Beyond the publishing groups mentioned above, some publishers with rich assets and competitive advantages also formed publishing groups by spinning off a number of subsidiary companies. Examples of this type of publishing group include People's Posts and Telecommunications Publishing House, Shanghai Literature & Art Publishing House, Publishing House of Electronics Industry, China Light Industry Press, China Machine Press, and Hebei Education Press.

The People's Posts and Telecommunications Publishing House releases 1,500 book titles annually and owns a dozen magazines with annual sales of 13 million copies. It also owns a book distribution center, an electronic network, the Oriental Saiweisi Property Management Corporation Limited, the Hongmai Information Consulting Firm, the Guomei Advertising Agency, and the commercial building at Beijing's Wangfujing Oriental Plaza. Its annual gross sales of all publications have exceeded RMB350 million and its total assets are close to RMB500 million.

The Shanghai Literature & Art Publishing House owns another three houses, eleven magazines, and one newspaper. Its annual output is 600 titles. Its monthly magazine, *Stories*, ranks first in national circulation.

Before 1949, many large Chinese publishers set up branches in markets outside of where their headquarters were located, and in those times, The Commercial Press had a branch in each province of China. China implemented a planned economy for the first 30 years after the country's new government was formed in 1949 and publishers mainly operated from their home bases with editing, designing, printing, and distribution all done locally. Publishers rarely developed business outside their local area, let alone set up branches elsewhere. Geographically, China is a vast country with a widespread population and so, publishers were also distributed evenly in numbers in each province with the exception of Beijing. However, creative minds and talents became heavily concentrated in the bigger cities like Beijing, Shanghai, Shenzhen, and other economically developed regions along the East Coast. Correspondingly, a large part of the book market became concentrated in these areas. Conducting business in a market environment outside a publishing company's home base has become necessary for some publishers in order to meet market demands, and is an important step towards a market economy for the book publishing industry.

At present, more than a dozen publishers have set up branches outside of where their headquarters are located. They are the Hainan Publishing House, Hebei Education Press, Jieli Publishing House, Yangtze River Literature and Art Publishing House, Guangxi Normal University Press, Guangxi People's Publishing House, Lijiang Publishing House, Shaanxi Normal University Press, Sichuan Children's Publishing House, Hunan Fine Arts Publishing House, The Commercial Press, Higher Education Press, and Shandong People's Publishing House. The Guangdong, Shanghai Century, and Jiangxi Publishing Groups have also opened up branches in Beijing. Six children's books publishers including Tomorrow Publishing House, Zhejiang Juvenile and Children's Books Publishing House formed a strategic alliance named East China Children's Publishing Group and have set up a joint-stock publishing company in Beijing. Publishing companies with branches in locations and markets beyond where they are headquartered are likely to be more competitive and efficient publishers. Beijing, Shanghai, and Shenzhen are the primary choice for opening up branches as these big cities hold prominent positions in culture, finance, and economic strength. That said, most of the publishers chose to open branches in Beijing first.

Many branch companies are independent profit centers. Jieli Publishing House not only moved their editorial department to Beijing, but also relocated the rest of their publishing businesses to the capital except its publishing operations for textbooks and supplement material. Now Jieli's president is based in the Guangxi headquarters while its editor-in-chief works in Beijing. Jieli now publishes 100 titles per year. The Shanghai Century Publishing Group also set up a branch called the Horizon Media Co., Ltd. in Beijing and this branch has published up to 100 titles including *The Marketing Revolution of Coca-Cola* and *Experiencing Microsoft.*

As publishing has become more market-oriented, a group of publishing gurus with editorial acumen and market savvy took center stage in China. They include Li Pengyi, President of the Foreign Language Teaching and Research Press; Nie Zhenning, President of the People's Literature Publishing House; Wang Yamin, President of Hebei Education Press; Li Yuanjun, President, and Bai Bing, Editor-in-Chief, of Jieli Publishing House; Zhang Shengyou, President of the Writers Publishing House; Zhou Baiyi, President of the Yangtze River Literature and Art Publishing House; Zhao Jiqing, President of the China Light Industry Press; Zhang Yanyang, President of Jindun (Golden Shield) Publishing House; Chen Xin, CEO of Shanghai Century Publishing Group; Yang Deyan, President of The Commercial Press; Ren Huiying, CEO, and Yu Xiaoqun, Vice-President of

Liaoning Publishing Group. The most prominent publisher in modern Chinese history is Zhang Yuanji, who led The Commercial Press from the 1930s to 1950s.

Figure 2.4
Picture of Zhang Yuanji

Under his leadership, The Commercial Press became one of the largest publishing companies in Asia.
(Photo provided by The Commercial Press)

There is a substantial imbalance in publishing and distribution capacity among the 34 provinces and regions of China. The top 10 most developed regions for publishing are Beijing, Shanghai, Jiangsu, Guangdong, Shandong, Liaoning, Hubei, Zhejiang, Hunan, and Sichuan. In 2002, the top 10 regions with annual book sales surpassing the RMB1.56 billion mark were Beijing, Jiangsu, Guangdong, Shandong, Sichuan, Henan, Zhejiang, Hunan, Hebei, and Shanghai. In general, the regions along the East Coast are well developed in the book trade while the inland and Western regions lag behind.

Beijing remains the center of book publishing, far exceeding the provinces in terms of scope, human resources, or market size. Forty percent of publishing houses are located in Beijing. Together, they publish 73,840 titles annually, accounting for 40%

of the country's total title output. Annual book sales in Beijing are RMB5.35 billion (about US$64.58 million), representing 12.3% of total book sales. Excluding the national publishers with headquarters in the capital, Beijing has 17 local publishing houses, releasing 3,009 titles per year, which accounts for 1.8% of the country's total output, with revenues of RMB1.26 billion (about US$151.81 million), representing 2.9% of annual book sales. Of the 17 local Beijing publishers, eight belong to the Beijing Publishing Group, which together publish 1,500 titles per year and also owns four magazines. Its annual sales were RMB200 million (about US$24.1 million) in 2002.

Shanghai is the second most developed region in publishing after Beijing. There are about 40 publishers in Shanghai, or 7% of the country's total. Shanghai publishers released a combined 14,500 titles a year, accounting for 8.5% of China's annual title output. Shanghai publishers achieved annual sales revenue of RMB1.56 billion (about US$187.95 million), accounting for 4% of the industry total. Shanghai is also the home of the Century Publishing Group and the Shanghai Literature and Art Publishing House, both of which have made great impact in the development of the industry. Jiangsu and Guangdong provinces are also two competitive regions after Shanghai.

2. Book Categories

Title output has increased impressively in the Chinese mainland in recent years. In 2002, there were 170,000 titles in print. Of these, 100,700 were new titles while the rest of the 70,300 titles were revisions or reprints. 2002 saw a 10% increase in the number of titles over 2001. (See Figure 2.5.)

Books published in the Chinese mainland include printed books, textbooks, and picture books. The title output and unit sales of picture books are counted towards the industry total. In 2002, 142,952 non-textbook titles were published, accounting for 84% of book output, of which 91,350 were first editions. In addition, 25,817 textbooks were published accounting for 15% of total, of which 8,163 were new titles. For picture books, 2,193

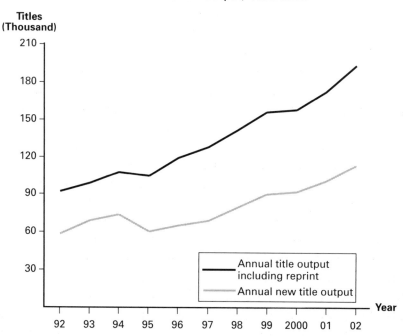

Figure 2.5
Total Chinese Book Output, 1992–2002

titles, of which, 1,180 were new titles, were published, accounting for 13% of the industry total.

In the Chinese mainland, books are classified into 22 categories as follows:

- Art
- Agricultural Science
- Astronomy and Earth Science
- Aviation and Space Sciences
- Biology
- Culture, Science, Education, and Sports
- Economics
- Engineering
- Environment
- General Natural Sciences
- History and Geography
- Languages

- Literature
- Marxism, Leninism, Mao Zedong Thought, and Deng Xiaoping's Theories
- Mathematics, Physics, and Chemistry
- Medical Science
- Military Affairs
- Philosophy
- Political Science and Law
- Social Sciences
- Transportation
- General

If the 22 categories were roughly summed up into two categories of social sciences and natural sciences, the ratio of social science books to natural science books would be 7:3. Though the government adopts these 22 categories, Chinese publishers tend to divide books into eight or nine categories: social sciences, science and technology, literature and art, children's books, Chinese classics, education, academic, and reference and encyclopedia. There are also publishers who follow Western practices and group books into three general categories: trade, professional, and educational. At present, it is not common in China to classify books by mass-market paperbacks and book club books. In this respect the publishing industry differs from that in the West.

B. Trade Books

Trade books refer to books that are sold mainly in bookstores. They include the following: literature, art, lifestyle, children, popular science, and humanities.

1. Literature and Art

In the Chinese mainland, art books include books on fine arts, photography, calligraphy, and drama. In 2002, about 21,000 literature and art titles were published, representing 12% of the country's annual title output. For literature, about 11,200 titles were published, of which 8,690 were new titles. Fiction titles represented 6.5% of the total annual title output. For art, about 10,100 titles were published, of which 6,940 were new titles. Illustrated titles accounted for 6% of China's annual title output. The total sales of literature and art books is RMB240 million per year, representing only 5% of total sales.

Fiction is very popular and there are many genres of fiction available. However, the market for literature and art books is gradually shrinking due to the increasing diversity of entertainment consumption. Less than 10% of fiction titles account for 60% of the total sales. The fiction bestsellers are priced at an average of RMB18–20 (approximately US$2.30). A novel with sales of 50,000 copies is regarded as a bestseller while a title with sales 100,000 is considered a national bestseller. In recent years, foreign fiction titles that sold over 100,000 copies include: *The Bridges of Madison County*, *The Horse Whisperer*, *The Unbearable Lightness of Being*, *The Lord of the Rings*, *Fragrant Chrysanthemum*, and *Norwegian Wood*.

There are 50 publishers specializing in literature and art. The most well-known are the People's Literature Publishing House, Writers Publishing House, Shanghai Literature and Art Publishing House, Shanghai Translation Publishing House, Yilin Press, Lijiang Press, China Youth Press, Huacheng Press, Yangtze River Literature and Art Publishing House, and Hebei Educational Press.

The People's Literature Publishing House is the most prestigious literary publisher in China. It has the largest back catalog and produces 500 titles each year. The People's Literature Publishing House has compiled and published series of both the complete and selected works of the finest Chinese and foreign literary writers in multiple volumes. For foreign literature, it has translated and published *The Complete Works of William Shakespeare*, *The Complete Works of Honore De Balzac*, *The Complete Works of Henrik Johan Ibsen*, and *The Complete Works of Miguel de Cervantes*. It is also the authorized Chinese publisher of the *Harry Potter* series. It publishes a number of influential literary periodicals including *Modern Times* and *Facts on File for*

Contemporary Literature. The Writers' Publishing House, affiliated with the Chinese Writers' Association, is another literary powerhouse with an impressive business operation. Its *Notes from Mountains, The Horse Whisperer* (translation) and *Sophie's World* all took the publishing market and literary world by storm.

Shanghai Translation Publishing House, Yilin Press, and Lijiang Press are publishers specializing in foreign literature. In recent years, Shanghai Translation and Yilin both have had impressive results by introducing contemporary foreign literature. Shanghai Yiwen has acquired rights to and published the works of William Faulkner, Ernest Hemingway, W. Somerset Maugham, Erich Maria Remarque, Heinrich Boll, William Golding, Günter Grass, Haruki Murakami, Milan Kundera, and Imre Kertész. Yilin Press has acquired rights to and published the works of Joseph Heller, J. D. Salinger, Bernhard Schlink, Junichi Watanabe, and Mizuno Toshikata. Hubei Education Press has caught people's attention by producing several dozen multi-volume complete and selected works of foreign literary masters with high editorial and production standards.

More than 10,000 illustrated titles are issued in the Chinese mainland each year, of which 6,000 to 7,000 are new titles. The annual sales for art books is in the range of RMB110–120 million a year. Areas with largest selection are illustrated books, techniques of fine arts, art collections, photography albums, and applied arts. Chinese paintings, oil paintings, calligraphy, and photography are primary sellers for the illustrated book market. Large format art and photography collections have also become major sellers in recent years.

The art books that set the highest standards are the 60-volume *The Complete Collection of Chinese Fine Arts*, *The Selected Collection of Chinese Fine Arts*, and *The Complete Collection of Chinese Folk Arts* jointly published by the People's Fine Arts Publishing House, Cultural Relics Press, China Architecture & Building Press, Shanghai People's Fine Arts Publishing House, and Shanghai Fine Arts Publishers.

Other defining art titles with high artistic and production standards include *The Art of Dunhuang Caves* and *Chinese Brick*

Inscriptions by the Jiangsu People's Fine Arts Publishing House, *The Complete Collection of Chinese Jadeware* and *The Art of Chinese Tangshan Leather-Silhouette Shows* by Hebei Fine Arts Publishing House, *Contemporary Chinese Wooden Printing Masterpieces* and *The Complete Collection of Qi Baishi* by Hunan Fine Arts Publishing House, *The Art of Chinese Opera Facial Make-up* and *The Art of Chinese Witch Masks* by Jiangxi Fine Arts Publishing House, *The Chinese Cartoon Series* and *The Chinese Ancient Villages Series*, *The Complete Collection of Famous Chinese Painters Series* by Hebei Education Press, *The Art of Lacquerware of Chu, Qin and Han Dynasties, Hubei Volume* by Hubei Fine Arts Publishing House, *The Pictorial History of One Century of Chinese Oil Paintings* (1840–1949) by Guangxi Fine Arts Publishing House, *The Best Epigraphs of all Dynasties: Beijing University Library Permanent Collection* by Cultural Relics Press, *The Complete Longmen Stone Cave Images and Inscriptions: Beijing Public Library Permanent Collection* by Guangxi Normal University Press, *Eternal Three Gorges* by the People's Fine Arts Publishing House, and *Selected Paintings of Nima Zheren, the Panchen Lama's Private Painter* by China Intercontinental Press.

Picture books are gaining market share as Chinese consumers have more disposable income, while the working pace is increasing and reading takes on more diversified forms. The Chinese book market has entered the era of "picture reading". More and more picture books of all kinds and subjects have entered the market. Various nostalgic picture albums of the past and photography collections portraying a new, modern age are becoming increasingly popular.

In addition to general art books, comic books and graphic novels have become a huge market. In the past decade, comic books and graphic novels from Taiwan, the United States, Europe, and Japan have dominated the market while locally produced comic books and graphic novels only account for 5% of sales. The popular American comic books are *Garfield, Snoopy, Superman,* and *Batman.* The popular European comics are *Father and Son, The Adventures of Tintin,* and *The Wonderful Adventures of Nils.* The Japanese manga comics *RoboCat, Crayon Shin Chan, Ninja Turtles, Slam Dunk,* and *Fighter Ken Street* have captured the largest number of readers.

Previously, the majority of readers for comics were young people. In recent years, however, as adult comic books and graphic novels became available in a greater variety, the number of adult comic book readers has increased exponentially. The best-selling Taiwanese graphic novels are mostly for adult readers. The most popular cartoonists are Cai Zhizhong, Zhu Deyong, and Ji Mi. *Cartoons of Chinese Classics* by Cai Zhizhong which depict Lao Zi, Zhuang Zi, and Confucius portraying the Chinese cultural tradition in a humorous and refreshing way have set a single artist sales record of 20 million copies. Cai's cartoons are also licensed to many other countries and he has become the highest paid Chinese cartoonist in the world. The American, European, and Japanese comics attract mostly younger readers. Disney's *Mickey Mouse* has done very well in China. The biweekly *Mickey Mouse* magazine, a joint venture of the People's Posts and Telecommunications Publishing House and the Egmont Group, has monthly sales of 700,000 copies.

The most famous comic publishers in the Chinese mainland are the China Picture-Story Book Publishing House, Shanghai People's Fine Arts Publishing House, and Hebei Fine Arts Publishing House. To develop the comic book and graphic novel market and support Chinese authors and cartoonists, Hebei Fine Arts Publishing House invested several million RMB to develop the Chinese mainland's first cartoon and comic book production facilities supplying creative, technical and sales services. Hebei Fine Arts has since become the publishing powerhouse for the Chinese mainland's comic books and graphic novels. In addition, the private company Sunchime is another influential and high-volume comic book producer.

There are about 30 publishers specializing in arts and photography publishing. Among the most prominent of these are the People's Fine Arts Publishing House, Jiangsu Fine Arts

Publishing House, Zhejiang Photography Press, China Photography Press, Liaoning Fine Arts & Photography Press, and Hebei Education Press.

The China Fine Arts Publishing Group is the largest publishing group specializing in art book publishing. It consists of the People's Fine Arts Publishing House, China Picture-Story Book Publishing House, Rong Bao Zhai, and the Zhaohua Juvenile and Children's Publishing House. It is affiliated with the China Publishing Group. The China Fine Arts Publishing Group primarily publishes fine art books and children's books, and engages in art-related business ventures. It has fixed assets of RMB70 million and it publishes 600 titles in the form of books, periodicals and electronic publications. Its annual gross sales based on cover prices is RMB110 million, with net revenues of RMB70 million and net profits of RMB9 million. People's Fine Arts Publishing House is the largest publisher of illustrated books. Rong Bao Zhai is located in the west section of Liu Li Chang Street outside of the He Ping Men (Peace Gate) in Beijing. It is a world-renowned Chinese cultural establishment specializing in the "four treasures of the study" (i.e. brushes, ink sticks, ink-stones, and paper), antiques, and publishing. It is a place frequented by artists and scholars from the Chinese mainland and abroad for the cultural exchange. Founded in 1672 (in the early years of the Qing Dynasty), Rong Bao Zhai has a history spanning more than three centuries. It has engaged in the businesses of art supplies (for the "four treasures of the study"), authentic paintings and calligraphy by Chinese art masters, antiques, art collectibles as well as letter and poem paper. Its watercolor woodblock printing technique is also known worldwide. Rong Bao Zhai has many subsidiaries including a publishing house, a Chinese art auction house, and an export trading company.

It has offices in Japan, Hong Kong, Singapore, the U.S., and South Korea.

Chinese publishers specializing in music include the People's Music Publishing House, Shanghai Music Publishing House, and the Hunan Literature & Art Publishing House.

2. Lifestyle Books

Lifestyle books cover fashion, home, cooking, entertainment, games, travel, self-help, health, sports, pets, hobby, collecting, or any subject related to everyday living. As living standards improve quickly, lifestyle books are becoming a fast growing sector.

There are 20,000 different lifestyle titles available in the market. Many lifestyle books have become favorites of the bestseller lists. In the past two years, health books have become quite popular. *Dr. Hong Shaoguang on Health* series by China's famous medical expert Hong Shaoguang has sold over one million copies. Travel is another popular category with all variety of self-guided tour books, travel guides with special themes, and picture travel guides becoming steady sellers. The China Travel & Tourism Press, the country's largest specialized travel publisher, publishes 400 new titles each year alone. Maps and atlases related to tourism and travel are the most popular. The fast growth of the Chinese tourist population, the exponential increase of private car and home ownership, the growing number of people opening up their own businesses, and the growth of overseas travel all have contributed to the demand for maps and atlases. City sightseeing maps, road atlases, and theme maps and atlases have become the three bestsellers in the map and atlas market.

The outstanding performers in this market are the most competitive publishers. Prominent publishers in the lifestyle book market are the China Light Industry Press, Jindun (Golden Shield) Publishing House, Shanghai Scientific and Technical Publishers, Liaoning Science and Technology Press, Jiangsu Science and Technology Publishing House, China Travel & Tourism Press, Guangdong Travel & Tourism Press, People's Medical Publishing House, People's Sports Publishing House, China Textile Press, China Architecture and Building Press, Beijing Sports University Press, China Agriculture Press, and the Beijing Publishing House.

The China Light Industry Press has been a fast growing publisher in recent years. Its sales revenue jumped to RMB230 million in 2001, up from RMB50 million in 1998. Its gross sales, operating revenue and profits have all increased by 60% annually. It has stellar brands in both books and magazines. Its fashion magazine, *Rayli*, licensed from Japan, is the most famous. Its well-known book lines include: *Rayli Pocket Books, Everyone's Gourmet, Road to Health, Everyday Dining, Eating in China, Chinese Crafts*, and *Interior Decoration and Design*. (See also Chapter 3-B.)

Jindun (Golden Shield) Publishing House, affiliated with the General Logistics Department of the People's Liberation Army, is another publisher with stellar performance. On one hand, it fulfils its main mission by serving the needs of the logistics and training divisions of the army and civic service personnel. On the other hand, it targets the mass market, especially readers in small towns and the countryside. It has focused on farmers through titles on the popular sciences and established book series in pragmatic areas such as: health, horticulture, animal husbandry, cooking, sewing, and knitting. It publishes thousands of titles each year with annual gross sales totaling over RMB200 million. Ninety percent of its 3,000 general interest titles get reprinted. On average, each title has a print run of some 100,000 copies. One title on how to rear pigs set the sales record of seven million copies sold. Jindun enjoyed the reputation that "wherever there are rural cooperatives, there are Jindun books." This is a vast rural population with very low purchasing power, but Jindun has achieved great success by mainly serving these rural readers. To achieve such record sales with such a unique publishing line is quite a remarkable feat.

At present, there are 10 publishers specializing in maps and atlases. The leading publishers are the China Atlas Publishing House, Planet Earth Maps Press, Chengdu Atlas Publishing House, the People's Transportation Publishing House, and Guangdong Atlas Press. The China Atlas Publishing House is affiliated with the Chinese National Cartography Bureau and is the largest map and atlas publisher with assets of RMB700 million whose publications account for 80% of the map and atlas market. It has 28 business divisions and branches in Shanghai,

Wuhan and Xi'an along with a number of other business ventures, with a total of 800 employees. In the past five years, its annual gross sales have averaged RMB600 million and its maps and atlases have also been licensed and translated into many other languages and sold abroad.

3. *Children's Books*

In 2002, 7,400 children's titles including 4,200 new titles were published and 2.3 billion copies were sold. Total sales of children's books reached RMB1.5 billion, representing 3.3% of national sales. The Beijing OpenBook Market Consulting Center has estimated that sales of children's books account for 8% of the national retail market. Children's books in the Chinese mainland are sub-classified as children's arts and literature, encyclopedias, cartoons, books for toddlers and beginning readers, books for young readers, books for young adults, children's classics, children's intelligence development, hanging cards, hanging pictures, and handcrafts. The first four categories account for 60–70% of the children's book market.

Generally speaking, children's books are priced quite low. About 55% of children's books are less than RMB10 (about US$1.20) for retail and 30% are priced between RMB10 and 20 (about US$1.20–2.41). Children's books sold in high volumes have an average cover price between RMB6 and 8. In additional to perennially favorite titles, new bestselling children's titles come up every year. For example, *Flower Season, Rainy Season* has sold one million copies in recent years and *Boy Jia Li* and *Girl Jia Mei* have sold 300,000 copies each. Pure children's literature, fiction, stories, fairy tales, classics, and science fiction titles can all become bestsellers. Children's publishing companies have also acquired the rights of many foreign titles, which have further diversified the sector. The *Harry Potter* series acquired by the People's Literature Publishing House has sold five million copies in Chinese translation. The *Goose Bumps* series acquired by Jieli Publishing House sold 260,000 copies in Chinese translation. Nonetheless, there exist some problems in children's book publishing, primarily the insufficient number of native Chinese authors, duplicated book titles, staggering growth, and market disorder caused by price wars. For example, there are 349 editions of the *Tales of Hans Christian Andersen* and 500 editions of *Ten Thousand Whys*.

In the Chinese mainland, there are 30 publishers specializing in children's books. There are also 3,000 editors and an equal number of professional writers for children's books. The leading children's publishers are the China Children Publishing House, Juvenile and Children Publishing House, Zhejiang Children's Books Publishing House, Jieli Publishing House, Jiangsu Juvenile and Children's Publishing House, Tomorrow Publishing House, Sichuan Children's Publishing House, Hunan Juvenile and Children's Publishing House, 21st Century Publishing House, and Anhui Juvenile Publishing House. In recent years, more publishers have entered into the area of young adult publishing. People's Literature Publishing House, Jilin Fine Arts Publishing House, Zhejiang Education Publishing House, and Children's Fun Publishing Co., Ltd. (a Sino-foreign joint venture) are the newcomers with impressive performance. China Children Publishing House, Juvenile and Children Publishing House, and Zhejiang Youth Publishing House have the broadest back catalogs and each of them have 1,000 titles in print. These three are top ranked in both unit and RMB sales for children's books. Jiangsu Juvenile and Children's Publishing House, Sichuan Children's Publishing House, Tomorrow Publishing House, and Jieli Publishing House all have annual gross sales surpassing RMB200 million. Zhejiang Children's Books Publishing House and Jieli Publishing House are the leaders in children's publishing.

The China Children's Press & Publication Group (CCPPG) is the only publishing group specializing in children's books and has the largest scale and scope in children's publishing. It is affiliated with Central Committee of the Communist Youth League. CCPPG publishes 1,000 titles annually in the form of printed books, audio, visual and multimedia publications with annual gross sales surpassing RMB400 million.

CCPPG owns the China Children's Fun Publishing House,

five juvenile newspapers including the *Chinese Teenagers' News*, the *Chinese Teenagers' News City Kids Edition, China Children's News, China Middle School Student News, China Children's Pictorial*, and 10 periodicals including the *Middle School Student, We Love Science, Children's Literature, Chinese Children, Toddler Pictorial, Infant Pictorial, Chinese Teenage Readers Digest* and *China Cartoons*. It also has a website (www.ccppg.com.cn). CCPPG also plays a leading role in the China Children's Newspaper & Periodical Professionals Association, the China Children's Publications Working Committee and the Chinese Board on Books for Young People.

The Chinese mainland has 360 million people aged 18 years and below, of which 300 million are below 14 years of age. The population of those 18 and younger in the Chinese mainland surpasses the entire population of the United States. According to publishing experts, children's book revenues are expected to double over the next 10 years, reaching RMB3 billion. Therefore, children's book publishing should have great potential for growth in the years to come.

4. Books on Social Sciences and Popular Sciences

In 2002, about 45,000 titles were published in the Chinese mainland on philosophy, politics, economics, military affairs, languages, history, geography, and education. Annual sales of social science books are RMB3.2 billion, accounting for 7% of total book sales. If professional books are excluded, the market share of social science books would be reduced.

There are 60 publishers specializing in social science books. The most well-known social science publishers are SDX Joint Publishing Co., Ltd., People's Publishing House, China Social Science Publishing House, Peking University Press, Shanghai People's Publishing House, Academia Press, China Renmin University Press, Guangdong People's Publishing House, Jiangsu People's Publishing House, Central Party Literature Publishing House, Sichuan People's Publishing House, and Hebei People's Publishing House.

SDX Joint Publishing Co., Ltd. is affiliated with the China Publishing Group. It is headquartered in Beijing with distribution and branches in 10 cities including Shanghai, Zhengzhou, Hangzhou, Jinan, Shenyang, Harbin, Kunming, Nanning, and Nanjing. Its annual title output is 500 with annual sales of RMB80 million. It is best known for its translations of the finest contemporary Western works in philosophy and the humanities. It also publishes similar subjects for laymen, reference books and culturally related titles. SDX Joint Publishing Co., Ltd. is the most prestigious and influential publisher in the social science field. Its magazines, *Du Shu (Reading)*, *SDX Weekly,* and *Music Lovers*, also have great social influence and are regarded as leaders in their categories. *Du Shu (Reading)* is the most popular magazine among Chinese intellectuals.

The People's Publishing House was the first well-known publisher of philosophy and social sciences. It specializes in Marxism, Leninism, Mao Zedong Thought, Deng Xiaoping's Theories, the history of the Communist Party of China, and other social science and related works. It published 360 titles with annual sales of RMB180 million (about US$21.69 million) in 2003. Its magazines *Xinhua (New China) Monthly*, *Xinhua (New China) Digest*, and *People* are all well known among readers.

The Chinese Academy of Social Sciences (CASS) is China's highest research institution for social sciences and is regarded as one of China's leading think-tanks. CASS has five publishing houses: the China Social Sciences Publishing House, China Social Science Documentation Publishing House, Modern China Publishing House, Economics Management Publishing House, and Local Records Publishing House. China Social Sciences Publishing House (CSSP) is the most influential and publishes 400 works per year, many of which are the fruit of the labors of first-rate scholars involved in priority projects of the country and CASS. The most famous academic works include *Modern China Series*, *World Civilization Series, Selected Works of Chinese Social Science Scholars, The New Cambridge Modern History, Translation Series of Foreign Masterpieces on Ethics, Series of Famous Foreign Works on Business Administration*, and *Modern Western Thoughts Series*.

Books on popular science have had modest growth over the last 10 years. According to a research report on popular science publishing from 1990 to 2001 published by GAPP, the Chinese mainland published 25,500 popular science titles over that decade, of which 19,100 were by Chinese authors, (accounting for 75% of the total market), while 6,400 were translations (accounting for 25%). In 2001, 4,400 popular science titles were published with 27.85 million copies sold and earning profits of RMB29.48 million. Most of the popular science books are natural science or technology related. Presently, there are 1,490 popular science editors.

Among all popular science books, medical books rank first, representing 12% of the total, while agriculture titles account for another 10%. In addition, there is a lot of variety in young adult popular science books, including earth studies and environmental titles. The great popular science books published in recent years were the *First Driving Force* series by Hunan Science & Technology Press, the *Finest Works by Science Masters* series by Shanghai Scientific and Technical Publishers, *Library of Thinking Thrice* by Jiangxi Education Publishing House, the *World Famous Labs* Series by Hebei University Publishing House, the *Academician Popular Science* series by Higher Education Press, the *Sciences and Humanities* series by SDX Joint Publishing Co., Ltd., *History of Scientific Discoveries* by Henan Scientific and Technology Publishing House, the *Grand Perspectives on Environments* Series by Shanghai Translation Publishing House, *Outlook of Global Environment* by China Environmental Science Press, *Complete Book of Chinese Organic Living* by Northeast Forestry University Press, *What We Can Do for the Planet Earth* by Guangxi Education Publishing House, and the *Interpretation of Life* series by Beijing Children's Publishing House and Beijing Education Publishing House. The grand-scale *Academician Popular Science* series is completely written by academics of the Chinese Academy of Sciences and Chinese Academy of Engineering.

Publishers making rapid progress in acquiring the translation rights for popular science books are the World Publishing Corporation, Zhejiang Science and Technology Publishing

House, Hunan Science & Technology Press, and Kaiming (Enlightenment) Publishing House. The Hunan Science & Technology Press translated and published works by Stephen W. Hawking to catch the "Hawking fever" in the Chinese mainland in recent years. Illustrated editions of *A Brief History of Time* and *The Universe in a Nutshell* sold 150,000 copies each. The newly acquired *A Brief History of Time* (children's edition) is in translation. Hawking's biographies have also had impressive sales. However, due to the limited budget and shortage of qualified science translators, many excellent foreign popular science books cannot be introduced into the Chinese mainland quickly enough at this point in time.

Half of the popular science titles in the Chinese mainland have print runs below 5,000 copies and only a minority of them have print runs over 10,000 copies.

C. Professional Books

1. Overview

In the Chinese mainland, professional publishing refers to natural sciences (habitually regarded as science and technology), parts of the social sciences, and ancient Chinese classics. Natural science titles typically include titles covering mathematics, physics, chemistry, astronomy, geology, biology, medicine, agriculture, forestry, the environment, industry, and communications. In 2002, 37,940 natural science titles were published, of which 24,500 were new releases. Annual sales of science and technology books were RMB3.5 billion, representing 8% of the total book market. If academic books on social sciences are taken into account, sales of professional books are RMB5 billion to RMB6.5 billion, representing 16% of the total sales.

To encourage scientific and technological development and to promote professional book publishing, China has set up a National Book Foundation for academic works on science and technology. The highest grant of RMB10,000 is awarded to academic, fundamental theory, and applied technology works.

Some local governments and publishers have also established similar academic awards and book grants.

The well-known professional publishers in science and technology are China Science Publishing Group, Publishing House of Electronics Industry, People's Posts and Telecommunications Publishing House, People's Medical Publishing House, Tsinghua University Press, China Architecture & Building Press, China Machine Press, China Communications Press, China Cartographic Publishing House, Shanghai Scientific and Technical Publishers, and Jiangsu Science and Technology Publishing House. (See Figure 2.6.)

The China Science Publishing Group is affiliated with the Chinese Academy of Sciences. It is the largest comprehensive professional publishing group that specializes in science and technology. Its subsidiaries include the Science Press, Beijing Hope Computer Co., Beijing Kehai High Technology Corp., China Science and Technology University Press, and China National Sci-Tech Information Beijing Co. It publishes books and journals by Chinese and foreign authors on sciences and

Figure 2.6

Top Science and Technology Publishers with Sales Over
RMB100 million in 2002

Rank	Publisher	Sales*
1	China Cartographic Publishing House	285
2	Science Press	284
3	Tsinghua University Press	280
4	China Light Industry Press	252
5	People's Medical Publishing House	245
6	China Machine Press	211
7	Planet Cartographic Publishing House	164
8	Publishing House of Electronics Industry	157
9	China Architecture & Building Press	132
10	Shanghai Scientific & Technical Publishers	123
11	People's Posts and Telecommunications Publishing House	109
12	Jiangsu Science and Technology Publishing House	103

millions of RMB

technology, operations management, and basic scientific theories. Its publications also cover popular science, reference materials, and encyclopedias. At present, Science Press publishes 2,000 titles a year and 180 journals, including 29 in foreign languages. In 2003, its sales were RMB740 million (about US$89.16 million). It has branches in Shanghai, Wuhan, Shenyang, Changchun, Chengdu, and Shenzhen. It also has a full press operation in New York, which is the only overseas publishing operation set up by a publishing house from the Chinese mainland. The All China Scientific and Technological Terms Examination and Approval Committee and the Scientific Publishing Foundation Committee of the Chinese Academy of Sciences are both part of this publishing group.

Chinese classics are a unique part of Chinese book publishing. China is not only one of the oldest ancient civilizations, but also one of the few nations whose civilization has been continuously sustained from pre-history until the present. There are between 100,000 and 150,000 ancient Chinese books still preserved to this day. Classifying these ancient books and historical records has become a unique and important task of the publishing industry. At present, 500 of these classic titles are reissued each year. There are 22 publishing houses and 600 editors specializing in this area. The most prestigious classics publisher is the Zhonghua Book Company. The central government has a National Chinese Classics Classification and the Publication Planning Committee, whose office is affiliated with the GAPP. Each year, the government allocates special funds to catalog and publish ancient Chinese books. The most important classics that have been classified and published are: *The Complete Collection of the Oracle Bone Inscriptions, The Great Tripitaka of China, Yong Le Encyclopedia, The Complete Four Treasures, The Collection of Documents on Dunhuang Grottoes and Turpan, The Complete Collection of Song Dynasty Poems*, and *Historical Records of the Qing Dynasty*.

In addition, a significant number of books on traditional Chinese medicine and military strategy have been published. The English and Chinese editions of the *Library of Chinese*

Classics series, which is soon to be published, is the first comprehensive and systematic introduction of Chinese classics to the world.

2. *Engineering and Computer Books*

As computers become increasingly popular, computer books have become one of the fastest growing book categories over the past 10 years. The number of computer books for both professional and general readers has increased by a large margin both in variety and market share. At present, there are 25,000 to 29,000 computer titles available on the market. Multimedia, Internet, programming, software guides, and basic computer science are the major subjects in the computer books market. The leading publishers specializing in information technology include the Publishing House of Electronics Industry, People's Posts and Telecommunications Publishing House, China Machine Press, Tsinghua University Press, Hope Electronics Press, China Youth Press, China Waterpower Press, Science Press, Peking University Press, and Higher Education Press. The Publishing House of Electronics Industry is the most influential publisher in this field. It is affiliated with the Ministry of Information Industry and is also the first publisher in the Chinese mainland that has adopted the ISO 9000 quality control system. It mainly publishes books and textbooks on communication technology, journals on electronic and telecommunication technology, and books in electronic format. It also engages in other business ventures such as online publishing and network communications as well as information technology teaching and training programs. Its publishing range not only encompasses all the various subjects of information technology but also covers transportation, business and economics, foreign languages, and other fields. In 2001, it published 900 titles in print editions and 350 titles in electronic format with sales reaching RMB320 million.

Machine building and architecture are other major areas of professional publishing. Major publishers in this field are China Machine Press, China Architecture and Building Press, China

Communications Press, Beijing Institute of Technology Press, China National Defense Industry Press, Liaoning Science and Technology Press, Shanghai Scientific and Technical Publishers, and China Building Material Press. China Machine Press is the leader of this field. It publishes books on mechanical engineering, automobile engineering, electrical engineering, electronics, instrument making, automation, computer technology, and business and management. It publishes 1,000 titles a year and has published 15,000 titles since its inception with annual sales of about RMB300 million. China Architecture and Building Press is the largest professional architecture publisher with an output of 1,600 titles a year. Its headquarters is in Beijing and it has branches in Shanghai and Guangzhou. It has a competitive distribution network and has its own chain stores in Beijing, Shanghai, and Guangzhou as well as its own online bookstore.

3. Medical Books

Medical books account for a large proportion of natural science titles. At present, 7,100 medical titles are published each year, second only to engineering and electronics titles in the total output of professional books with annual sales of RMB1 billion. Medicine, preventive medicine, and pharmaceutical titles are the top selling categories. Clinical medicine, illustrated plates, medical textbooks, and medical test guides are all important as well.

The print run for medical books is small. Generally, the first print run is 3,000–5,000 copies, and for some titles, the initial print run can be as low as 1,000–2,000 copies. Except for medical textbooks, it is very rare for a medical title to have over 10,000 copies printed. But medical books are priced much higher than general books, therefore, RMB revenues for medical books are considerable. To take the four-volume *Campbell's Operative Orthopedics, 9th edition*, for example, rights for the Chinese edition were acquired and it was published by Shandong Science and Technology Press in February 2001. It is priced at RMB980 (US$118.07). The original English edition was priced at US$480, about four times the price of the Chinese edition. Normally, the average U.S. cover price is 10 times the price of a Chinese edition. Science Press published the English reprint edition with the cover price of RMB734 (about US$88), which is one-fifth the cost of the original U.S. edition.

In recent years, the rights to more and more foreign medical titles have been acquired. Chinese medical publishers have a special interest in books on the latest medical technologies that are much needed, such as books on MRI and PTCA. For example, the *Illustrated PTCA* was licensed from Japan by China Science and Technology Press. In addition, Chinese publishers are also interested in books on medical practices and those written by international medical authorities such as *Cecil's Textbook of Medicine, Williams Obstetrics,* and *Campbell's Operative Orthopedics.*

At present, there are six million medical professionals in the Chinese mainland and medical colleges plan to increase enrolment. Therefore, medical books have great market potential.

There are about 50 Chinese publishers engaging in medical publications, a dozen of which are the leading professional medical publishers, such as the People's Medical Publishing House, People's Military Medical Press, China Medico-Pharmaceutical Science & Technology Publishing House, Peking University Medical Press, China Press of Traditional Chinese Medicine, Peking Union Medical College Press, People's Military Medical Press, and Second Military Medical University Press. In addition, some science and technology presses and a few trade publishers have also published a good number of medical books. The important players include Science Press, Shanghai Scientific and Technical Publishers, Jiangsu Science and Technology Publishing House, Liaoning Science and Technology Press, Shandong Science and Technology Press, Zhejiang Science and Technology Press, Hunan Science and Technology Press, Tianjin Science and Technology Press, Tianjin Science & Technology Translation Company, Beijing Science and Technology Press, Shanghai Scientific and Technological

Literature Publishing House, and Jindun (Golden Shield) Publishing House. The People's Medical Publishing House alone captures half of the medical book market while the rest take 20% of the market share.

People's Medical Publishing House is affiliated with the Ministry of Heath. It is the largest and most competitive and diversified medical publishing house in the market. It publishes academic medical works, medical textbooks, medical reference books and popular medical science titles ranging from modern medicine and pharmacology to traditional Chinese medicine. Its publishing programs are comprehensive and include titles on all imaginable medical subjects. As of 2002, People's Medical Publishing House had 500 different medical textbooks available, of which 60 textbooks were for modern medical education courses and 70 were named as the key textbooks by the Ministry of Education and as textbooks of national excellence. Its *Internal Medicine, Surgery, Obstetrics & Gynecology, Pediatrics, Anatomy & Embryology*, and *Physiology* titles have print runs of over 1.5 million copies each. Some of its medical textbooks went through many revisions and have become time-honored course books in the Chinese mainland. Over the past 50 years, People's Medical Publishing House has published 20,000 books and printed 67 million copies, with 1,000 titles published and 10 million copies distributed each year. Its current annual sales have surpassed RMB500 million (US$60.24 million).

4. Business and Law Books

Business and law books for professionals (excluding those for general readers) do not have a big market in the Chinese mainland. According to an estimate by the Beijing OpenBook Market Consulting Center, business and law books, including those for general readers, accounted for only 8% of the retail book market.

Among the professional business books, accounting, taxation, finance, medical insurance, and management titles sell well. For example, *Tax Planning, Tax Exemption Cases,*

Solutions to Complicated Tax Issues, Intermediate Accounting, and *Intermediate Investment* are popular titles. Business textbooks also have substantial sales followed by business-related standardized test guides. As the Chinese mainland implements an annual national test for registered accountants, study guides on accounting and taxation have taken a more important position. Test guides and supplementary readings on accounting, taxation, auditing, and economics have impressive sales. Books on personal finance such as investment guides, have the largest retail market share among all business books.

The important business book publishers are the China Financial & Economic Publishing, China Financial Publishing House, Economic Science Press, Economic Management Press, China Taxation Press, Peking University Press, Tsinghua University Press, China Renmin University Press, Dongbei University of Finance and Economics Press, Shanghai University of Finance and Economics Press, and Li Xin Accounting Press. China Financial & Economic Publishing House and the six university presses mentioned above dominate the business textbook market for higher education. Imported business textbooks including reprint editions are very popular and many of them are preferred over similar Chinese books.

Personal finance for general readers always hold an important position. There are over 300 titles on various topics of stocks available on the market. At the Beijing Book Building, the largest bookstore in the country, 200 personal finance titles are on display. It is estimated that if each personal finance title has a print run of 30,000 copies, two in ten stock investors will own a stock investment guide.

Books on law and politics are regarded as one category. In 2002, the Chinese mainland published 7,100 titles on law and politics, of which 5,400 were new titles. There are 112 million copies of law and politics books in print with a retail value of RMB1.77 billion. 3,550 titles on law with a total retail value of RMB885 million was published each year.

Law books in the Chinese mainland can be sub-categorized into legal theory, legal practice, legal documents, and legal text guides. Outside legal theory, all the other three sub-categories account for the largest percentage of the legal book market.

The most well-known law book publishers are the Law Press, China Legal Publishing House, The People's Court Press, China University of Political Science and Law Press, China Democratic and Legal Publishing House, China Prosecution Press, China Fang Zheng Press, Peking University Press, China Renmin University Press, Jilin People's Publishing House, Higher Education Press, and Chinese People's Public Security University Press.

Law Press is the largest and most influential publisher of legal titles. It publishes in seven areas: legal documents, case law, legal education, legal academic research, law testing, general law, and legal journals. It owns China's first Attorney Club, along with the China Law Book Co., Ltd. and a comprehensive online legal bookstore. Law Press publishes 600 titles each year, with annual sales of RMB100 million (US$12.05 million) and annual pre-tax operating profits of RMB30 million (US$3.61 million), has dominated the legal book market for years.

As the Chinese mainland builds its legal system, an interest in law books has grown steadily each year and this market is expected to continue to expand. Medical doctors and lawyers are part of the high-income class, therefore, law and medical books are priced relatively high. Some law and business book publishers hold trade fairs in Beijing each January to promote books and provide consolidated order services to their distributors.

D. Educational Publishing

1. *Overview*

Educational publishing constitutes the largest industry segment in terms of market share. In 2002, more than 25,800 textbooks were published, of which 8,163 were new titles. There were 11,995 textbooks for the college level and higher, accounting for 46% of all textbooks published. Primary and secondary (including high school and secondary vocational) schoolbooks took second place with 8,260 textbooks published. Textbooks and teaching materials for vocational schools and continuing education ranked third. Textbooks generate a whopping revenue of RMB20 billion (US$2.41 billion). College and secondary/ higher vocational school textbooks contribute to RMB3 billion (US$361.45 million) in revenue, representing 15% of the educational book market. Ninety-three percent of the 568 publishers in the Chinese mainland participated in the publication of teaching and study guides to grab a share of this huge market.

Figure 2.7
Size of Educational Book Categories

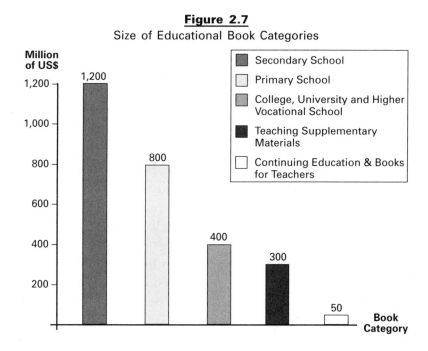

In addition to textbooks, teaching guides and supplementary materials also have a large market. According to an estimate by the Beijing OpenBook Market Consulting Center, 13,300 new teaching guides and supplementary materials were published in 2001, with a total of 66,720 different ones available in the market in the same year. Education and university presses are the main forces in publishing reference, teaching supplements, and study-related books. The active players in this section are the Longman Book Company, Jilin Educational Publishing House, Shaanxi Normal University Press, Northeast Normal University Press, Guangxi Normal University Press, Beijing Normal University Press, and Jiangsu Education Publishing House.

Educational publishers can be classified into three categories: those affiliated with the Ministry of Education such as the Higher Education Press and Educational Science Press; those affiliated with the provincial government such as the educational publishing house in each province; and those affiliated with universities such as the university presses. Of these, provincial educational publishing houses hold a very important and special position.

Each province has one education publishing house that is responsible for publishing textbooks as well as teaching and study guides for its province. In the old days of the planned economy, these houses did very well by publishing, printing and distributing textbooks and teaching and study aids to meet local demand on a monopolistic basis. Some provincial educational publishers have accumulated assets well above hundreds of millions RMB and have enjoyed far better earnings than publishers in other sectors, making them the richest publishers historically. Even today, educational publishers in Jiangsu, Zhejiang, Guangdong, Anhui, Shandong, Fujian, Hebei, Shanghai, Hubei, Shanxi, and Liaoning provinces still enjoy handsome annual gross sales in the hundreds of millions RMB. With the transformation to a market economy, many of the preferential policies enjoyed by the provincial educational publishers are gradually being phased out, decreasing their market share. Those who could not adapt to the market economy are losing ground. However, some who altered their publishing strategies in a timely fashion and who were reactive to the market changes have become competitive players. The publishers who have fared well are the Hebei Education Press, Liaoning Education Press, Hubei Education Press, and Jiangsu Education Publishing House.

2. *Higher Education and University Presses*

Higher education publishing is a sector that is considered to be closest to a market economy and is least restricted, enjoying the fastest growth in recent years. There are 16 million college students, with another 4.5 million students in community colleges, schools for continuing education, and vocational schools. According to the Chinese mainland's five-year development plan, the number of college students in campuses throughout the country is to reach 16–17 million by 2005. This number does not include the students in community colleges. At present, the annual RMB sales of college textbooks is RMB2.5 billion. By 2005, sales are expected to be higher still.

The leading higher education publishers are the Higher Education Press, Foreign Language Teaching and Research Press, Tsinghua University Press, Shanghai Foreign Language Education Press, China Renmin University Press, Peking University Press, and Publishing House of Electronics Industry. All these publishers have achieved annual sales of over RMB100 million and the first six have topped RMB300 million.

The Higher Education Press is affiliated with the Ministry of Education and is the most powerful establishment in the higher education publishing market with assets of RMB1 billion (US$120.48 million). With huge annual gross sales of RMB1 billion, it dwarfs all the other 568 Chinese educational publishers targeting the college segment. It ranks first in both sales revenues and sales of college textbooks in seven disciplines: foreign languages (mostly English), business, electronics, science and engineering, law, humanities, and public health and medicine. The Higher Education Press was founded in 1954 and has published 30,000 textbook titles since 1978 with a current annual title output of 3,800. It has printed 90 million books in total. At present, the Higher Education Press has reached an agreement with three university presses, including Zhongshan University Press, to form the Higher Education Publishing Group.

Figure 2.8
Organizational Structure of the Higher Education Publishing Group

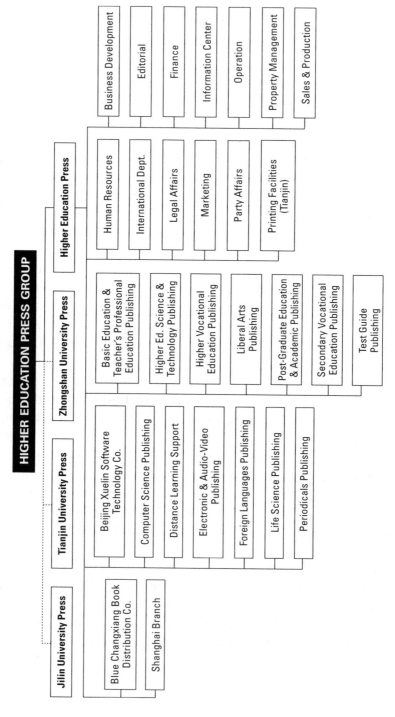

If the deal goes through, the new organization is expected to become one of the most competitive publishing groups in the Chinese mainland.

There are more than 1,000 universities in the Chinese mainland. Among 101 university presses, 24 are affiliated with leading national universities, and 77 are attached to local universities. Unlike their U.S. and U.K. not-for-profit counterparts, these university presses operate as profit centers just as commercial presses. However, with the exception of a dozen, the revenue level of a typical university press is well below the book industry's average. Among the 50 publishers surpassing RMB100 million in revenue, only 14 are university presses. These top performers are the Foreign Language Teaching and Research Press, Tsinghua University Press, Shanghai Foreign Language Education Press, People's Education Press, Guangxi Normal University Press, Fudan University Press, Peking University Press, China Central Radio and Television University Press, East China Normal University Press, South West Normal University Press, and Shaanxi Normal University Press.

The Tsinghua University Press publishes 2,000 titles in printed books, audio, and electronic formats annually, of which 800 are new titles. It has 1,200 sales outlets throughout the country, annual unit sales have reached RMB13 million, and annual gross revenues have surpassed RMB400 million. Its *C++ Programing Design* has cumulative sales of four million copies, setting a new record for science and technology titles.

In addition, Tsinghua University Press has acquired the reprint rights for 200 foreign titles each year. It has a long history of publishing reprints of original textbooks in varying disciplines. The Beijing Normal University Press is another impressive performer among the university presses with an annual output of 340 titles and gross sales of RMB300 million.

3. Elementary and High School

The elementary and high school (ELHI) textbook publishing market totals RMB17 billion, representing 40% of national book sales revenues. In 2002, 12,000 kinds of ELHI textbooks, reference books, after-class and home schooling materials were published, of which 3,530 were high school textbooks and 4,730 were elementary school textbooks. At present, there are nearly 218 million ELHI students, of which 122 million are elementary school students and 95.96 million are high school students. The market for high school books is 50% larger than that of elementary school books. According to China's education laws, nine years of free education is universally provided.

The state sets up national committees to examine and approve the ELHI textbooks compiled by various publishers. Any unit or group that wish to publish ELHI textbooks for those in the national nine-year free compulsory education system must submit their plans to the provincial education bureau for a feasibility review. Upon provincial approval, the proposal must be submitted to the Ministry of Education's Committee for ELHI Textbooks for validation. The People's Education Press, leading national universities, science and research units at the ministry level, and national academic bodies can directly submit their complete sets of ELHI textbooks to the Ministry of Education for evaluation. Approved textbooks can then be published and distributed nationwide. At present, six complete series of ELHI textbooks have been adopted nationwide and over 75 single-subject ELHI textbooks are in use.

There are three major ELHI textbook developers in the Chinese mainland. The first are the provincial textbook research units such as the Jiangsu Provincial Teaching and Research Committee and the Hebei Teaching Science Academy. The second are course research and development units established by normal universities (e.g. the Textbook Writing and Compiling Committee of Beijing Normal University Course Center). The third are schoolbook publishers such as the People's Education Press and Yu Wen Press. Developing a single textbook requires a RMB50,000–80,000 initial investment. The central government has final control over the list price and the profits of ELHI textbooks. A publisher cannot earn more than 5% profit nor can it include the initial investment in their pricing calculations.

As the restrictions for textbook development are now being relaxed, more and more publishers are jumping on the bandwagon. People's Education Press is the leader with 50 years of experience in ELHI textbook development and publishing. It is affiliated with the Ministry of Education and is primarily engaged in research on curricula, writing, compiling, publishing, and distributing general textbooks, textbooks of specific subjects, and related material. Before 1996, the People's Education Press participated in developing the syllabi of all ELHI subjects and has compiled and published nine series of national ELHI textbooks. It has millions of readers and has printed tens of billions of textbooks. Its publishing scope encompasses textbooks for kindergarten, elementary and high schools to colleges and universities, and textbooks and related materials for vocational schools, special education, secondary education for adults, and ELHI teachers' training materials. It also owns printing factories and the China Educational Publications Import & Export Corporation. It publishes 1,000 titles a year and has annual revenues approaching RMB1.2 billion, the highest among all publishers. Beijing Normal University Press, Jiangsu Education Publishing House, and the East China Normal University Press also have performed solidly in developing ELHI textbooks. Teaching materials catering to local needs are primarily published by provincial educational publishers.

4. Foreign Language and Reference Books

As part of the overall educational book market, reference and language learning books have a substantial share. Over the past 50 years, there have been 10,000 dictionaries published. Famous language and reference books include the *Encyclopedia of China* by Encyclopedia of China Publishing House, *Ci Hai* (Chinese Idioms) by Shanghai Encyclopedia Publishing House, *Ci Yuan* (Word Origins), *The English-Chinese Dictionary*, *Xinhua Dictionary*, and *Modern Chinese Dictionary* by The Commercial Press. The concise *Xinhua Dictionary* has sold over 300 million copies and the medium sized *Modern Chinese Dictionary* has sold 40 million copies, both outselling any other dictionary in the same category. *Xinhua Chinese Dictionary* is regarded as the most saleable book after the *Holy Bible*. At present, there are 20 dictionary and reference publishers publishing 500 reference titles annually.

Language reference books represent the largest share of the reference book market. The best-known reference publishers are The Commercial Press, Shanghai Lexicographical Publishing House, Encyclopedia of China Publishing House, and Sichuan Lexicographical Publishing House.

Figure 2.9
Night View of The Commercial Press

The publishing house with the longest history in China: The Commercial Press. *(Photo provided by The Commercial Press)*

The Commercial Press was founded in 1897 in Shanghai and is the oldest Chinese publishing house. In the 1930s, it was the largest publishing company in Asia and the powerhouse of China's educational and academic publishing. In 1954, The Commercial Press moved to Beijing. Over the past 100 years, The Commercial Press has published 30,000 titles. At present, it engages mainly in the translation and publication of academic works on philosophy and social sciences and compiling and publishing dictionaries and linguistic reference books. It also publishes research works, textbooks, and popular titles as side ventures. Its *World's Best Known Academic Works* is the most extensive and influential series of foreign philosophy and social sciences published in Chinese in the past 50 years. The Commercial Press publishes 200 titles per year and its retail sales reached RMB400 million (US$48.19 million) in 2002. The now independent Commercial Presses of Hong Kong, Taipei, Singapore, and Kuala Lumpur were all subsidiaries of The Commercial Press in Shanghai before 1949.

The Chinese mainland is not only a country with the largest Chinese-speaking population, but it is also the country with the largest English-learning population. At present, the number of English learners has surpassed 30 million with some elementary and high schools adopting bilingual education. Shanghai plans to train 10,000 bilingual teachers, adopt bilingual education in 500 schools, and provide bilingual education to 500,000 students. As the Chinese mainland continues to open to the world, the learners of foreign languages, especially English, will increase more rapidly.

English learning books are the fastest growing sector of the educational book market. At present, English learning books make up 6–8% of the retail book market. Basic English, dictionaries and test guides are the three major components of English learning books. Among the 560 publishers, 80% have published books in English, and a number have become great foreign language presses. The most important publishers in this area are the Foreign Language Teaching and Research Press (FLTRP), Shanghai Foreign Language Education Press, The Commercial Press, and World Publishing Corporation. In addition, the Foreign Languages Press, Shanghai Translation Publishing House, Higher Education Press, China Renmin University Press, World Affairs Press, Shanghai Jiao Tong University Press, and Tsinghua University Press also have a good share in the English language book market.

FLTRP founded by the Beijing Foreign Studies University is the most famous university press in China. It primarily publishes textbooks, dictionaries, and teaching guides and supplementary materials in foreign languages along with several periodicals. At present, FLTRP has assets of RMB500 million, a 80,000 square meter distribution center valued at RMB300 million, and 15 information centers across the country. It publishes 1,600 titles annually and in 2002 had gross sales reaching RMB800 million (US$96.39 million). The state-of-the-art FLTRP office building with a floor space of 17,000 square meters is named one of the "Top 10 New Buildings in Beijing" in the 1990s and is regarded as a landmark for the book publishing industry. The Shanghai Foreign Language Education Press has also shown remarkable performance with annual sales of RMB400 million.

Figure 2.10
FLTRP Office Building

(Photo provided by FLTRP)

Magazine Publishing in the Chinese Mainland

A. Brief Introduction to Magazine Publishing

1. Overview

According to the statistics provided by the General Administration of Press and Publication (GAPP), by the end of 2002 there was a total of 9,029 magazine titles published. The average print run was 20,406 copies per issue and the total print run was 2.951 billion copies, i.e. two copies per capita. Magazine advertising revenue reached approximately RMB2.65 billion (US$319.28 million), an average based on the official figure of RMB1.5 billion to RMB3.8 billion, the estimate of the Beijing Hui Cong Media Research Center. Although magazine publishing in the Chinese mainland is a relatively big industry, it still lags behind established magazine publishing industries and compares strongly only with other developing countries. Nevertheless, the Chinese mainland's magazine market is growing with impressive speed.

Magazines are generally divided into seven categories based on coverage, such as natural sciences (science and technology), philosophy and social sciences, cultural and educational, literature and art, children's, pictorial, and general interest magazines. (See Figure 3.1.) Natural sciences magazines are the most numerous, with 4,457 titles in 2002, accounting for about 49.4% of the total. The other six categories of magazines ranked in descending order are: philosophy and social sciences magazines (2,318 titles, about 25.7%), cultural and educational magazines (about 957 titles, about 10.6%), general interest magazines (547 titles, about 6%), literature and art magazines (539 titles, about 6%), children's magazines (149 titles, about 1.7%), and pictorial magazines (62 titles, about 0.7%). A quarter of these magazines are published by national publishers and the others by regional publishers.

Of the seven categories, children's magazines have the largest average print run with nearly 167,200 copies per issue, 110,000 copies more than general magazines which rank second. The average print numbers for other magazines is 53,200 copies per issue for general interest, 31,900 for cultural and educational, 29,800 for philosophy and social sciences, 29,300 for literature and art, 14,200 for pictorial, and 7,500 for natural sciences.

Monthly magazines are the most common. Of the various types of magazines such as the monthly, the bimonthly, the biweekly, the 10-day periodical, the weekly and the quarterly,

Figure 3.1

Seven Magazine Categories in the Chinese Mainland

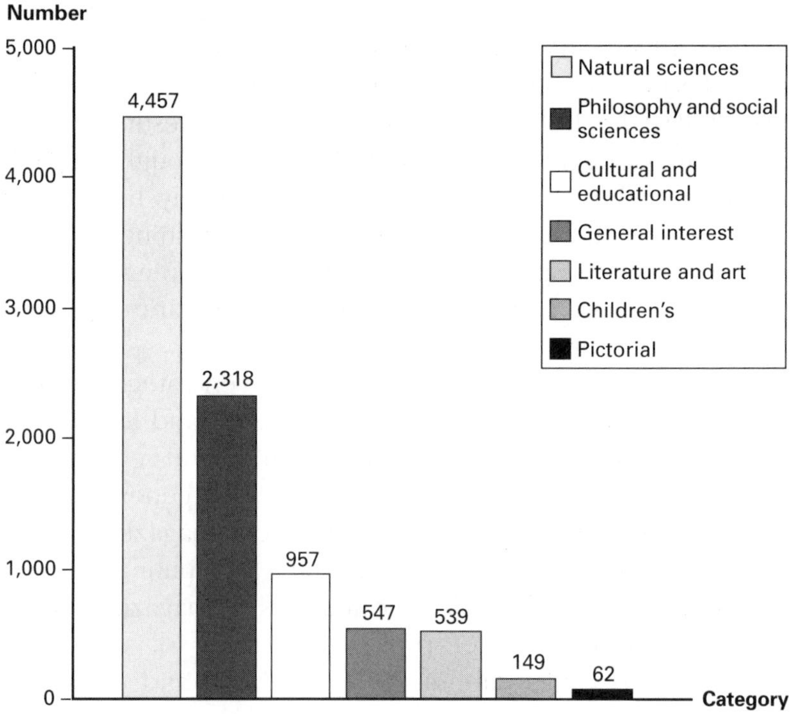

Source: *GAPP*

the monthly magazine is most popular with 3,094 titles, accounting for 34.3% of total magazine publications. This is followed by the bimonthly and quarterly, which account for 30.9% and 26.3% of the total. In major cities, TV and news weeklies are becoming more popular, while entertainment and leisure magazines still mostly have a monthly print cycle.

Publishing capacity varies in different regions. Generally speaking, big cities and coastal regions are well developed and take the lead in many aspects such as editing, distributing, and printing. Well-developed regions include Beijing, Guangdong, Shanghai, Hubei, Liaoning, Shandong, Henan, Anhui, Zhejiang, and Jiangsu; of which Beijing, Shanghai, Guangdong, and Shanghai are the strongest.

The Beijing region is the national center of politics and culture and ranks first both in the number of magazines and circulation volume. There are more than 2,370 magazines based in Beijing with a total printing volume of more than 809 million copies, accounting for 26.7% and 27.9%, respectively, of the national total. Of the 133 magazines with an average print run of over 250,000, 39 are published in Beijing, accounting for nearly one-third of the total. Thirty-eight of these are produced by national publishers.

Outside Beijing, Guangdong and Shanghai boast the strongest publishing capacity, producing 351 and 616 magazines respectively, ranking third and second. Guangdong magazines have a total average print run of 15.84 million, with the Shanghai magazines weighing in at 14.12 million copies, ranking second and third respectively. Of the 133 magazines with an average print run of over 250,000, 11 are based in Guangdong and 6 in Shanghai, ranking second and sixth respectively. Five Guangdong magazines have an average print run exceeding one million. More importantly, most popular magazines in Guangdong and Shanghai are commercial magazines subscribed to or bought by individuals, with a few distributed through industrial distribution channels. Prominent magazines in Guangdong and Shanghai are *Gu Shi Hui* (*Stories*), *Jia Ting* (*Family*), *Ren Zhi Chu* (*The Origins of People*), *Family Doctor*,

Foshan Literature and Art, Shaonan Shaonu (Teenagers), Shanghai Gushi (Shanghai Stories), Gushi Dawang (King of Stories), Shanghai Style, and *Shanghai TV.*

In an effort to encourage the publication of excellent magazines, the government and trade organizations have established various periodical awards, of which the National Periodical Award offered by GAPP is the most prestigious. Other major awards are the National Excellent Social Sciences Periodical Award, the National Excellent Sciences and Technology Periodical Award, and the 100 Major Social Sciences Periodicals Award. Comprehensive publishing awards at the national level such as the Taofen Publishing Award and the 100 Best Publishers also cover periodical publishers.

Well-known magazine publishing personalities include President and Editor-in-Chief of the Trends Magazines Wu Hong and Liu Jiang, President of *Rayli* Zhao Jiqing, *Nan Feng Chuang (Southwind Through Window)* Editor-in-Chief Qin Shuo, *Cai Jin (Finance and Economy)* Editor-in-Chief Hu Shuli, *SDX Weekly* Editor-in-Chief Zhu Wei, *Zhi Yin (Bosom Friend)* Editor-in-Chief Hu Xunbi, *Modern and Ancient Legends* President Shu Shaohua, *Du Zhe (Reader)* Editor-in-Chief Peng Changcheng, *Stories* Editor-in-Chief He Chengwei, *Chinese National Geography* President Li Quanke, *Women of China* President Han Xiangjing, and Chairman of *The Journal of Chinese Medical Association (Internal Medicine)* You Suning. Private publishers are emerging in the Chinese mainland and some of them have become quite successful.

As well as these mass-distributed magazines, there are about 10,000 in-house magazines or periodicals that mostly belong to various companies and organizations and are distributed internally free of charge. Some of them print a considerable number of copies, such as *Konka News* of the famous electronic enterprise Konka Group, which has a circulation of 300,000 copies. The *Vanke Weekly* of the Vanke Group, also has considerable circulation volume and exerts some national influence.

2. Distribution and Advertising

In terms of distribution channels, magazines in the Chinese mainland can be divided into two categories: the "commercial magazines" which are voluntarily subscribed to or bought by readers in the market, and "non-commercial magazines" which are distributed within an organization or industry. Distribution within an organization or industry is done in three different ways: first, the Ministry of Education requires students to subscribe to certain magazines as supplementary learning materials; second, members of organizations such as the Communist Party of China, the Youth League and trade groups subscribe to their organizational magazines; third, magazine sponsors require subscriptions by members of certain organizations or industries by using higher administrative or executive power. Of the three, the latter two are typically non-market-oriented operations (the subscription fees are mostly covered by public funds), while the first also has the trace of a command economy to some degree. In 2003, the central government adopted severe measures to curtail these practices, and 667 magazines and newspapers, including 395 magazines, went out of business and 94 magazines and newspapers turned to free of charge distribution.

The Post Office acts as a major distribution channel for most magazines. The limitations are obvious, and the major problems include the fact that the Post Office controls the subscription lists. Therefore, the magazine publishers do not know who their subscribers are and are unable to get feedback, and the service quality and capacity of the Post Office is becoming more and more questionable. There are no other well-developed distribution channels and a lack of professional sales agents.

In 2002, there were 133 magazines with an average print run of more than 250,000 per issue and 24 magazines with circulation over 1 million. Of these, *Gu Shi Hui* (*Stories*), *Xiaoxuesheng Daokan* (*Pupil's Journal*), *Ban Yue Tan* (*China Comment*), and *Du Zhe* (*Reader*) have an average print run of

Figure 3.2

Magazines with Circulation More Than One Million Copies in 2002

Rank	Title	Frequency	Circulation ('000)	Category	Price (RMB)	Reader Group	Headquarters Location	Sponsor
1	Gu Shi Hui (Stories)	Monthly	3,450	Pop literature	2.50	Readers in rural areas, pop literature fans	Shanghai	Shanghai Literature & Art General Publishing House
2	Ban Yue Tan (China Comment)	Biweekly	3,200	Current affairs and politics	2.70	Party and government organizations, individuals	Beijing	Xinhua News Agency
3	Shishi (Current Affairs)	Bimonthly	3,000	Current affairs and politics	2.00	Party and government organizations, individuals	Beijing	Publicity Dept., CCCPC
4	Du Zhe (Reader)	Biweekly	2,800	Digest	3.00	Population in cities and towns, similar to that of America's Reader's Digest	Lanzhou, Gansu Province	Gansu People's Publishing House
5	Xiaoxuesheng Daokan (Pupil's Journal)	Monthly	2,280	Education	1.60	Primary school students in Hunan province	Changsha, Hunan Province	Department of Education, Hunan Province
6	Zhi Yin (Bosom Friend)	Biweekly	2,230	Lifestyle	3.50	Female readers	Wuhan, Hubei Province	Hubei Women's Federation
7	Chu Zhong Sheng (Junior High Students)	Monthly	2,210	Education	1.60	Junior high students	Changsha, Hunan Province	Department of Education, Hunan Province
8	Guangdong Zhibu Shenghuo (Guangdong Life in Party branches)	Monthly	1,440	Party	3.00	Party members in Guangdong	Guangzhou, Guangdong Province	Organization Dept. of Guangdong Provincial Party Committee

Source: *GAPP*

Figure 3.2 (Cont'd)

Rank	Title	Frequency	Circulation ('000)	Category	Price (RMB)	Reader Group	Headquarters Location	Sponsor
9	Jia Ting (Family)	Biweekly	1,400	Lifestyle	3.50	Mainly female readers	Guangzhou, Guangdong Province	Guangdong Women's Federation
10	Ren Zhi Chu (The Origins of People)	Monthly	1,400	Lifestyle	4.00	General readers	Guangzhou, Guangdong Province	Guangdong Family Planning Committee
11	Xiaoxuesheng Daodu (Pupil Reading Guide)	Monthly	1,250	Education	2.80	Primary school students	Hefei, Anhui Province	Department of Education, Anhui Province
12	Qingnian Wenzhai (Youth Digest)	Biweekly	1,240	General readers	3.00	Young people	Beijing	China Youth Press
13	Zhongguo Shuiwu (China Tax News)	Monthly	1,230	Trade information	8.00	Tax professionals	Beijing	State Administration of Taxation
14	Dangyuan Tekan (Party Member Special)	Monthly	1,200	Party	2.00	Party branches and individual party members in Liaoning Province	Shenyang, Liaoning Province	CPC Liaoning Provincial Committee
15	Dangdai Xiaoxuesheng (Contemporary Pupil)	Biweekly	1,200	Education	2.20	Primary school students	Jinan, Shandong Province	Shandong Education Press
16	Shaoxian Duiyuan (Young Pioneer)	Monthly	1,160	Education	1.20	Primary school students	Guangzhou, Guangdong Province	Communist Youth League of China Guangdong Provincial Committee

Figure 3.2 (Cont'd)

Rank	Title	Frequency	Circulation ('000)	Category	Price (RMB)	Reader Group	Headquarters Location	Sponsor
17	Xiaoxuesheng Shidai (Pupil Times)	Monthly	1,160	Education	1.80	Primary school students	Hangzhou, Zhejiang Province	Zhejiang Educational Newspaper and Periodical Office
18	Guangdong Di'er Ketang (Guangdong Second Classroom)	Biweekly	1,160	Education	1.00	Primary school students and junior high students	Guangzhou, Guangdong Province	Guangdong Education Magazine House
19	Xiaoxuesheng Tiandi (Pupil's World)	Monthly	1,120	Education	1.50	Primary school students	Wuhan, Hubei Province	Department of Education, Hubei
20	Xiaoxuesheng Bidu (Pupil's Must Read)	Monthly	1,080	Education	1.50	Primary school students	Shijiazhuang, Hebei Province	Hebei Educational Newspaper and Periodical Office
21	Gong Chan Dangyuan (Communist Party Members)	Monthly	1,020	Party	3.00	Party branches and individual party members	Shenyang, Liaoning Province	CPC Liaoning Provincial Committee
22	Nongmin Wenzhai (Peasant's Digest)	Monthly	1,020	Digest	1.80	Peasants, farmers	Beijing	China Rural Periodical Press
23	Qiu Shi (Searching Truth)	Biweekly	1,000	Politics and current affairs	5.80	Party and government leaders. The most influential party and political magazine	Beijing	CPC Central Committee
24	Dang De Shenghuo (The Life of the CPC)	Monthly	1,000	Party	3.00	Party branches and individual party members	Harbin, Heilongjiang Province	CPC Heilongjiang Provincial Committee

over 2 million per issue, with *Gu Shi Hui* (*Stories*) the largest with 3.712 million copies per issue. Over the past 10 years, the total circulation volume of magazines in the Chinese mainland has been almost constant at about 2.8 billion.

Of the magazines listed in Figure 3.2, many of them are distributed within an organization or industry, i.e. "non-commercial" magazines, such as the magazines for primary school students and Communist Party members. The ranking of leading commercial magazines based on free market sales is shown in Figure 3.3.

Currently, there is no true professional reading survey company, but the Business Publication Audit (BPA) has already commenced operations. BPA has authorized Global China (Beijing) Media Consulting Co., Ltd. to be its local agent, conferring newspapers distribution and sales level certificates to publishers, and more than 30 media companies have adopted the BPA protocol.

Magazine advertising takes only a small share of total advertising expenditure. It has never exceeded 3% of the total and lags far behind that spent on TV, newspaper, and radio advertising. The statistics in 2000 provided by the China Advertising Association showed that advertising percentages taken by TV, newspapers, radios, and magazines were 23.7%, 20.6%, 2.2% and 1.6%, respectively. In 2002, magazine advertising was about 2% of total. However in recent years magazine advertising revenue has increased rapidly with an average annual growth rate of 25%. According to Hui Cong Media Research Center, magazine advertising revenue reached RMB4.9 billion (US$590.36 million) in 2003. The magazine categories with the highest advertising revenues are fashion, business, IT, and lifestyle (in descending order).

The seven major categories of magazines can be divided into three groups based on their editorial content and publisher: general magazines, professional magazines, and university journals. General magazines refer to commercial magazines that are totally market-oriented and subscribed to and bought by individual customers. These include literature and art magazines,

Figure 3.3

Commercial Magazines with Circulation Over One Million Copies in 2002

Rank	Title	Year of Establishment	Type	Circulation ('000)	Category	Price (RMB)	Reader Group	Headquarter Location	Sponsor
1	Gu Shi Hui (Storries)	1963	Monthly	3,450	Pop Literature	2.50	Readers in rural areas and pop literature fans	Shanghai	Shanghai Literature & Art General Publishing House
2	Du Zhe (Reader)	1981	Biweekly	2,800	Digest	3.00	Readers mainly in cities and towns, like that of America's Reader's Digest	Lanzhou, Gansu Province	Gansu People's Publishing House
3	Zhi Yin (Bosom Friend)	1985	Biweekly	2,230	Lifestyle	3.50	Female readers	Wuhan, Hubei Province	Hubei Women's Federation
4	Jia Ting (Family)	1982	Biweekly	1,400	Lifestyle	3.50	Mainly female readers	Guangzhou, Guangdong Province	Guangdong Women's Federation
5	Ren Zhi Chu (The Origins of People)	1989	Monthly	1,400	Lifestyle	4.00	General readers	Guangzhou, Guangdong Province	Guangdong Family Planning Committee
6	Qingnian Wenzhai (Youth Digest)	1981	Biweekly	1,240	General readers	3.00	Young people	Beijing	China Youth Press
7	Nongmin Wenzhai (Peasant's Digest)	1984	Monthly	1,020	Digest	1.80	Peasants, farmers	Beijing	China Rural Periodical House

cultural and educational magazines, children's magazines, and pictorial magazines. Professional magazines include social sciences and natural sciences magazines as well as some cultural and educational magazines, and both have small readership. University journals belong to the category of professional magazines but their publishers are very different in structure, and are therefore grouped in a separate category.

3. Major Trends in Magazine Publishing and Major Problems

Magazine publishing in the Chinese mainland has entered into a stage of change and rapid development. Currently, the major features of magazine publishing are the different reader profiles divided by reader groups, the establishment of large publishing groups, investment in many new titles, and increasing cooperation with international companies and adoption of international standards and practices.

The different reader profiles are related to both different reader groups and varying editorial content. Identifying the target reader group has become the primary factor in determining the success of a magazine and, accordingly, editorial content must have focus in order to attract the desired readers. The previous broad reader profiles that had no distinction in age or background no longer apply. For instance, women's magazines currently have different areas of focus such as upmarket fashion, pop culture, and entertainment. Other magazines mirror this pattern. A new trend has emerged, and that is to identify the target reader profile in order to target the right readers.

Another new trend in magazine publishing is the formation of magazine publishing groups. Some well-managed magazines with their own star products have begun to expand their market share by launching new magazines or acquiring others, and thus forming magazine groups. Now there are several magazine publishing companies operating on this scale such as *Jia Ting* (*Family*), *Zhi Yin* (*Bosom Friend*), *Trends*, and *Modern and Ancient Legends*, and some of them have become the leading representatives of the magazine publishing industry. As the market economy continues to develop, this trend will continue.

More commonly, capital from various sources has begun to be invested in magazine publishing. As the state-owned monopoly is broken, capital from other industries and private sources will enter into this market. In addition to media groups, some industrial enterprises have also begun to invest in magazine publishing, such as 999 Group (a famous medicine manufacturer) investing in the *New Weekly* and the Chengcheng Group (a printing and real estate enterprise) investing in *Hope*. Also, it is not uncommon for private companies and individuals to invest in magazines. For instance, Hong Huang has invested in several magazines including *Mingpai Shijie • Le* (*Famous Brand World • Enjoy*), *iLOOK*, and *Seventeen*.

The third trend is that in both investment and management magazine publishers have engaged in international cooperation and have taken the lead among all the different publishing sectors in this respect. Currently, capital from foreign countries, Hong Kong and Taiwan have found their way into magazine publishing with the establishment of joint ventures and alliances. More than 50 magazine titles are now issued with foreign involvement. Many internationally well-known magazines have also published Chinese editions, and some of them have achieved unusual success. Meanwhile, several Chinese magazines have ventured abroad. For example, *Chinese National Geography* launched a Japanese edition, the *Big Front Teeth*, a product of the cooperation between Hong Kong publishers and *Dongfang Wawa* (*Oriental Babies*) of Jiangsu Juvenile Children's Publishing House, has circulation in Hong Kong and Southeast Asia, and *Zhi Yin* (*Bosom Friend*), *Nu You* (*Woman's Friend*), and *Du Zhe* (*Reader*) launched overseas editions in both North America and Australia.

The Chinese mainland's magazine publishing industry also has many problems, of which the most obvious include the lack of sound distribution channels and independent distribution agents. Also, problems lie in that there are insufficient regulations governing competition and service quality of the Post Office needs urgent improvement.

4. Professional Magazines

There are about 7,000 professional magazines now in circulation. Most publishers of these magazines are research institutes and these magazines have small circulations because of their specialized content. These magazines have distribution of between 2,000 and 3,000 copies per issue, with social sciences magazines having a slightly larger circulation than those of the natural sciences. Also, they carry little advertising except for some advertisements regarding professional information.

The 2,300 social sciences magazines cover various disciplines including philosophy, politics, economics, religion, law, history, and archeology; and each of the disciplines generally has more than one magazine. For instance, in history and archeology there are several dozen magazines including *Historical Research, Research on Chinese History, Modern Chinese History Studies, World History, Taiwan Studies, The Western Regions Studies, Dunhuang Studies, Literature and History, Archeology, Cultural Relics,* and *Xun Geng* (*Root-Seeking*).

Prominent social sciences magazines with international influence are *Cultural Relics, Archeology, Dunhuang Studies, Social Sciences in China, Philosophical Research, Confucius Studies, China Tibetology, Tibetan Studies, Qiu Shi* (*Searching Truth*), *Study of the History of CPC, Study of World Religions, Economic Research Journal, Educational Research, Strategy and Management, Zhongguo Junshi Kexue* (*China's Military Science*), *China Legal Science, Zhongguo Yuwen* (*Chinese Language Studies*), *Wenxue Pinglun* (*Literature Review*), and *Journal of the Library Science in China. Xinhua Digest* and *Chinese Social Sciences Digest* are the most authoritative digest magazines.

Cultural Relics was first published in January 1950 and covers cultural relics, archeology, history, ancient characters, art history, and scientific and technological history. As one of the major magazines specializing in cultural relics and archeology in China, it boasts the highest circulation for magazines in this category and ranks first among them in terms of overseas circulation. *Archeology* was first launched in 1955 by the Institute of Archeology, Chinese Academy of Social Sciences and ranks first among archeology magazines. It enjoys overseas distribution to more than 20 countries and regions and has always been the leading Chinese magazine in terms of overseas circulation. *Social Sciences in China*, a bimonthly magazine published by Chinese Academy of Social Sciences since 1979, focuses on presenting the most important research in philosophy and social sciences. The publisher of *Social Sciences in China* also publishes *Social Sciences in China Quarterly* in English and the *Historical Research* bimonthly, the most authoritative magazine on history. It also translates and publishes the *International Social Science Journal*.

There are a great number of natural sciences magazines, accounting for nearly 50% of total magazine titles. In terms of subjects, magazines on industrial technology have the highest number of copies sold, accounting for about 40% of this sector, followed by medicines and hygiene, accounting for 16%, and agriculture, accounting for 13%. In addition, there are some scientific and technological magazines published in the languages of national minorities, accounting for 10–15% of the total number of minority languages magazines.

Many natural sciences magazines have achieved international influence, and prominent ones include *Science in China, Chinese Science Bulletin, Acta Mathematica Sinica, Engineering Science, Engineering Mechanics, China Agricultural Science and Technology, Chinese Medical Journal, Chinese Journal of Surgery, Acta Physiologica Sinica, Acta Botanica Sinica, Chinese Journal of Geophysics, Acta Metallurgica Sinica, Acta Seismologica Sinica, Acta Mechanica Sinica, Journal of China Coal Society, Acta Genetica Sinica, Journal of Population, Environment and Resources in China,* and *Rare Metal Materials and Engineering.*

Many scientific and technological magazines issue English language versions, such as the *Chinese Journal of Aeronautics, Chinese Journal of Chemistry, Chinese Journal of Geochemistry, Chinese Physics Letters, Chinese Journal of Oceanology and Limnology, Journal of Rare Earths,* and *Life Sciences and*

Environmental Sciences. According to the Institute for Scientific Information of the United States, 67 of these magazines had entered the world famous SCI periodical index system by 2001.

Universities and colleges also publish their own journals. Currently, there are about 3,000 various journals, generally divided between both social and natural sciences. Prominent titles include the *Journal of Peking University, Tsinghua Science and Technology, Journal of Nanjing University, Chemical Journal of Chinese Universities*, and the *Journal of Literature, History and Philosophy*.

B. General Interest Magazines I

General interest magazines are the most market-oriented and can be divided into two categories based on the different revenue sources, the first earning the revenues mainly from subscriptions and the other primarily from advertising. Magazines relying on subscription revenue are mostly digests, literature and art magazines, and lifestyle magazines. This category of magazines caters to the interests of ordinary people and carries no specific regional uniqueness. While using the Post Office as their major distribution channel, they also develop their own distribution channels to increase circulation. Social groups with low to middle incomes and students in the cities and towns constitute the bulk of the readers of these magazines. Prominent examples are *Gu Shi Hui (Stories), Du Zhe (Reader), Qingnian Wenzhai (Youth Digest), Zhi Yin (Bosom Friend), Globe*, and *Shang Jie (Business World)*. These magazines do not have a large amount of advertising income and most advertisements are small in size.

The magazines relying on advertising attract mostly readers with middle to high incomes, and the editorial content is more focused and layout more fashionable. With exquisite design and excellent printing, these magazines sell at high prices. Good examples of this type of magazines are *Cosmopolitan, Rayli, Fortune* (China), and *Auto Magazine*. Advertisements in these magazines display images of excellent quality and an exquisite style and are mostly full page.

Magazines can be further classified into sub-categories including fashion and style, business, electronic information, lifestyle, news and digest (learning), of which fashion and style, business, and news are the most popular.

1. Female Fashion Magazines

In recent years, fashion magazines have had the fastest growth and the greatest impact. The women's magazine market has had the greatest expansion since most of these fashion magazines focus on topics of interest to women and attract female readers. Well-known women's fashion magazines include *Rayli*, *Trends Cosmopolitan*, *Elle* (China), *Hong* (*Madame Figaro*), *Marie Clarie* (China), *Shanghai Style*, *Hope*, and *Shape*. The *China Book Business Report*, based on its survey of publishers, listed five women's magazines among the 10 most popular magazines in 2002. Currently, the most prominent women's fashion magazines are *Rayli*, *Trends Cosmopolitan* and *Elle* (China), and they all rank high in terms of circulation, with more than 200,000 copies for each issue. *Rayli* and *Trends* have further developed into magazine publishing groups.

Trends Magazines, under the supervision of the National Tourism Bureau and sponsored by the China National Tourism Association, is a prominent magazine group. Its first magazine, *Trends (Shi Shang)*, was launched in 1993 and became popular among the white-collar workers with its fashionable approach, promotion of refined living, superior quality, and high retail price. Not long after its debut, this magazine began to make rapid progress through cooperation with the International Data Group (IDG) and the Hearst Corporation, buying the rights to famous magazines such as *Cosmopolitan*, and adapting these magazines to fit the local market. Now, Trends Magazines Group consists of 12 magazines including *Cosmopolitan*, *TRENDSHOME*, *Bazaar*, *CosmoGIRL!*, *Autostyle*, and *Cultural Geography*. (See Figure 3.4.) The group also owns two subsidiaries in Shanghai and Shenzhen, two advertising companies, one printing plant, and one distribution company, in

Figure 3.4

Organizational Structure of Trends Magazines Group

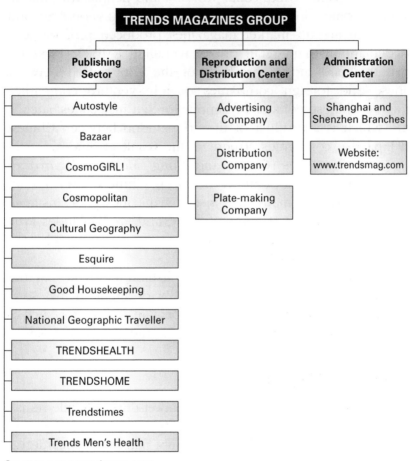

Source: *www.trendsmag.com*

addition to several joint ventures with IDG. In 2002, Trends Magazines had four magazines in the list of the 10 monthlies with the most advertising revenues as published by the *China Press and Publishing Journal*. Trends Magazines is known for organizing various large fashion extravaganzas, and Hearst has signed a proposal for strategic cooperation for the next 30 years.

Rayli and *Elle* (China) are also famous names published by the China Light Industry Press and Shanghai Translation Publishing House, respectively.

These women's magazines share some features. First, their readers are mainly white-collar workers and people with middle to high incomes, in other words the "petty bourgeois." Second, all of them are up market magazines produced professionally and demanding high retail prices averaging RMB20 (US$2.41). Third, they are mostly products of the cooperation between Chinese and foreign companies or joint-venture companies. Some are Chinese editions of famous foreign magazines, such as *Rayli*, which is a product of the cooperation between Chinese and Japanese companies. Trends is the result of Sino-American cooperation, and *Elle* (China) and *Hong (Madame Figaro)* are products of the cooperation between Chinese and French companies. Lastly, many are sister magazines. For instance, Trends has *TRENDSHOME* and *Bazaar*, and *Rayli* includes *Rayli Women's Glamor, Rayli Lovely Vanguards*, and *Hong (Madame Figaro)* has *Figaro Girl*.

With the emergence of many new fashion magazines, market competition has intensified. It is worthy of attention that some male magazines are beginning to appear in this sector such as *Trends Men's Health* and *Mangazine* as the industry expands.

2. Business Magazines

Business magazines are also highly market-driven. While female readers dominate the fashion magazine world, men dominate business magazine readership. Prominent magazines include *Cai Jing (Finance and Economy), Shang Jie (Business World), IT CEO & CIO in Information Times, Chief Executive China, Securities Market Weekly, Global Entrepreneur, China Entrepreneur, China Marketing, Manager, Contemporary Manager,* and *New Fortune.* Chinese editions of foreign business magazines also have attracted many readers including *BusinessWeek China, Harvard Business Review* (China), and *Forbes* (China).

A majority of business magazines are monthlies, with a small portion being biweeklies and weeklies. Their prices are generally between RMB10 and 15 (US$1.20–1.81) and the most popular have a circulation of about 100,000 copies with comparatively good ones distributing about 60,000 copies.

Cai Jing (Finance and Economy), a monthly magazine launched in 1998 by the Stock Exchange Executive Council, is the most famous and original business news magazine. It has a professional team with both veteran business reporters and new talents and has won support from China's famous economists such as Wu Jinglian and Wang Dingding. This magazine has impressed the business world as well as that of standard news reporting with an independent and unique style, insightful and trenchant editorials, and clear and stimulating views. The *Wall Street Journal* commended *Cai Jing* as "the leading business publication in China," and the *South China Morning Post* praised it as "a magazine deserving high respect." *Cai Jing* has cooperated with many famous magazines of its type in the world. In 2002 it started to cooperate with Britain's *Economist* to publish the Chinese edition of *World (Review)*.

IT CEO & CIO in Information Times is similar to *Cai Jing* in its feature articles but its readers are mainly IT professionals. It currently has a circulation of about 110,000 copies per issue, and is published by a Sino-American joint venture, China Computer World Publishing & Servicing Company.

Shang Jie (Business World) and *China Marketing* boast the highest circulation among business magazines. *Shang Jie* is published by the Office of Restructuring Economic Systems under the Chongqing Municipal Government and prints about 350,000 to 400,000 copies per issue, with a retail price of RMB6.50 (US$0.78). It attracts readers among company managers, small and medium-sized private enterprise owners, ordinary clerks, students, and military personnel. *China Marketing* is published twice a month from Zhengzhou in Henan Province and prints about 250,000 copies per issue. Its readers are mainly those in the sales profession. Many famous foreign business magazines have entered into the market and are published in Chinese. The pioneer is *BusinessWeek China*, which is produced similarly to local Chinese magazines using a sixteen-page format and coated paper with color printing. The number of pages of each issue is 70 and retail price is RMB10 (US$1.20).

Harvard Business Review (China) and *Forbes* (China) are the new rising stars. *Harvard Business Review* (China), first started in

2003 with cooperation from the Social Science Documentation Publishing House. It contains 30% local content and is published almost simultaneously with the English edition. Its retail price is RMB70 (US$8.43), the most expensive of this type of magazine in the country, almost seven times higher than the price of many other magazines. Nevertheless, it is still preferred by many readers, and its monthly circulation already has reached 60,000 copies according to a BPA survey. This magazine also has a Chinese website (www.hbrchina.com). *Forbes* (China) was launched in 2003 in Hong Kong with the Chinese mainland as the target market with a retail price of RMB15 (US$1.81) and now is distributed mostly free of charge. *Forbes* formally established a news center in Shanghai in November 2002 and sent its senior editor, Russell Flannery, to China to assist in the publication of *Forbes* (China), which contains about 50–80% of overseas content, with the remaining 20–50% local. Currently, the circulation goal is 75,000 copies in the three regions of Beijing, Shanghai, and Guangdong with China National Publications Import & Export (Group) Corporation taking charge of subscription and retail sales. Now *Forbes* (China) continues to recruit talent in Beijing and Shanghai and in order to promote the magazine has launched a Chinese website (www.forbeschina.com).

3. Lifestyle Magazines

Lifestyle magazines in the Chinese mainland follow closely the style of Trends. However, they focus more on reaching out to the mass audience unlike Trends which target niche markets. In terms of professionalism, a big discrepancy exists in terms of taste and quality. These publications are not as attractively laid out as Trends magazines. Such lifestyle magazines target mainly at the working class, and based on content, can be split into two main categories: lifestyle and health, and fitness and leisure.

The popular lifestyle magazines in the Chinese mainland for lifestyle and health includes *Zhi Yin* (*Bosom Friend*), *Jia Ting* (*Family*), *Nu You* (*Woman's Friend*), *Family Doctor*, *Miss*

Fashion, City Life, Health, Fashion L' Officiel, Lady, CITY, Chengshi Jufu (City Women), City Pictorial, Modern Daily Necessities, Chic, Shenghuo Zhixun (Life Information), Mum & Baby, LIFE Monthly, Beauty, Makeup, and Modeling, and *China Health.*

The revenues for these magazines come mainly from subscriptions. Its business strategy is to retail at a low price and to sell in large quantities. It is usually priced between RMB3.50 and RMB8.00 (US$0.42–0.96) but the sales volume can reach hundreds of thousands of copies. For instance, *Zhi Yin (Bosom Friend), Jia Ting (Family), Ren Zhi Chu (The Origins of People), Family Doctor, Urban Beauties, Life, Lnyouth, Woman Life* has achieved sales of 500,000 copies. Among this, *Zhi Yin* and *Family* has weekly sales of 2.23 million and 1.4 million copies, respectively. They are one of the most favored by readers and is now part of Magazines, Inc. Lifestyle magazines, such as *Family, Miss Fashion, City Life, Health, Fashion L' Officiel,* and *Lady* also have substantially high advertising revenues of over RMB20 million (US$2.41 million).

Zhi Yin Group Corporation, or in its full name Hubei Zhiyin Periodical Publishing Group Corporation Ltd., is located in Wuhan, Hubei Province. The flagship magazine *Zhi Yin* was first published in 1985 as a monthly. In terms of distribution volume, *Zhi Yin* ranks the sixth among all magazines and the third out of commercial magazines. The Zhi Yin Group currently owns six magazines, one newspaper, five subsidiary companies, one website, and one college, with total assets of over RMB300 million and tangible assets of RMB150 million. It employs more than 280 people with sales of RMB270 million and profits of more than RMB70 million per year. *Zhi Yin* pays great attention to editorial content and pays its authors RMB1,000 per 1,000 Chinese characters (a high fee for the Chinese mainland). Of all magazines *Zhi Yin* has the honor of having the most number of stories to be republished elsewhere and also adapted for TV shows and films. The other magazines of the *Zhi Yin* group are *Zhi Yin* (Overseas edition), *Business Focus, Dagong (Look For Job) Magazine, Happy Life, Fortune EQ, Liang You (Good*

Friend), and its subsidiary companies cover advertising, distributing, printing, and real estate development.

The *Family* Periodical Group is located in Guangzhou in Guangdong Province and its first magazine, the biweekly *Family*, belongs to the Guangdong Women's Federation and was first published in 1982. For several consecutive years, the group has generated profits over RMB34 million, and it owns three subsidiary magazines, *Child*, *Elegance*, and *Personal Financial Management*; a female professional college; and some other subsidiary companies. *Nu You* of Shaanxi Province also established a magazine group. Other than the flagship magazine *Nu You*, which has a circulation of nearly 400,000 copies, the group also publishes *Nu You • Cute*, *Nu You • Love*, and *Nu You • Style*. In addition, it issues *Nu You • Woman Friend* in Australia and New Zealand and *Nu You • New You* in North America.

Sports and leisure magazines have gained much popularity in recent years, and prominent magazines include *Sports & Leisure, New Sports, Soccer World, Sports Vision, The World of Weiqi, Bo Sports Magazine (Striving), Yun Dong Jing Xuan (Pick of Sports), Golf, Chinese Martial Arts, The World of Ping-Pong, Fitness & Beauty, Ba Xiaoshi Yiwai (Sparetime), National Park of China, Traveler, Chinese National Geography, Deep: Scientific Exploration, Human and Nature, National Geographic Traveler* (published by Trends Magazines), *Direct VIP, Traveling Scope, Tourism Times, Cultural Geography, Deep: Civilization, China Aviation Tourism Guide, Tours to West China,* and *Tibet Tour.*

These magazines can be classified into two groups. *Bo Sports Magazine, Yun Dong Jing Xuan, Golf, Sports & Leisure, Chinese National Geography* and *Direct VIP* belong to the upmarket group, with cover prices of about RMB15 (US$1.81) or higher, of which *Golf* is the most expensive with a list price of RMB40 (US$4.82). The rest are pop magazines with a list price of about RMB6 (US$0.72).

Chinese National Geography was first published in September 1949 in Beijing by the Institute of Geographic Sciences and Natural Resources Research, Chinese Academy of

Sciences, and The Geographical Society of China. It is printed on imported full-color art paper, has 100 pages, different versions including simplified Chinese, traditional Chinese, Japanese, and English, and is retailed in Taiwan, Hong Kong, and Japan. By September 2003, its total circulation had reached 518,000 copies (386,000 in simplified Chinese, 85,000 in traditional Chinese, and 47,000 in Japanese). The magazine publishes a version for youths and children as well as an audio-visual version. It also operates a website, www.cng.com.cn (including a Japanese version), and another website for youths and children, and has organized the Geographical Society of Chinese in the World and the Chinese National Geography Foundation, while also preparing to establish a Chinese National Geography Museum. The current president of the magazine is the famous researcher Li Quanke, a scientist who once climbed Mount Everest.

C. General Interest Magazines II

1. News Magazines

In the past there were not many news magazines, and the earliest was *Outlook Weekly*, published by the Xinhua News Agency. With the growth of readers' purchasing power, recent years have witnessed a boom of various weeklies, including news weeklies. Currently, prominent news magazines are *Sanlian Life Weekly, New Weekly, Newsweek, Nan Feng Chuang (Southwind Through Window), Xinmin Weekly, China Comment, Outlook Weekly, Society Observation, Qing Nian Shi Xun (Youth Times), China Youth Biweekly, Oriental Outlook, Shenzhen Weekly*, and *Phoenix Weekly*.

These magazines are mostly located in Beijing, Guangdong and Shanghai and are published by news agencies. For instance, *China Comment, Outlook Weekly*, and *Oriental Outlook* belong to Xinhua News Agency; *Newsweek* belongs to China News Agency; *Qing Nian Shi Xun* belongs to China Youth newspaper; *Xinmin Weekly* belongs to *Wenhui-Xinmin* United Press Group; and *Phoenix Weekly* belongs to Hong Kong's Phoenix TV.

For distribution, while a few of these magazines depend on subscriptions through the Post Office, most of them rely on both subscriptions and retail sales. *China Comment* and *Outlook Weekly* with circulations of 3.2 million and 300,000 copies respectively, rely heavily on the Post Office distribution, and their subscribers are mostly state-owned organizations and enterprises. The circulation of *China Comment* ranks second amongst all magazines in the country. Other magazines focus more on retail sales including *Sanlian Life Weekly, New Weekly, Newsweek, Nan Feng Chuang (Southwind Through Window), Xinmin Weekly* and *Qing Nian Shi Xun*. For advertising revenue, the magazines relying on retail sales depend more on advertising revenue. Observations of the Beijing Hui Cong Research Center show that in 2002 the news magazines such as *Sanlian Life Weekly, New Weekly, Newsweek, Xinmin Weekly* and *China Comment* all earned more than RMB10 million from advertising.

In recent years news magazines such as *Nan Feng Chuang, Sanlian Life Weekly,* and *New Weekly* have become quite well known. *Nan Feng Chuang,* sponsored by the Department of Publicity of the Guangzhou Municipal Party Committee of CPC and first published in 1985, attracts readers with its boldness, objectivity, and authoritativeness, and has been regarded as a "barometer of our times" and a magazine with a strong sense of responsibility. About 90% of its readers are management professionals, lawyers, doctors, teachers, public service workers, and other mainstream professionals. *Sanlian Life Weekly* is descended from the former *Life Weekly,* a magazine published by the famous news reporter and publisher Zou Taofen in the 1920s, and has attracted a large group of readers with its characteristically acute viewpoints and stimulating editorials.

Some news magazines are also published in foreign languages, such as *Beijing Review* (English), *China Today* (English), and *People's China* (Japanese), all belonging to the China International Press Group Limited. With businesses focusing on publishing, printing, and distribution, the China International Press Group Limited owns five magazines, *Beijing Review, China Today, China Pictorial, People's China,* and *China Report* in different language versions including English,

French, Spanish, Japanese, and Chinese. It also operates a website with various language versions. In addition, it has seven publishing houses including the Foreign Languages Press and New World Press, one import and export company, and a large media company (China Intercontinental Communication Center), with total annual publication of nearly 1,000 titles in more than 20 languages and distribution covering more than 190 countries and regions. The China International Book Trading Cooperation, a subsidiary of the China International Press Group Limited, is the country's second largest book import and export company. China Intercontinental Communication Center produces audio and video products (including films and TV programs) and publications in various languages, and annually distributes several hundred hours of films and TV programs as well as more than 100 book titles throughout the world.

2. *Educational and Digest Magazines*

Among the many general interest magazines, learning and digest magazines have also attracted many readers. Learning magazines comprise magazines focusing on general knowledge and popular science as well as youth issues, such as *China Youth*, *Shenzhen Youth*, *Lnyouth*, *World Affairs*, *Globe*, *Speech and Eloquence*, *Naval & Merchant Ships*, *Radio*, *Ordnance Knowledge*, *Newton: Scientific World*, *Scientific American* (Chinese edition), *Science Fiction World*, *Nongcun Baishitong* (*All-Knows Magazine for the Countryside*), *The World of English*, *English Language Learning*, *College English*, *Studio Classroom*, and *English Square*. Of these magazines, many win over readers with specialized focuses. *Speech and Eloquence*, published in Changchun of Jilin Province, has a circulation of more than 650,000 copies; *Science Fiction World*, published in Chengdu of Sichuan Province, and *Ordnance Knowledge*, published in Beijing, both achieve circulations of over 300,000 copies. *English Language Learning* and *The World of English* are English learning magazines published in the Chinese mainland with a comparatively long history and have exerted considerable influence, while *Studio Classroom*, although with a long publishing history in Taiwan, is a newcomer in the Chinese mainland and yet has already attracted a large readership.

According to existing copyright law, if writers do not specifically indicate "no republication without consent," the articles can be republished on the condition of providing payment to the authors (note: such republication is allowed only in newspapers and magazines). Therefore, there are many digest magazines which always attract many readers. Prominent digest magazines include *Du Zhe (Reader), Qingnian Wenzhai (Youth Digest), Nongmin Wenzhai (Peasant's Digest), Overseas Digest, ESWN (East South West North), Youth Vision,* and *Overseas Tidings Magazine,* of which *Du Zhe, Qingnian Wenzhai,* and *Nongmin Wenzhai* all have circulations of more than one million.

The most famous digest magazine in the Chinese mainland is *Du Zhe,* with its headquarters located in Lanzhou in Gansu Province and published by the Gansu People's Publishing House. In 2002, *Du Zhe* distributed 2.7 million copies per issue, ranking fourth of all magazines in the Chinese mainland and second among commercial magazines. This magazine is published as a biweekly with a list price of RMB3 (US$0.36), and other than the flagship, other titles are produced such as *Du Zhe* (Rural edition), *Du Zhe Collections, Du Zhe* (Uyghur edition), and *Du Zhe* (Braille edition). By the end of 2003, their combined circulation had reached eight million copies. According to the statistics provided by the International Federation of the Periodical Press (FIPP), *Du Zhe* globally ranked fourth in circulation only behind America's *Readers' Digest, National Geographic* and *Time,* and first in Asia. In August 2003, the *Du Zhe* magazine and Big Way Media, Inc. in America signed an agreement to publish *Du Zhe* (North American edition) with a list price of US$2.50 and Big Way Media will produce 5,000 copies for the first issue.

3. Literature and Art Magazines, Children's Magazines and Pictorials

As people's lifestyles have become more diverse, literature, art and many other cultural magazines popular in the past have begun to face a decline in circulation. In the past, every provincial writer's association or cultural federation issued at least one, or even several literary magazines, and currently there are still several hundreds of such magazines. However, in the new market environment only a few of these magazines operate successfully and are able to attract many readers while many struggle for survival. Some find financial support from private companies, a generally adopted method among many mediocre magazines in order to keep the business running, while some try to explore new strategies or face the possibility of going out of business.

Literature magazines in the Chinese mainland can be divided into two categories: serious and pop. Currently, prominent serious literature magazines include *Harvest, Dang Dai (Contemporary Time), People's Literature, China Writer, Poetry Magazine, The Star Poetry Monthly, Play Monthly, Chinese Poetry and Verse, October, Zhongshan Literature, Da Jia (Great Master), People's Liberation Army Literature and Art, The Selected Works of Taiwan & Hong Kong, Translations, Foreign Literature, Prose, Du Shu (Read), Essay, Panorama, Shu Wu (Book House), Fiction Monthly, Selected Stories, Journal of Selected Novelettes, Journal of Short Short Stories*, and *Journal of Selected Essays*. Most of these magazines are monthlies or bimonthlies.

Harvest, a bimonthly magazine, is the most influential literature magazine, with a distribution volume of more than 100,000 copies per issue, the highest distribution figure of its type and a retail price of RMB12 (US$1.45). In addition, *People's Literature, China Writer & Poetry Magazine*, and *Selected Stories*, sponsored by the China Writers' Association, also exert a comparatively large influence. The *Translations* bimonthly and the *Foreign Literature* quarterly specialize in introducing foreign literature. *Translations*, published by Yilin Publishing House located in Nanjing in Jiangsu Province, provides the greatest number of contemporary foreign literary works.

Du Shu, Essay, Panorama, and *Shu Wu* to some degree can be considered as literature magazines but their coverage also goes beyond literature and enters into the area of social sciences and some other social aspects, with many of their articles tending towards political criticism. Of more than a dozen titles of this type in China, *Du Shu* is the most influential. Like *SDX Weekly*, *Du Shu* is issued by the SDX Joint Bookstore, and with the pursuit of "free thought and humanistic concern," the magazine publishes articles brimming with the ideas and insights of contemporary Chinese intellectuals, and thus it reflects the views and thoughts of the Chinese intelligentsia. *Du Shu* is printed in 32 pages with a list price of RMB6 (US$0.72) and distributes about 100,000 copies, the highest of this type.

There are several dozen pop literature magazines, including *Du Shu Hui* (*Stories*), *Modern and Ancient Legends*, *Shanhai Jing* (*Mountain and Sea Classics*), *Folk Narrations*, *Shanghai Stories*, *Gushi Dawang* (*King of Stories*), *Teahouse Tale Monthly*, *Foshang Literature and Art*, *Traditional Chinese Fiction*, *Martial Arts Stories*, and *Popular Literature Digest*. These magazines focus on presenting various stories, legends, sagas and jokes, with students and readers in towns and rural areas as their target audience. The retail prices of these magazines are comparatively

Figure 3.5

The First Issue of *Du Shu*

(Photo provided by Shen Changwen)

low, about RMB3 (US$0.36), and the magazines are filled with vivid and interesting content and popular descriptive styles, which are often able to attract a high readership. Among these, *Stories, Modern and Ancient Legends,* and *Shanhai Jing* are the most popular.

Du Shu Hui, sponsored by the Shanghai Literature & Art General Publishing House, had a circulation of 3.5 million copies per issue in 2002, ranking first among all magazines. According to the statistics provided by the International Federation of the Periodical Press in 1998, in that year the circulation of *Du Shu Hui* ranked fifth of its type in the world. This magazine is printed in 32 pages with a retail price of RMB2.50 (US$0.30) making total revenue from each issue some RMB8.75 million (US$1.05 million).

Modern and Ancient Legends belongs to the Modern and Ancient Legends General Publishing House in Wuhan in Hebei Province, and enjoyed a circulation of 260,000 copies in 2002. Now the general publishing house issues several versions of *Modern and Ancient Legends,* including monthly, biweekly, story, romance, martial arts, and digest versions, *Hubei Pictorial,* and *Home of Dramas,* with a total distribution volume of nearly 2 million copies and annual sales of more than RMB50 million (US$6.02 million). It employs about 100 people and owns its own distribution company, advertising company, printing company, and cultural development company.

There are about 140 art magazines, covering various artistic fields. Prominent titles include *Popular Cinema, Look: (Going to Movies), World Cinema, Film Literature, TV Shows, Chinese Beijing Opera, Theater Arts, Qu Yi (Variety Shows), Dancing, Music Lovers, Songs Monthly, Opera, Light Music, The Beatles, Music Trends Magazine, Comedy World, China Audio & Video, Art, Art Panorama, World Art, Sculpture, Chinese Oil Painting, Chinese Calligraphy, Chinese Photography, Portrait Photography, Chess Magazine, Collectors, The World of Art,* and *Foreign Literature and Art.*

Many of these magazines were and are still the most authoritative magazines of their kind. For instance, *Popular*

Cinema was previously the most popular magazine among film magazines, and today the "Popular Cinema One Hundred Flowers Award" is still one of the most important film awards in the Chinese mainland. *Art* is the most authoritative magazine among art magazines and *Qu Yi* the most prominent among magazines on traditional variety shows. Nevertheless, as market competition becomes more intense, the gap between magazines of the same type narrows. For example, *Look* has become a new leading film magazine.

There are several hundreds various junior and children's magazines. Such magazines with comparatively high distribution volumes are *Xiaoxuesheng Daokan* (*Pupil's Journal*), *Xiaoxuesheng Shidai* (*Pupil Times*), *Xiaoxuesheng Tiandi* (*Pupil's World*), *Dangdai Xiaoxuesheng* (*Contemporary Pupil*), *Guangdong Di'er Ketang* (*Guangdong Second Classroom*), *Zhongxuesheng Tiandi* (*The World of Middle School Students*), *Zhongxuesheng* (*Middle School Students*), *Gushi Dawang* (*King of Stories*), *Little Friend*, *Xin Shaonian* (*New Juvenility*), *Juvenile Literature and Art*, *Little Torch*, *Little Star*, *Shaonan Shaonu* (*Teenagers*), *Juren* (*Giant*), *Zhongxue Shidai* (*Middle School Times*), and *King of Children's Stories*. Since many of these magazines are sponsored by educational departments at the provincial level and schools in the province organize subscriptions, magazines such as *Pupil's Journal*, *Pupil Times*, and *Pupil's World*, can distribute more than a million copies even without resorting to commercial distribution. Of these magazines, some have also enjoyed good sales with their excellent editorial content, such as *Shaonan Shaonu* (*Teenagers*) sponsored by the Guangdong Writers Association, which has a circulation of some 350,000 copies per issue.

More than 60 pictorial magazines cover three sectors including news, culture and entertainment, and cartoons. News pictorials include *China Pictorial*, *Shanghai Pictorial*, *Nationality Pictorial*, and *People's Liberation Army Pictorial*; culture and entertainment pictorials include *City Pictorial*, *World Screen Pictorial*; and *World Affairs Pictorial*; while prominent cartoon magazines include *Youmo Dashi* (*Humorous Master*),

Mickey Mouse, Manhua Dawang (*Cartoon King*), *Picture Stories, Cartoon Monthly, China Cartoon,* and *Ying Er Hua Bao* (*Infant Pictorial*). Of the three, culture and entertainment and cartoon magazines are comparatively more market-oriented. The *Humorous Master,* published in Hangzhou in Zhejiang Province, distributes nearly 400,000 copies, the highest among cartoon magazines. *Mickey Mouse,* a Sino-U.S. joint venture, has a distribution volume of about 350,000, ranking first among children's cartoon magazines.

4. Information Technology Magazines

With an increase in readership, information technology magazines have been generally treated as general interest instead of professional magazines. Currently, there are more than 100 magazines covering information technology. Prominent titles include *China Computer Users, Internet Weekly, Microcomputer, PC World China, PC Magazine, Computer Fan, Chip, China Computer Magazine, PopSoft, Software Magazine, PC Shopper Weekly, Play, Ruan Jian Guang Pan* (*Software and CD-ROM*), *Financial Computer of China, NetComm World, DigiTIMES, Internet Information World, International Broadband Network, Digital Power, Computer,* and *Computer Master.*

The popularity of the PC and the promising future of the internet industry have helped this type of magazine gain high advertising revenue, ranking behind only fashion, business, and professional magazines. According to the Beijing Hui Cong Research Center, in 2002 *China Computer Users, Internet Weekly,* and *Microcomputer* all had advertising revenue of over RMB43 million (US$5.18 million), with *China Computer Users* earning RMB55.8 million (US$6.72 million). These magazines are usually issued by scientific research institutes and electronics companies and they normally distribute over 100,000 copies. For example, *Microcomputer* distributes 300,000 copies and *China Computer Magazine* 150,000 copies.

Audio-Video and Electronic Publishing, and Publishing Research in the Chinese Mainland

A. The Audio and Video Industry

1. *Overview*

According to *The 2003 China Statistical Data Collection of Press and Publication* prepared by the General Administration of Press and Publication (GAPP), by the end of 2002 there were 292 audio-video publishing companies in the Chinese mainland. Of these 221 were independent publishers specializing in audio-video production (i.e. only producing audio-video products) and the other 71 were the audio-video departments of larger publishing houses. A total of 12,296 audio titles were produced, with total output of 226 million copies and total distribution of about 200 million copies, while 13,576 video titles were produced with 218 million copies duplicated and 174 million copies distributed.

Most of the audio-video publishers in the Chinese mainland do not operate on a large scale. In terms of total assets, a majority of them (149), have assets of just RMB1–10 million (US$120,482–1.21 million), accounting for 52% of the total number of publishers. If those with assets less than RMB1 million were included, the percentage would be 60% of total. Another 83 publishers possess assets between RMB10 and 50 million (US$1.21–6.02 million), accounting for 30% of the total number, and a further 25 have assets of more than RMB 50 million (US$6.02 million), accounting for 10% of the total number, and only 16 publishers have assets of more than RMB100 million (US$12.05 million).

122 are literary and art publishers, accounting for 42% of the total, followed by 65 educational publishers, 60 social sciences publishers, and 45 science and technology publishers. Audio-video publications on literature and art are the most market-oriented and are regarded as mass-market products. Recent years have seen an increasing demand for educational products, and as a result such products have taken a one-third market share. The prices of audio-video products in the Chinese mainland are inexpensive. One CD costs about RMB20; a tape about RMB8–18; a VCD about RMB10–28; and a DVD about RMB15–30. In general, the prices are about one-eighth to one-fifth of the U.S.

Audio-video products basically cover five media: cassettes, videotapes (including LD), compact disks, video compact disks, and digital video disks. VCDs and cassettes have the largest market share, accounting for 52% and 42% of the total, respectively. CDs are third on the list taking about 5%, and DVDs close to 1%. (See Figure 4.1.) In 2002, only about 663 videotapes titles were released with a total of 430,300 copies duplicated. This represents only 0.2% of the total market, signaling the extinction of this medium.

Figure 4.1
2002 Market Share of Audio-Video Media

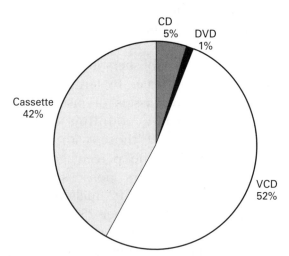

Source: Wang, J. 1998, 'The Production Scale and Structure of the Audio and Video Industry in China,' in *China Press and Publishing Journal*, 20 February.

The large difference in production structure between the Chinese mainland, Europe and the U.S. mainly stems from the consumption standard and the development of consumer electronic products. Before videotape players became popular in China, video compact disks emerged in the market. Although the VCD is not a replacement of the videotape in Europe and America, it had many advantages in China. Because they are much cheaper than a VCR player, VCD players quickly entered the homes of millions of Chinese families. Moreover, because a computer, another increasingly popular product, can also play VCDs, the VCD gained more momentum to become a mass-market medium. Several factors contribute to the fact that cassettes sell much better than CDs. First, the price is cheaper than that of a CD. Second, the number of various portable cassette players is much higher than that of portable CD players. Third, the main customers of cassettes are students and people in towns and rural areas, representing a huge population; while the main customers of CDs are the city youth, whose number is much smaller.

The development of the audio-video industry in the Chinese mainland over the last 10 years has shown a fluctuating pattern. Before the mid-1990s, the industry grew rapidly, and then it began to decline to its lowest point in 2000. Currently, it seems that the growth has resumed, and in the years 2000 to 2001, 24 audio-video publishers achieved sales of over RMB10 million (US$1.21 million), indicating that some strong audio-video publishers can maintain stable operations and sales numbers. According to Wang Ju, Executive Vice Secretary-General of the China Audio-Video Association, there are 89 audio-video publishers in debt, accounting for 31% of the total publishers, a figure that has reduced from the past (Wang 2003).

In terms of overall capacity in audio-video production, state-owned companies are not a match for the growing private companies. For instance, 70% of singers sign contracts with private producing companies, and almost all popular singers have contracts with private companies. Private companies are stronger in the distribution sector as well. Compared with book and magazine publishing, audio and video publishing in the Chinese mainland is short of high quality professionals, such as high-level managers and project designers, and it is in great need of more industrial regulation. In addition, piracy still casts a very large shadow over the industry.

To encourage the production of excellent audio and video products, the Chinese mainland has set up various publishing awards. The most authoritative award is the National Audio and Video Productions Award, established by GAPP, and there are also the China Record Golden Disc Prize by China Audio and Video Association and the China Golden Record Prize by China National Radio. The China Audio-Video Association is working on the compilation of the first comprehensive yearbook on the audio and video industry, *China Audio and Video Yearbook 2002* (First Issue), which was published in May 2004.

2. *Various Companies*

The audio-video publishing market is largely divided into three stages: the early, middle, and the last stage. The early stage refers to producing and publishing, the middle stage to duplication and the last to wholesale and retail distribution. Four kinds of companies, production, publishing, duplicating, and distribution are engaged in the three stages. Private companies dominate production, which a few publishing houses engage in, and they are mostly music studios that have many contracts with singers and composers, and provide new products to publishers for production. Generally, these companies will not be involved in publication, duplication, and distribution except for participating in product promotion in the distribution stage.

In theory, the production stage should be handled entirely by formal publishing houses, which are also responsible for sales. But in reality, many companies in the distribution sector also engage in the publishing and wholesale business, and most of these companies are private enterprises that cannot be pigeonholed as a "production company." Known as "production and distribution companies," these companies generally conduct the production and distribution businesses, even though they are generally not involved in producing original works. The second stage in the production process is duplication, which is mostly controlled by specialized duplication companies, and yet some large publishing companies and distribution companies also have their own duplication units. In the distribution stage, well-to-do distribution companies have also developed into production and distribution companies, and there are almost no large companies that specialize in distribution alone.

Prominent performers have emerged from all the different types of companies. Well-known producers include Rye Music Ltd., Modern Sky Entertainment Co., Ltd., Beijing Star Maker Music Entertainment Co., Ltd., Kirin Kid Productions Ltd., Dadi Records, Zhushu Entertainment Ltd., Northern Brother Culture Development Co., Ltd., Mandolin Culture and Art Development Co., Ltd., Jingwen Entertainment Group Ltd., Kingring Records, Shanghai New Stars Music Production Co., Ltd., Chia Tai Ice Music Production Ltd., Aoqi Music, Tian Xing Culture and Entertainment Co., Ltd., Beijing Victory Culture and Art Development Center, and New Bees Records. A majority of these companies consist of about 10 people, and their business focuses on discovering and exploring singers and launching original works.

In the publishing sector, about 20 publishers have achieved sales over RMB10 million (US$1.20 million) recently, of which 50% are educational publishers. The top five companies with the highest sales in 2001 are the China Record Shanghai Corporation (RMB61.66 million, or US$7.43 million), China Record Shenzhen Corporation (RMB60 million, or US$7.23 million), People's Education Electronic & Audiovisual Press (RMB59.98 million, or US$7.23 million), Beijing Foreign Language Audiovisual Publishing House (RMB46.2 million, or US$5.57 million), and Shanghai Foreign Language Audiovisual Publishing House (RMB42.44 million, or US$5.11 million). Other major publishing companies include China Record Corporation, Pacific Audio & Video Co., Shanghai Audiovisual Press, Jiangsu Electronic & Audiovisual Press, China Audio & Video Publishing House,

China International Television Corporation, China Musicians Audiovisual Publishing House, Beijing Culture and Art Audiovisual Publishing House, China Film Audio and Video Publishing House, and Jiuzhou Audiovisual Publishing Corporation.

The China Record Corporation (CRC) was formed in 1949 and is the national audio and video publisher with the longest history and largest size. It has headquarters in Beijing and subsidiaries in Shanghai, Chengdu, Shenzhen, and Guangzhou. It owns Beijing Record Plant, CRC Audio and Video Production Center and Recording Base, CRC Huaxia Performing Management Co., Ltd., *Audio and Video World* magazine, CRC Audio and Video Co., Ltd., CRC Music Network, and Shanghai UDO, etc. and has a total of about 3,500 employees. CRC possesses a highly professional production team and advanced production equipment. In the 50 years since formation, it has issued over 56,000 titles with total distribution of 870 million copies, covering all artistic categories. Currently, CRC has accumulated about 120,000 master recordings, of which over 40,000 are the only existing ones on folk music performances of up to 50 years old, and therefore it is the most authoritative audio and video publisher in the country with the greatest number of music titles and with the most diverse record categories.

The Pacific Audio & Video Co. and Shanghai Audiovisual Press are located in Guangzhou and Shanghai respectively. Pacific is the first Chinese company with a complete set of world-class recording, kinescoping equipment, and a modern audio-video production line. As a large, comprehensive audio-visual publishing enterprise, it owns a 10,000 square meter building on the shores of Liuhua Lake. Pacific has the honor of publishing the very first Chinese stereo sound recording tape, and the first Chinese picture-recording collections. Shanghai Audiovisual Press is also a comprehensive company covering producing, publishing, duplicating and distributing and has earned a well-established name in the market. In addition, China International Television Corporation, under China Central Television, is also a fast growing company in recent years thanks to its rich programming catalog.

In production and distribution, major companies in recent years include Guangdong Zhong Kai (Zoke) Cultural Development Co., Ltd., Guangzhou Beauty Culture Communication Ltd., Guangdong Face Audio & Visual Production Co., Ltd., Guangdong Jiajia Audio-Video Productions Co., Ltd., Guangzhou Impact Audio-Video Industry Co., Ltd., Guangzhou Art-land Human Being Culture Communication Co., Ltd., Guangdong Freeland Movie and Video Production Co., Ltd., Guangzhou Hong Xiang Audio-Video Productions Co., Ltd., Tianjin Taida Audio and Video Distribution Center, Dongguan Dongfanghong Movie and Video Production Co., Ltd., Huizhou Dongtian Audio-Video Co., Ltd., Sunchime Group, Starwin Culture Communication Co., Ltd., and Tianyi Audio and Video Limited Company. Most of these companies are private companies that have developed their business by making alliances with state-owned audio-video publishing houses. Many of them have well-developed nationwide distribution networks, own branches and duplication companies and have engaged in other various business fields related to audiovisual products, films and TV programs besides just publishing and distributing. Most of them have headquarters in Guangdong. Now Guangdong Zoke, Guangdong Beauty, Guangdong Face, Guangdong Impact, and Sunchime have become major brand names in audio-video publishing.

Guangdong Zoke has established subsidiaries or offices in various provinces and major cities. In Beijing, in cooperation with Jiuzhou Audiovisual Publishing Corporation it established Beijing Jiuzhou and Zoke Cultural Development Co., Ltd. This company engages in publishing and copyright trading and has a subsidiary in Hong Kong. Zoke owns nearly 5,000 hours of programming, including films, TV shows, children's encyclopedias, traditional operas, and local music. It has sold hundreds of films and TV shows in the form of VCDs and DVDs, including *Xiao Ao Jianghu* (*The Legendary Swordsman*), *Da Zhaimen* (*The Big Household*), *The Imperial Dynasty of Kang Xi*, *Qingshenshen Yumengmeng*

(*Romance in The Rain*), *The Lion Roars, Wanee and Junah*, *Zhouyu De Huoche* (*Zhouyu's Train*), *Infernal Affairs*, and *Black Mask II*. Guangzhou Zoke is a leading company in the audio and video market in the Chinese mainland.

Guangzhou Beauty and Guangdong Face operate in a similar form and scale as Guangdong Zoke. Guangzhou Beauty produces about 300 movies and TV shows a year, amounting to over 3,000 total productions. Guangdong Face owns over 2,000 various audio-video products, and set a record by paying RMB17.8 million (US$2.14 million) for the domestic audio and video copyright for the movie, *Hero*.

Sunchime Cartoon is known for creating native cartoons, and is a subsidiary of Sunchime Group, whose business covers audio and video publications, electronic publications, and education. Now programs produced by Sunchime Cartoon represent 50% of the total cartoon production, and its star program *3,000 Whys of Blue Cat* has been aired in over 1,000 TV stations including CCTV and Taiwan's Eastern Television. Books related to the program have also been a major success. Sunchime has invested over RMB120 million (US$14.46) in cartoon production.

B. Electronic Publishing

There is no clear-cut definition of electronic publishing, and the electronic publishing discussed in this book focuses mainly on two types: first, the tangible electronic publications in the form of CD-ROMs, CD-Is, etc. and second, online publications, i.e. the electronic books and magazines provided by Internet digital communications, excluding news publications such as online newspapers.

In 2002, there were about 102 electronic publishers producing 4,713 different electronic publications with a total reproduction of 96.81 million copies; nearly 20,000 electronic book titles were downloadable and more than 10 websites providing download services for these e-books.

As in the case with online publishing in the other parts of the world, online publishing in China also experienced a recent decline, but now the tide has started to turn.

Online publishing takes on mainly three forms. First, websites disseminate e-books, which can be downloaded by readers for a fee or free-of-charge. Second, websites send e-books through e-mails to subscribers for a fee or free of charge. Third, websites provide customized services through print-on-demand (POD). All of these forms are still young and far from being popular, but a few websites already operate on a considerable scale and are gaining popularity.

Major online publishing websites currently include www.china-pub.com, www.chnebook.com, www.cnbook.com.cn, www.eobook.com, www.chinesebook.com.cn, www.ebook.com, and www.jinke.com.cn. All of these websites have more than 1,000 titles, with an average price around RMB5–10 for works under copyright protection.

The website www.china-pub.com was launched by a professional publishing company China-pub.com Inc. in cooperation with the Huazhang Co. of China Machine Press. It focuses on selling computer and foreign language books and has a huge customer base. Prominent players in publishing management include www.chnebook.com of Hunan Publishing Group, www.cnbook.com.cn of Liaoning Publishing Group and www.eobook.com of Jiangsu Publishing Group. The website, www.peoplespace.net, a pioneer in exploring online publishing, provides fee-based downloads of over several dozen books, including *War and Anti-War* and *Fifty Years of Chinese Economic Development*. However, it has made little progress recently.

Producers of electronic readers, also known as e-readers or e-books, include the Liaoning Publishing Group, Tianji Jinke Electronics Co., Ltd. (a joint venture between Nankai University and Hong Kong Pangjing Group), Shanghai Webon Digital Technology Co., Ltd., and Eshutang Scientific and Technological Development Co., Ltd. They have developed their own products, even though they have not yet gained mass popularity. The Liaoning Publishing Group has the most number of products such as Q-Reader, electronic school bag, and electronic musical score book. Q-Reader is a popular product, which has similar functions as American rocket e-Book, with a 6-inch black and white touch-sensitive LCD, five degrees of background light shades adjustable to ambient light supporting night-time reading without additional light, two adjustable font sizes, and a total weight of about 400g. It adopts the internationally used Open eBook (OEB) format and is compatible with html documents and able to convert other formats into OEB for reading. As for hardware configuration, it has a 32MB memory which can store 50–60 books with about 20 million characters and is able to upload new books from the Internet.

In electronic publishing technology and services, Beijing Founder Electronics Co., Ltd. of Peking University has launched Apabi ebook network publishing solutions, the first comprehensive electronic publishing solutions in the Chinese mainland. The solutions contain Apabi Maker for designing formats of electronic books, Apabi Publisher Server for publishing houses, Apabi Retail Server for online bookstores, and Apabi Rights for readers. Founder Apabi eBook Solutions has prepared the way for publishing houses to quickly start online publishing with their electronic book files.

To encourage excellent electronic publishing products, GAPP has established the biennial National Electronic Publications Award. In addition, the industry is also very active in competing for international prizes, for instance, it has participated in the "Möbius Prize of International Multimedia" held in Moscow for eight years, sponsored by the European Union and International Federation of Multimedia Associations. Many Chinese works have won prizes, and in 2001 the award ceremony was held in China.

C. Internet Publishing

While the future of Internet publishing in China and the rest of the world still seems elusive and uncertain, online bookstores are beginning to see signs of hope turning into reality. Online bookstores in the Chinese mainland are just getting started.

There are about 300 online bookstores in operation, of which several dozen have established their own distinctive features and sphere of influence. Active players in this field include www.joyo.com, www.dangdang.com, www.bol.com.cn, www.bookbuilding.com, www.bookmall.com.cn, www.ewen.cc, www.chnebook.com, www.eobook.com, www.book321.com, www.modernbooks.com, www.huabeibook.com, www.peoplespace.net, www.bookyesite.com, www.bayakala.cn, www.book 800.com, www.sybook.com, www.jingqi.com, and www.dragonsource.com.

Private companies, IT enterprises, bookstores, and publishing houses run most of the online bookstores, which are mostly located in the big cities of Beijing, Shanghai, Guangzhou, Chengdu, Shenzhen and Nanjing. Generally speaking, online bookstores share four major features. First, most of them deliver books directly to customers. Second, there are various ways of payment, including online payment as well as cash. Third, the majority of online bookstores have their own warehouses. Fourth, some online bookstores cooperate with bookstores, and this enables customers to pick up books they bought online from the nearest partner bookstore.

Because payment by credit cards has not become popular and labor costs are very low, many companies provide express delivery services to customers. For instance, two-thirds of Dangdang.com customers make their payment as they receive books via express delivery. Only 10–15% of customers make online payment by credit cards. Other websites are similar. If customers live in the same city where the website company is located, the company could have the books delivered to them within two days. Generally, those websites with such services have their own delivery team of more than 10 people or even several dozen, while bigger companies could have as many as a hundred or more.

Within the last four to five years, online bookstores have experienced ups and downs, and now they are beginning to regain their strength. Gone are the days of the phenomenal boom when 20 dotcoms can emerge every day, but the Internet continues to gain more influence with an expanding market. In 2003, *China Internet Weekly*, an authoritative journal of the online industry listed Joyo.com and Dangdang.com among

"China's Top 10 Flagship Internet Companies," showing that online bookstores in the Chinese mainland have made impressive growth and achieved recognition within the Internet industry.

Joyo.com was formed in 2000 by two famous IT companies in China, Kingsoft Corp. and Lenoro Group Ltd. (formerly Legend Group Ltd.), and later the internationally well-known capital firm Tiger Technology Fund became its third-largest shareholder. Joyo.com set up its headquarters in Beijing and has subsidiaries in Shanghai and Guangzhou, with a total of nearly 200 employees and selling mostly fashionable cultural products including audio and video products, books, software, games, and gifts. Joyo.com is known for its superior quality and fast delivery and thus, the company has won over more than 5.2 million registered customers, becoming the retail website with the largest number of logins and highest sales. In 2003, Joyo's revenues reached RMB160 million (US$19.28 million), of which book sales accounted for 55%. Joyo.com has received many honors, such as winning the title of "China's Excellent Cultural Website" offered by the Organizing Committee of the National Network Cultural Project, ranking among "China's Top 10 Flagship Internet Companies" and "Top 100 Internet Companies with the Most Investment Values." In 2003, online shopping customers rated Joyo.com as the most satisfying company among all Chinese business-to-customer (B2C) webs (surveyed by Sina.com, the most famous website in China), and Cheng Nian, Vice-President of Joyo.com, became one of the *China Business Post's* "Top 10 People in China's Economy."

Dangdang.com claims to be the largest online Chinese bookstore in the world and was formed in November 1999 by the International Data Group of the U.S., Luxembourg Cambridge Holding Group, Softbank Corporation of Japan, and the Science and Culture Corporation of China. It provides over 200,000 Chinese book titles and more than 10,000 audio and video products with logins of over 800,000 and about 4,000 orders daily, which over half are for DVDs or CDs. In 2002, Dangdang.com's sales reached RMB35 million (US$4.22 million), and its gross profit reached 25%, very close to Amazon.com's 28%. It had planned to get into the black by 2003.

As well as Joyo.com and Dangdang.com, Bol.com.cn also deserves attention. Bol.com.cn is owned by Bertelsmann AG and has its headquarters in Shanghai. It claims to be of one of the three largest online bookstores in China. Launched in end 2000, it now has over 300,000 products with 200,000 daily logins, daily orders of between 3,000 and 4,000, and annual sales of RMB40–50 million (US$4.82–6.02 million). Bol.com.cn currently has around 530,000 regular customers and it provides after-payment delivery service to 16 cities.

Modernbooks.com was the earliest online bookstore, and Peoplespace.net also once enjoyed popularity, but now both of them have fallen into mediocrity.

Compared with their counterparts in Europe, the U.S., Hong Kong and Taiwan, the online book industry has its advantages and disadvantages. With more improvements taking place in the financial service system, people are beginning to have more trust in online sales. Yet, there still are two major obstacles impeding the development of online sales. First, most people are not used to online payment. It is popular among young people to pay with credit cards, but that is mostly in stores, not online. Second, online bookstores do not have sufficient supplementary sales networks in small and medium-sized cities.

However, online bookstores in the Chinese mainland have their own advantages, which include the following:

First, there is a demand and need for online publishing and distribution. At present, books with a small readership, especially academic books, have difficulties with both publication and distribution, and this situation actually invites the development of online publication and distribution. Internet publishing, especially with the technology of POD, could help interested readers and publishers find each other.

Second, conditions are favorable to provide express delivery. In developed countries, express delivery is more expensive because labor is more expensive, but that is not a problem in the Chinese mainland. The existence of surplus human resources makes labor costs very low, and it therefore would not cost companies much to provide express delivery. In Beijing, for example, even when the bookstores request professional delivery companies to deliver books, the cost is only RMB10 within 25 kilometers, and RMB20–30 within 40 kilometers. If the bookstores themselves deliver the books, it costs only RMB4 every time, therefore, bookstores generally provide free delivery service if a customer spends over a certain amount (usually it is about RMB50, or US$6.02). In short, book delivery cost is not high at all. Currently, several dozen of express delivery companies have emerged in Beijing, such as Zhaijisong Express, Pony Express, and Little Red Hat, all doing very well. Competition in this field has been relentless, and it has forced the state-owned Post Office system to compete and begin to provide express services with low charges.

Third, the cost of warehousing is also relatively low. It is a must for online bookstores to have their own warehouses in order to provide fast delivery at a low cost. In the land-rich Chinese mainland where there are many available spaces in city suburbs, it is convenient and cost-efficient to build warehouses.

Fourth, the number of Internet users in the Chinese mainland is increasing rapidly, and more Internet users are taking advantage of e-commerce. According to the latest survey by the Internet Society of China, by the end of 2003 there were already more than 78 million Internet users, ranking second in the world, and the number of people paying online with various credit cards also recorded a significant increase. More importantly, it is becoming popular to transfer money via cell phones. There are nearly 260 million cell phone users, ranking first in the world, and the number of people paying through cell phones is growing daily. Of 30 million short messages in the world, nine million messages are sent in China. In 2003, the revenue of China Telecommunication reached RMB381.4 billion (US$45.95 billion), growing 14.5% over the last year. Online payment services were recently introduced, and this is definitely a blessing to online bookstore sales.

Fifth, the ·government is giving full support to the Internet industry. Government offices at various levels have adopted many measures to promote the development of the Internet industry. The projects such as the "Government Online Project" and "Enterprises Online Project" have been fully implemented. Also, the registration for public service examinations, university admissions and services for student study and counseling all have been processed with Internet technology, and this facilitates the development of online bookstores. In 2003, during the period of the SARS outbreak, GAPP recommended 20 online bookstores to the people nationwide, and the sales of various online bookstores went up rapidly at that time.

The development of online bookstores in the past five years in the Chinese mainland shows that it is not feasible to follow the exact Amazon.com business model. However, if parts of the model are used in tandem with the features distinct to the market, it may be possible to build a "new Amazon" that is likely to succeed. The success of Joyo.com has proven that this is possible.

D. Publishing Research, Education, Information Service, and Trade Organizations

1. *Publishing Research and Education*

Publishing research, education, and information services have developed a definitive structure that is the most comprehensive of any Chinese language publishing industry in the world.

Specialized research institutes and higher educational institutions are major players in publishing research. At present, there are about 10 various publishing research institutes, including both private and state-owned. Their focus is on editing, marketing, and publishing history. Prominent players are the Chinese Institute of Publishing Science, Beijing OpenBook Market Consulting Center, Beijing Hui Cong Media Research Center, Periodical Research Institute under Beijing Institute of Graphic Communication, and Global China (Beijing) Media

Consulting Co., Ltd. The Chinese Institute of Publishing Science is the largest.

The Chinese Institute of Publishing Science, a comprehensive publishing research organization with a total staff of over 80 people, was founded in 1985 by GAPP. It consists of several research units on publishing theory, three magazine editing units, one publishing house, one information center, and a website. It issues magazines such as *Publishing Research, Publishing World* and *Media*. Its subsidiary, China Book Publishing House, is well known for publishing various professional books, including recent influential books such as the *Blue Book of China Publishing*, the *Blue Book of International Publishing* and *Research on Publishing Groups*. The Periodical Research Institute under the Beijing Institute of Graphic Communication was formed by the China Periodical Association and Beijing Institute of Graphic Communication and focuses on researching both domestic and foreign periodicals. It has completed many projects commissioned by the government and trade organizations.

Both Beijing OpenBook Market Consulting Center and Beijing Hui Cong Media Research Center are private companies that provide commercial information services. OpenBook has over 40 employees and focuses on providing data and information on the book market. It produces related reports through monitoring the retail market and then selling the reports to publishing houses. Its surveys and investigations cover about 120 medium-to-large bookstores in 70 cities with total sales of about RMB220 million (US$26.51 million), accounting for 14% of total retail sales. Beijing Hui Cong, a subsidiary of Hui Cong International Information Co., provides mostly periodical market data. It owns a well-developed newspaper-magazine media data bank, a newspaper and magazine database, monitoring over 1,100 newspapers and magazines in 72 cities. It monitors advertisements as well as content, with the total amount of monitored advertisements representing 90% of the national advertising total in newspapers and magazines and covering 26 trades or industries with more than 3,000 product categories. Besides conducting commissioned research, Beijing Hui Cong also publishes information materials such as *Research on Media Advertising Market in China* in cooperation with the Public Opinions Research Institute of Renmin University. Both companies have their own websites, www.openbook.com.cn and www.media.sinobnet.com.

In addition, some universities and periodical publishers have established publishing research units, such as the Editing Research Office of Henan University, the Publishing Research Institute of Beijing Normal University, and the Periodical Research Office of the *Nu You* magazine.

Publishing education has reached a considerable scale in the Chinese mainland and covers three levels: elementary, intermediate and advanced. Now more than 30 higher educational institutions have begun to train students in specialties including editing, printing, distribution, and publishing, with prominent schools including: Wuhan University, Nanjing University, Peking University, Tsinghua University, Henan University, Beijing Normal University, Fudan University, Nankai University, and the Beijing Institute of Graphic Communication. (See Figure 4.2.) Formed in 1978, the Beijing Institute of Graphic Communication is the first institute of higher education specialized in printing. It has also established a publishing department and other departments related to publishing. The China Museum of Printing is also located at this institute. Since 1978 (when the Chinese mainland started reforms), more than 11,000 students have chosen publishing or publishing-related subjects and have graduated from various professional schools, colleges and universities. In addition, GAPP and many press and publication bureaus at the provincial level have established training centers focusing on training publishing professionals. In order to improve professional skills and professional standards, an examination system for publishing professionals has also been implemented.

Figure 4.2

Universities with Majors in Editing and Publishing
(including undergraduate and graduate degrees)

University	Location	Degree
Anhui University	Hefei	Bachelor
Beijing Broadcasting Institute	Beijing	Bachelor
Beijing Institute of Graphic Communication	Beijing	Bachelor, Masters
Beijing Normal University	Beijing	Bachelor, Masters, Doctorate
Chang'an University	Xi'an	Masters
China Renmin University	Beijing	Bachelor, Masters
College of Liberal Arts, Shanghai University	Shanghai	Bachelor, Masters
Fudan University	Shanghai	Bachelor, Masters
Guangxi Normal University	Nanning	Bachelor
Guangxi University for Nationalities	Nanning	Bachelor
Hangzhou University of Commerce	Hangzhou	Bachelor
Hebei University	Shijiazhuang	Bachelor
Hebei University of Economics and Business	Shijiazhuang	Bachelor
Henan University	Luoyang	Bachelor
Inner Mongolia University	Huhhot	Bachelor
Inner Mongolia University for Nationalities	Huhhot	Bachelor
Kunming University of Science and Technology	Kunming	Bachelor
Nanjing University	Nanjing	Bachelor, Masters
Nankai University	Tianjin	Bachelor, Masters
Northeast Normal University	Changchun	Bachelor
Northwestern University	Xi'an	Bachelor
Ocean University of Qingdao	Qingdao	Bachelor
Peking University	Beijing	Bachelor, Masters, Doctorate
Shaanxi Normal University	Xi'an	Bachelor
Sichuan Academy of Social Sciences	Chengdu	Masters
Sichuan University	Chengdu	Bachelor
Siping Normal Institute	Siping	Bachelor
Tsinghua University	Beijing	Bachelor, Masters
University of Science and Technology of China	Hefei	Bachelor, Masters
Wuhan University	Wuhan	Bachelor, Masters
Xi'an Jiaotong University	Xi'an	Masters
Zhejiang University	Hangzhou	Bachelor, Masters

Note: Some information comes from Wei Yushan, "Building the Professional Platform for Modern Publishing."

2. Publishing Information

Many media carry publishing information, especially newspapers, magazines, and websites. Currently, there are about 50 various newspapers and magazines specializing in the publishing industry. Influential newspapers include *China Book Business Report, China Press and Publishing Journal, China Reading Weekly, Wenhui Reader's Weekly, New Books Weekly,* and *China Books and Periodicals Vision*, with *China Book Business Report* being the most influential. *China Book Business Report*, a newspaper focusing on the publishing and distribution industry under the China Publishing Group and issued on Tuesdays, provides the most inclusive and recent information in the industry and is always the first choice for publishing advertisements. It also issues *Book Review Weekly*. *China Press and Publishing Journal* is a professional newspaper directly under GAPP. *China Reading Weekly* and *Wenhui Reader's Weekly* are newspapers specializing in providing publishing information with targeted readership of academia and publishing professionals, respectively. These three newspapers exert considerable influence in the publishing industry.

There are also many magazines specializing in the publishing industry. Many books, newspapers, and electronic and Internet publications also have their own trade journals. Prominent titles include *Information on Publication, Publishing Research, China Publishing Journal, China Editors, A Vast View on Publishing, Media, China Audio & Video, China Electronic Publishing, Publishing Science, Publishing Economy, Science, Technology and Publication, Publishing Square, China Juvenile and Children's Publishing, Friend of Editors, China Book Review, Publishing Work, National New Books, Weekly Bulletin of China's CIP* and *China Book Guide*. Of these, *Information on Publication* and *A Vast View on Publishing* always contains a large of amount of publishing information, and *Publishing Research* and *Publishing Science* are known for theoretical exploration, especially *Publishing Research*, the most authoritative magazine on publishing theories. *Media, China*

Figure 4.3
Major Publishing Media

Name	Sponsor	Issue Frequency	Features
China Book Business Report	China Publishing Group	Tuesday	The most prestigious newspaper on publishing. It owns the separately issued newspaper, the *Book Review Weekly*.
China Press and Publishing Journal	The General Administration of Press and Publication	Friday	It also issues the colored printed Book Information and Printing Business every other week.
China Reading Weekly	Guangming Daily Group, The Publishers Association of China	Weekly	Its readers include mostly scholars and publishing professionals.
Wenhui Reader's Weekly	Wenhui-Xinmin United Press Group	Weekly	Its readers include mostly scholars and publishing professionals. It focuses on humanities and is is printed in a quarto 32-page edition.
New Books Weekly	Sichuan Bureau of Press and Publication	Weekly	It provides mostly book publication information.
China Books and Periodicals Vision	China State Post Bureau	Weekly	It provides publishing information on both books and periodicals.
China Publishing Journal	The General Administration of Press and Publication	Monthly	It contains work guidance, information exchange, and publishing research.
China Editors	China Editors Association	Bimonthly	It focuses on theoretical research on publication and editing of books and periodicals.
Publishing Research	Chinese Institute of Publishing Science	Monthly	It is the most authoritative academic magazine on publishing.
Information on Publication	Promotion Committee of International Cooperating Publication of the Publishers Association of China, Chinese Institute of Publishing Science	Biweekly	It is known for its rich information and circulates in different regions through the Chinese publishing world.

Figure 4.3 (Cont'd)

Name	Sponsor	Issue Frequency	Features
China Book Review	The Publishers Association of China, China Book Review Institute and the Press and Publication Bureau of Liaoning Province	Monthly	It contains mostly book reviews, and also provides reports analyzing the domestic book market.
A Vast View on Publishing	Guangxi Bureau of Press and Publication, Guangxi Publishing Group	Monthly	A new publishing magazine with growing influence.
Publishing Economy	CNPITC	Monthly	It publishes research articles mostly on publishing economics and management.
Science, Technology and Publication	The Publishers Association of China, Working Commission of Science and Technology Publication of the Publishers Association of China, Post & Telecommunications Press	Bimonthly	Its purpose is to draw attention to the impact of science and technology on publications and application of science and technology to publishing.
Media	Chinese Institute of Publishing Science	Monthly	It focuses on exploring administration policy and management business in newspaper publications.
Friend of Editors	Shanxi People's Publishing House	Bimonthly	It is the earliest magazine on editing and focuses on the editing of books and periodicals.
Editors Bimonthly	Shanghai Municipal Editor Association, Academia Press	Bimonthly	It explores both editing theory and practices and strives to build a modern editing science.
University Publishing	China University Press Association	Quarterly	It focuses on the operation and management of university presses and related subjects.
Publishing Square	Fujian Bureau of Press and Publication	Bimonthly	It is a comprehensive magazine on providing publication information and has considerable influence in the publishing world.

Figure 4.3 (Cont'd)

Name	Sponsor	Issue Frequency	Features
Acta Editologica	China Editology Society of Science Periodicals, Science Press	Bimonthly	It focuses on the research of editing scientific and technological periodicals.
Publishing Science	Hubei Editology Society	Bimonthly	It focuses on the research and the theoretical building of editing and publishing science.
Publishing and Printing	Shanghai Publication & Printing Institute	Quarterly	It presents theoretical research on publishing and print engineering as well as the exploration and application of related technology.
News and Publishing Exchange	Shanxi Bureau of Press and Publication	Bimonthly	It provides guidance to news publishing professionals. Its readers and contributors are mostly from Shanxi province.
Press and Publishing Guide Journal	Shandong Bureau of Press and Publication	Monthly	It provides guidance to news publishing professionals. Its readers and article contributors are mostly from Shandong province.
China Juvenile and Children's Publishing	Working Commission of Juvenile Publication of the Publishers Association of China, Juvenile Committee of China Book & Periodical Issuing Association, International Board On Books For Young People (IBBY)	Monthly	It is a research magazine focusing on theories and practises of publishing books for juveniles and children.
China Audio & Video	China Audio & Video Association	Monthly	It presents publication of audio and video products.
China Electronic Publishing	Electronic Publishing Institute of the Publishers Association of China	Bimonthly	It provides information on the publications in new forms such as CD-ROMs and internet books.
Electronic Publishing	Printing and Printing Equipment Industrial Association of China	Monthly	It is a professional magazine containing trade information, technology, and application of technology.

Figure 4.3 (Cont'd)

Name	Sponsor	Issue Frequency	Features
Weekly Bulletin of China's CIP	GAPP Information Center	Weekly	Each week it provides the national catalog of books in publication.
National New Books	GAPP Information Center	Monthly	It mostly presents the national catalog of new books and some book reviews for important books.
Copyright	China Copyright Establishment Protection Center	Bimonthly	It contains research on copyright theory, law implementation, and management.
Publishing Work	The Newspapers and Periodicals Center of Renmin University	Monthly	It is the most prestigious publication digest.
Book Digest	Guangming Daily	Monthly	Its contents are extracted from various books.
Du Shu	SDX Joint Publishing Co., Ltd.	Monthly	The most influential reading magazine with scholars constituting the main readership, and it also has considerable influence among publishing professionals.
Books and People	Jiangsu Press & Publishing House	Bimonthly	It focuses on introducing books and also presents some reports analyzing the book market.
Read	Shanghai Joint Publishing House, The Publishers Magazine House of Shanghai	Monthly	It contains various columns covering literature, music, film, and network, TV. It presents many contemporary literature reviews.

Audio and Video, and *China Electronic and Net Publishing* focus on providing newspaper and magazine information, audio and video information, and electronic publishing information. *National Bibliography of New Books*, *Weekly Bulletin of China's CIP*, and *China Book Guide* are booklist providers, with the first two sponsored by The Information Center of GAPP. *Publishing Work* collects articles on publishing from various newspapers and magazines and is published by the Newspapers and Periodicals Information Center of Renmin University.

In addition to the professional information providers, many other magazines also have publishing coverage, such as *Du Shu*, *Panorama*, *House Book*, *Read*, *Books and People*, *Shu Yuan*, *Book Digest*, and *Digest of Chinese and Foreign Books*. These magazines also often carry publishing information and advertisements, especially *Du Shu*, which has significant influence among Chinese intellectuals and is therefore one of the first choices to carry advertisements for social science books. In addition, some chain bookstores, book clubs, and publishing groups publish their own magazines such as *Literary Landscape* of the Shanghai Century Publishing Group, *CNP Readers' Club* from the same organization, *Book Review* of www.cn-book.com, *Good Books* of Xishu, and Bertelsmann's catalog.

In the 50 years since 1949, there have been about 1,600 titles released specializing on publishing. Other than many monographs and translated works, there are also multi-volume educational, reference and research books such as *China Encyclopedia: Press and Publication*, *Historical Data of Chinese Contemporary Publishing*, *Publishing Historical Materials of People's Republic of China*, and *Textbooks for Book Distribution Major in Higher Educational Institutions*. Since 1980, The Publishers Association of China has issued the *China Publishing Yearbook* annually. In addition, there is the *Periodical Yearbook*, *Press Yearbook*, *China Book Publication Yearbook*, and the *Audio and Video Publishing Yearbook* which was published in April 2004.

Many TV and radio stations broadcast special programs dedicated to book reading, such as Reading Hour on CCTV and

Book-Reading on Hebei TV station. Moreover, many websites provide publishing information, the prominent ones being www.booktide.com, http://book.sina.com.cn, www.people.com.cn, www.magazinemarket.org.cn, http://av.ccnt.com.cn, www.cnave.com, www.ewen.cc, www.bayakala.com., www.21cbi.com, www.sinobook.com.cn, and www.ccopyright.com.cn. GAPP and the National Copyright Administration have also set up several information sites such as www.ppa.gov.cn, www.ncac.gov.cn, and www.chinabook.gapp.gov.cn.

3. Publishing Organizations

Many publishing organizations exist, covering various fields such as book publishing, newspaper and magazine publishing, audio and video publishing, electronic publishing, and copyright protection. Generally they have two different levels, the national and the regional. Major national organizations include The Publishers Association of China, China Periodicals Association, All-China Journalists' Association, China Audio and Video

Figure 4.4

Major Publishing Associations in the Chinese Mainland

Name	Year of Establishment	Leader	Telephone Number
China Audio and Video Association	1994	Liu Guoxiong	0086-10-65588610-13
China Book and Periodical Issuing Association	1991	Yang Muzhi	0086-10-65135071
China Copyright Protection Association	1990	Shen Rengan	0086-10-62357081
China Editors Association	1992	Liu Gao	0086-10-84027978
China Paper Association	1964	Qian Guijing	0086-10-68396639
China Periodicals Association	1992	Zhang Bohai	0086-10-64016886
China University Press Association	1987	Peng Songjian	0086-10-62752032
Music Copyright Society of China	1993	Wang Liping	0086-10-65232656
Printing and Printing Equipment Industries Association of China	1985	Li Shouren	0086-10-63490074/0057
The Printing Technology Association of China	1980	Wu Wenxiang	0086-10-68325195
The Publishers Association of China	1979	Yu Youxian	0086-10-65212827

Association, China Book and Periodical Issuing Association, China Editors Association, The Printing Technology Association of China, China Copyright Protection Association, China University Press Association, and China Youth Newspapers and Periodicals Association. Regional organizations are generally established at the provincial level or prefecture municipal level, such as Beijing Publishers Association or the Liaoning Publishers Association.

The major functions of publishing organizations range from organizing book fairs, trade fairs and conferences to training professionals and protecting members' legal rights. The Publishers Association of China, the largest publishing organization, has publishing units as members and over 30 working committees covering fields including science and technology, youth, women, copyright, and proofreading. It offers influential book awards such as the China National Book Award and Taofen Publishing Award. The All-China Journalists' Association is the largest organization of reporters, and China Periodicals Association, China Audio and Video Association, and the China Book and Periodical Issuing Association are the most influential organizations in their respective fields.

Book Distribution in the Chinese Mainland

A. Overview

The Chinese mainland's publication distribution market consists of four segments: books, magazines, newspapers and audio/video/electronic publications. If newspapers and electronic publications are excluded, books, magazines and audio-video publications have a total market of RMB95.6 billion. Books have a total market of RMB43.5 billion (US$5.24 billion), magazines (subscription and advertising) have a market of RMB17.25 billion (US$2.08 billion), and audio and video publications have a market of RMB20 billion (US$2.41 billion).

At present, the distribution of publications has not been entirely commercialized and there is a lack of a national distribution network and publication distribution is mostly regional with the retail market primarily based in big cities. Books, magazines, newspapers, and audio and video publications all lack national, modern, full-service distribution networks and that has limited potential sales. All market segments have their own distinctive retail sales models and distribution channels.

Sales of publications differ greatly between urban and rural areas, and also among the different regions. City residents are the primary consumer group, especially for books and magazines. The publication consumption per capita in major cities such as Beijing, Shanghai, Guangzhou, and Shenzhen far exceeds the levels of all other regions. About 400 million urban residents buy approximately 70% of all books and magazines. At present, publication sales are mainly concentrated on the developed coastal regions of Eastern China. In contrast, mid-western China accounts for a small percentage of the overall sales. Beijing, Guangdong, Jiangsu, and Shanghai are the largest markets. The sales outlets for books and periodicals are densely concentrated in the eastern provinces. Outlets become less concentrated in central China and are sparse in the western regions. Beijing, Shanghai, Jiangsu, Zhejiang, Fujian, Hunan, Shandong, Shaanxi, Hebei, and Anhui are the 10 provinces and regions where bookstores are most densely concentrated. (See Figure 5.1.)

Figure 5.1
2002 Book Sales: Top 10 Regions in the Chinese Mainland

Rank	Province/Region	Sales[1]	Regional Population[2]	Population Rank
1	Beijing	5,348	13.8	27
2	Jiangsu	3,531	74.4	5
3	Guangdong	3,254	86.4	3
4	Shandong	2,845	90.8	2
5	Sichuan	2,397	83.3	4
6	Henan	2,368	92.6	1
7	Zhejiang	2,068	46.8	10
8	Hunan	1,805	64.0	7
9	Hebei	1,805	67.4	6
10	Shanghai	1,563	16.7	26

[1] *millions of RMB*
[2] *millions*
Source: *GAPP*

1. The Book Market

In 2002, total book sales topped RMB43.49 billion (US$5.24 billion) in revenue and 7.027 billion copies sold. Among book categories, textbooks held the largest market share. Sales of textbooks for high schools and elementary schools reached RMB17 billion (US$2.05 billion), representing 39.5% of total. If textbooks for colleges and vocational schools are included, total sales of textbooks exceeded RMB20 billion

(US$2.41 billion). This means that textbooks take up nearly half of the book market. Non-textbook book sales were about RMB23.4 billion (US$2.82 billion), accounting for 53.5% of total sales. Books on culture and education held the second largest market share after textbooks and sales totaled RMB11.1 billion (US$1.35 billion), accounting for 25.6% of the total. Other large book categories were the natural sciences with sales of RMB2.36 billion (US$284.34 million), the social sciences with sales of RMB3.20 billion (US$385.54 million), literature and art titles with sales of RMB2.35 billion (US$283.13 million), and children's books with sales of RMB1.46 billion (US$175.90 million). (See Figure 5.2.)

Urban residents are the main consumers of books with rural consumption levels far lower. In 2002, the consumption of books per capita in the Chinese mainland was RMB33.86 (US$4.08) with 5.5 copies purchased per person. On the retail level, the ratio of urban to rural consumption was 3 to 1. That is to say, 400 million urban residents bought RMB32.62 billion (US$3.93 billion) worth of books, while 900 million rural

Figure 5.2
Book Categories by Market Share, 2002 (US$100 millions)

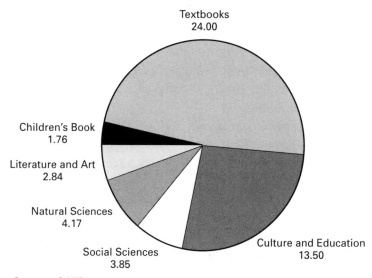

Source: *GAPP*

residents bought only RMB10.87 billion (US$1.31 billion) worth of books. The city residents purchased three times as much as those in the country. On a personal level, in one year a city consumer spent on average RMB82 on books, while a rural resident only RMB12.10. A city consumer spent 6.7 times as much on books as a rural consumer.

Books are sold through bookstores, schools, post offices, the Internet, wholesalers, and special outlets. Direct sales are rare. Among all the distribution channels, bookstores are the mainstay of book sales. The most common distribution flow is from wholesalers to retailers. Publishers sell their books to regional wholesalers, who then resell the books to various bookstores. At present, there is no national distributor and the majority of distributors are regional and distribute books within the confines of their respective provinces. Publishers also supply books direct to large bookstores, especially to superstores.

Textbooks for elementary schools, high schools, colleges and vocation schools are all sold through the schools. Most educational publishers sell to schools directly but publishers also sell college textbooks to students through 80 college bookstores. Postal sales and online sales also hold some market share and online book sales are growing steadily. Special outlets handle books purchases by companies.

Direct book sales is still in its nascent stages. A few private booksellers and joint ventures have tried to enter into direct sales but have had little success. In the late 1990s, some companies such as the Bright Prospect Culture Development Ltd. went into direct sales.

Sales from publishers and wholesalers are classified into "consignment sales," "firm sales" and "hybrid sales," based on the terms of book return and payment. For consignment sales, publishers automatically supply books to wholesalers, who will pay for the books that have been sold and return those unsold copies up to a number mutually agreed upon. For firm sales, publishers supply books to the wholesalers according to their mutually agreed number. Wholesalers will pay the publishers according to the dates specified on their contracts and keep the unsold copies. Under many circumstances, a wholesaler gets exclusive distribution rights of a title in exchange for firm sales (known as primary or exclusive wholesale). Hybrid sales are the combination of consignment and firm sales. Generally speaking, a wholesaler submits its firm order to a publisher, who will supply accordingly and then provide additional quantities as demanded. For the firm order component, the wholesaler will handle payment and returns according to the agreement with the publisher. For the extra copies supplied by the publisher, the wholesaler will treat them as consignment sales.

Presently, most deals between publishers and wholesalers are either consignment or hybrid sales. Of course, trade publishers will handle consignment, firm, or hybrid sales differently from educational publishers. The same is true with different types of books. Most publishers offer a wholesale discount of between 35% and 45%. The wholesale discount can be as high as 55% and sometimes a 70% discount is also possible.

Among publishers, distributors, and retailers, publishers bear most of the risk. Under most circumstances, booksellers can get the books first and pay later. The distribution market is not standardized and there is a wide array of credit terms. Some booksellers and distributors do not pay on time, deliberately delay payment, or even default on payment. All the potential risk is ultimately borne by the publishers. Sometimes, publishers also breach distribution agreements, especially when they have a super bestseller (nicknamed a "fast book"). Publishers will ignore the exclusive distribution contract with the regional distributor and supply the same book to other distributors in the region.

2. The Magazine Market

In 2002, total revenues of the magazine sector reached RMB12.35 billion (US$1.49 billion), this includes both retail sales revenue and revenue from advertisements. As there were no accurate statistics on subscription prices, we must go by the average magazine cover price. In 2002, over 2.951 billion copies of magazines were printed in the Chinese mainland. The average cover price per copy was RMB4.97. According to this price, total sales of magazines were RMB14.67 billion and the advertising revenue was RMB2.65 billion. (See Chapter 3 on Magazine Publishing.)

Magazine distribution differs substantially from book distribution. The primary magazine wholesalers are the national postal system, in-house distribution departments, and professional magazine distributors. Most magazines use the first two. There are only a limited number of specialized magazine distributors who are capable of just regional distribution.

In the past, the overwhelming majority of magazines used postal distribution and this is still true today. The postal distribution network (called the China Post) covers the entire nation. The China Post not only handles physical distribution, but also the flow of cash and information of the regional wholesale and retail trade. After receiving the distribution authorization from a magazine, it will seek subscriptions and distribute the magazine through its national post office network. China Post handles readers' payment for the subscriptions and after a holding period, it passes the payment on to the magazine after deducting a 40% commission fee based on the cover or subscription price.

In 2002, China Post had a nationwide network of 82,000 post offices and 240 regional postal bureaus. China Post recorded an annual revenue of RMB50 billion (US$6.02 billion). The average revenue per employee was RMB100,000. In addition, China Post also offers postal savings and remittance services and currently has about RMB400 billion (US$48.19 billion) under deposit. The State Postal Bureau publishes an annual concise catalog of newspapers and magazines. It also set up a website (www.chinapost.com.cn), where readers can subscribe to magazines and newspapers online. China Post also assigns a code number to each periodical for easy subscription. In addition, China Post publishes a weekly *Panorama of Chinese Books, Newspapers, and Magazines* to provide readers with timely information.

The second-tier wholesalers of magazines consist of local postal distributors, local syndicated distributors, and private individual distributors. At present, there is one wholesale market for newspapers and magazines in each region or large city where wholesalers and retailers operate. Half of all the Chinese magazines are traded at such wholesale markets. The transactions between wholesalers and retailers are done through cash. Retailers are not willing to make large orders and the small amount of the cash transactions is detrimental to a newly launched magazine.

The retail sales of newspapers and magazines rely mainly on newsstands, supermarkets, convenience stores, hotels, and restaurants while some bookstores also sell magazines. In addition, most post offices also sell newspapers and magazines. Hotels primarily sell high-end magazines and imported magazines which are supplied by the China National Publications Import & Export (Group) Corporation and Foreign Language Bookstores.

Currently in many large cities, there are a number of retail chains that own a network of newsstands. The most well-known are Shanghai Oriental Newspaper and Magazine Service Co., Ltd., Shanghai Subway Book and Magazine Service Co., Ltd., and Beijing Paper Tiger Book Co., Ltd. All of these distributors control hundreds of newsstands under uniform management and supply practices. For example, Shanghai Oriental Newspaper and Magazine Service Co., Ltd was cofounded by the Shanghai Postal Bureau, Liberation Daily, Wenhui-Xinmin Newspaper Syndicate and Shanghai Press and Publication Bureau. Shanghai Oriental has 2,600 employees and distributes 600 newspapers and magazines. On average, each employee earns RMB1,500 (about US$181) per month.

In addition to the above-mentioned distribution channels, more and more magazines have been relying on self-distribution in recent years. Most of them are high-end magazines such as *Rayli* and *Trends* that enjoy good retail sales and substantial advertising revenues.

The main model of self-distribution is to hire provincial agents to handle local distribution. For example, *Marie Claire* came up with the provincial distribution plan shortly after it was launched and advertised to hire distribution agents simultaneously in 27 provinces.

3. The Audio-Video Market

The audio-video market is not as well defined as that of books or magazines. According to Wang Ju, Executive Vice Secretary-General of China Audio-Video Association, the audio-video market has sales of RMB20 billion (US$2.41 billion) with two billion units sold. However, the *China Press & Publications Statistics* indicates that only 374 million audio/video tapes and discs were sold in 2002.

Audio-video product distribution shares some similarities with book and magazine distribution but also has its own distinctive features. China's audio-video distribution consists of privately owned chain stores, the Xinhua Bookstore system, audio-video superstores, and the postal system. Large bookstores and supermarkets all have audio-video sections and sell books and audio-video publications side by side. Some post offices also sell audio-video publications along with newspapers and magazines. In addition, audio-video publications have their own distribution channels and retail stores, which include professional audio-video chains, audio-video superstores, and independent audio-video stores.

Audio-video chains are the most distinctive features of the audio-video business. They are the fastest growing among chain operations of all publications including books, magazines, newspapers, and electronic publications. By 2002, there were 80 audio-video chains that owned 3,000 stores. Some notable audio-video chains are Jingwen Audio-Video Chain Co., Ltd., Shanghai Yamei Audio-Video Chain Co., Ltd., Shenzhen Boenkai Audio-Video Chain Co., Ltd., and the Oriental Audio-Video Chain Co., Ltd. The Jingwen Audio-Video Chain is affiliated with Jingwen Record Co., Ltd. and owns 300 audio-video stores. The Shanghai Yamei Chain now owns over 200 stores spread around Shanghai. Oriental Audio-Video Chain is another large chain affiliated with Shanghai Xinhua Distribution Group that owns about 160 audio-video retail outlets. Shenzhen Boenkai Audio-Video Chain owns 30 stores.

To operate a national audio-video chain store requires approval from the General Administration of Press and Publications. Seven companies have obtained permits to run national audio-video chains. They are the Shanghai Yamei Audio-Video Chain, Jingwen Audio-Video Chain, Xinhua Yizhan, Sunchime Film Studio Development Corporation, China Record Corporation, Guangdong Jingcai Wuxian Cultural Co., Ltd., Beijing Gehua, and Chinese Media.

Audio-video superstores (also called audio-video cities) are another unique feature of the audio-video market. Presently, there are 50 audio-video cities that are over 500 square meters in size. The biggest and most famous one is Guangdong Audio-Video City, with stores engaged in both wholesale and retail sales and stocks 55,000 titles. Its stores handle 70% of all audio-video wholesale trade. In 2002, the distribution volume reached RMB1.5 billion (US$181 million). More than 142 companies including many large audio-video distributors have set up counters at Guangdong Audio-Video City. The city even has a commercial website (www.cnave.com).

China's audio-video market was the first segment of the publication distribution market to open to foreign competition. In 2002, Sony Music Entertainment Inc. (U.S.) formed the Shanghai Epic Music Entertainment Co., Ltd. (SEME) with Shanghai Xinhui Disc Group and Shanghai Jingwen Investment Co., Ltd. SEME is the first cooperative joint venture which has obtained national distribution rights for audio-video publications. The three companies invested a total of US$30 million and now SEME has established a wide distribution network by partnering with 60 audio-video wholesalers and retailers. In addition, two Hong Kong-registered public companies, COM and Sun TV, acquired the Guangzhou Hongxiang Audio-Video Co., Ltd. and Media Pioneer Limited (affiliated with Jingwen Records). They have used the shells of these acquired Chinese companies to enter the Chinese audio-video market.

Private enterprises have taken the lead in the Chinese audio-video market. In 2002, China Audio-Video hosted the "Star Brand" appraisal and promotion event. Among the top 15 "Star Brands" of audio-video distributors, 14 of them are private enterprises. The top 15 distributors recorded annual sales over RMB1 billion (about US$121 million) and distributed over 30,000 backlist titles, one-third of which they own the copyrights to.

4. State-Owned and Private Distribution Companies

The Chinese mainland publication distributors consist of both state-owned and private companies. There are 248,600 people employed in publication distribution. Previously the state-owned distributors had almost the entire market and private distributors only accounted for a negligible part. In the past 10 years, however, private distributors have grown rapidly. Today, private distributors share the book distribution market with state-owned booksellers. In 2002, there were 71,824 bookstores and bookselling outlets, out of which 13,368 were state-owned, accounting for only 18.6% of the total number. The remaining 58,456 were private booksellers. However, the state-owned bookstores still have the upper hand in distribution volume and sales revenue with the state-owned Xinhua Bookstore System accounting for 76.7% of total copies distributed and 65.5% of total book sales in 2002. What needs to be noted is that the distribution of textbooks is completely contracted to state-owned companies and textbooks account for half of the entire book market. If textbooks are excluded, private enterprises sell more books than the state-owned companies.

The state-owned bookstores in the Chinese mainland are made up mainly of Xinhua Bookstores. The name "Xinhua Bookstore" originates from "Shaanxi Yan'an Xinhua Book Bureau" founded by the Communist Party of China. In 1949, most of the state-owned bookstores were named "Xinhua Bookstore" by Chairman Mao Zedong. Presently, the Xinhua Bookstore is not a unified national book chain. At the provincial level the Xinhua Bookstore is a specialized regional book distributor, which has a degree of control over Xinhua retail bookstores at the prefecture and county levels in the province. The provincial Xinhua bookstores are independent profit centers and are not subsidiaries of the Xinhua Bookstore General Store in Beijing. The General Store only plays the role of overall coordinator.

In recent years, the book distribution system has undergone rapid reform, notably with the formation of distribution groups and bookstore chains. The formation of distribution groups took place mainly among Xinhua bookstores within each province. In 1999, the Chinese mainland's first book distribution group, the Jiangsu Xinhua Distribution Group, was born. Soon afterwards, Guangdong, Sichuan, and Shanghai also formed their own book distribution groups. Today, seven book distribution groups have been approved by the General Administration of Press and Publication to operate on a trial basis. The original Xinhua Bookstore General Store has merged into the China Publishing Group. In January 2003, 3,000 Xinhua bookstores, each a single legal identity, formed a not-for-profit professional association—the China Xinhua Bookstore Association. By the end of 2002, the Xinhua network had 13,200 bookstores and 150,000 employees.

Private book distributors have been called Second Channel distributors in comparison with the state-owned Primary Channel distributors. Over the past 20 years, the Second Channel has grown from infancy to its adolescent stage and from chaotic to standardized operations. Highly educated professionals replaced the less qualified personnel within the Second Channel. The status of Second Channel has been changed from "underground" to "well-established." Today, the Second Channel holds half of the market share in book distribution.

As highly educated professionals entered the Second Channel, a number of well-run independent bookstores emerged and the image of private bookstores has improved substantially. Consumers now see private bookstores in a different light. There are quite a number of established private bookstores in the Chinese mainland. In Beijing, there are Guo Lin Feng Bookstore, Feng Ru Song Bookstore, Wansheng Bookstore, Sanwei

Figure 5.3
Major Book Distributors

Name	Year Founded	Total Assets*	Annual Sales*	Annual Profit*	Employees	Notes
Anhui Xinhua Book Distribution Group	2002	16.00	21.00	0.90	6,098	N/A
Beijing Book Distribution Group	2004	15.00	N/A	N/A	N/A	Consists of Beijing Xinhua Bookstore, China Bookstore, and Foreign Language Bookstore with 200 outlets.
Beijing National Railroad Media Investment Co., Ltd.	2004	N/A	N/A	N/A	N/A	Engages in book distribution order, fulfilment and information services. Has branches in 40 cities and alliances with booksellers in 123 cities.
Fujian Book Distribution Group	2002	N/A	N/A	N/A	N/A	N/A
Guangdong Xinhua Book Distribution Group	1999	9.80	16.70	0.45	1,746	The only equity ownership company in book distribution channels.
Hebei Xinhua Book Distribution Group	2002	19.50	32.76	1.00	7,500	Consists of 11 municipal Xinhua bookstores and 147 county-level Xinhua bookstores.
Hunan Xinhua Book Distribution Group	N/A	N/A	N/A	N/A	N/A	N/A
Jiangsu Xinhua Book Distribution Group	1999	32.16	61.57	2.02	8,323	Among the top 500 largest service enterprises in China.
Jilin Xinhua Book Distribution Group	2000	N/A	N/A	N/A	N/A	Has 47 solely owned subsidiaries.

millions of RMB

Figure 5.3 (Cont'd)

Name	Year Founded	Total Assets*	Annual Sales*	Annual Profit*	Employees	Notes
Liaoning Book Distribution Group	2000	N/A	N/A	N/A	N/A	Consists of four enterprises and Liaoning Province Xinhua Bookstore.
Shanghai Xinhua Book Distribution Group	2002	12.00	2.40	0.67	4,920	N/A
Sichuan Xinhua Book Distribution Group	2000	23.75	42.52	1.92	8,588	N/A
Xinhua General Bookstore Distribution Group	2003	N/A	N/A	N/A	N/A	Co-funded by Xinhua General Bookstore, China Publishing Industry Trading Corp, China Post Logistics Co., Ltd., and China Post Mail Order Co., Ltd.

* *millions of RMB*

Source: *GAPP*

Bookstore, and Long Zhi Mei Bookstore. In Shanghai, there are Penguin Bookstore and Jifeng Bookstore. Well-established private bookstores are also found in other parts of the Chinese mainland such as the Photosynthesis Book City in Xiamen, Wanban Book City in Shaanxi, Southwest Wind Bookstore and Xixi Fo Bookstore in Guiyang, Dongyu Bookstore in Shenyang, Lingyu Bookstore in Foshan, and Random Book Square in Wenzhou. In 2002, two privately owned superstores opened: Yongzheng Book Shopping Center in Guangdong Province's Dongguan, and Nanjing Book City. Both stores have sales floors of 12,000 square meters with 100,000 titles. They are by far the largest among all privately owned bookstores.

In addition, some private booksellers also engage in book packaging. These entrepreneurs have had great influence on the book publishing industry. They are concentrated in Beijing, Guangzhou, Chengdu, and Shenzhen. The most well-known are Beijing Zhihong Education Group, Beijing Reader's Cultural & Arts Co., Ltd., Zhenyuan Work Studio, Wuhan Jiuzhou Book Company Ltd., Shanxi New Century Educational Bookstore, Shaanxi Xuehai Book Distribution Center, and Guangzhou Xueyuan Book Group. Book industry insiders estimate that there are some 2,000 companies and studios involved in book packaging. They produce about 20,000 titles annually, accounting for 20% of all new books published. Industry insiders also estimate that there are 25 private booksellers whose annual book sales exceed RMB100 million (US$12.05 million). Many of them specialize in study guides and school supplementary readings. For example, Ren Zhihong, a high school teacher of Chinese language, founded the Beijing Zhihong Educational Group in 1993. The group specializes in publishing and distributing school guides and supplementary readings. Zhihong now employs 240 people and produces and distributes 600 new titles per year. Now the company has expanded its business to social science books, educational training, and educational information.

In addition to book packaging and distribution, many private entrepreneurs work in cover design, publishing consulting, and book marketing. Many private companies have made themselves the leaders in their fields. For example, Xiaokang Studio, Renshou Workshop and Jingren Studio in book design; Beijing OpenBook Market Consulting Center, and Beijing Hui Cong Media Research Center in book industry consulting; and Beijing Book Media Research Institute in book marketing.

At present, private entrepreneurs still face restrictions in certain fields and do not have the same privileges as state-owned companies. For example, private booksellers are not allowed to distribute textbooks and a few other book categories (mainly books on the Communist Party of China and political documents). On September 1, 2003, the General Administration of Press and Publication (GAPP) issued the new *Regulations on Publications Distribution Market*, which further reduced the restrictions on private booksellers.

B. Different Book Sales Outlets

There are about 71,800 book sales outlets including independent bookstores, book chains, online bookstores, and book clubs. The majority of bookstores are independent but in the past two years, book chains have grown very fast, but they are still regional and rarely operate across provincial borders. Online bookstores and book clubs only started recently but they also are growing fast. Independent bookstores include mini-bookstores, general bookstores, superstores, and professional stores. Superstores have much larger sales volume and revenues, and therefore have a greater impact on the market. As China has joined the WTO, various joint-venture bookstores are expected to emerge.

Large wholesale markets, trade fairs, and book fairs form an an important component of book sales. Modern distribution and fulfillment systems are being built and the international book trade volume grows each year, even though it is comparatively small now.

1. Book Superstores

Book superstores are called "Book Cities." They all have large retail spaces and carry a wide range of products with a large selection of titles. At present, there are 20 superstores larger than 10,000 square meters in the Chinese mainland. The most famous superstores are Beijing Book City, Beijing Wangfujing Bookstore, Shanghai Book City, Shenzhen Book City, North China Book City, Guangzhou Book City, Hubei Publishing and Culture Book Shopping Center, Nanjing Book City, Chongqing Book City, and Chongqing Liujiangmen Modern Book City. (See Figure 5.4.)

The majority of these superstores are operated by a provincial or municipal Xinhua Bookstore, or by another state-owned bookseller. They are not only huge in size, but are also equipped with modern facilities and offer a comfortable environment for shopping. They stock a wide range of products and a huge selection of titles. Their sales volumes are also very impressive. For example, Beijing Book City is 16,000 square meters in size, employs 700 people, and offers 230,000 titles. Eighty percent of new titles in the Chinese mainland are on the shelves here. In 2001, it had annual sales of RMB260 million (US$31.33 million), becoming the leader for single store sales in China. In September 2002, it set the one-day sales record of RMB2 million (US$240,964). In addition to traditional state-owned bookstores, other industrial groups have begun to invest in book sales and distribution in recent years. Notably, the Guangdong Nuclear Power Group invested in building two superstores in Chongqing: the Chongqing Linjiangmen Modern Book City and the Chongqing Shapingba Modern Book City. The former is 24,000 square meters large and claims to be the largest bookstore in size. The latter is about 10,000 square meters.

What is worth mentioning here is the emergence of privately owned superstores in recent years. The well-known private superstores are Dongguan Yongzheng Book Shopping Center in Guangdong Province, Nanjing Book City, and Zhidao Book Square in Beijing. All three are over 10,000 square meters in size and stock over 100,000 titles.

Figure 5.4
Book Superstores

Store Name	Size[1]	Stock[2]	Annual Sales[3]	Highest Daily Annual Sales[4]	Ownership	Primary Investors
Beijing Book City	16	230	320	3,072	Equity	Beijing Xinhua Bookstore
Beijing Wangfujing Bookstore	17.5	217	200	1,020	Equity	Beijing Xinhua and Foreign Language Bookstore Group
Changchun Book City	12	150	N/A	250	Equity	Jilin Provincial Xinhua Bookstore Group and Chuangchun Ronguang Co., Ltd.
Changchun United Book City	10	180	N/A	N/A	Equity	Chuangchun United Book City Co., Ltd.
Chongqing Book City	14	15	N/A	500	Equity	Chongqing Xinhua Bookstore Group
Chongqing Linjiangmen Modern Book City	24	17	300	293	Equity	China Guangdong Nuclear Power Group
Chongqing Shapingba Modern Book City	10.5	10	N/A	N/A	Equity	China Guangdong Nuclear Power Group
Dongguan Yongzheng Book Shopping Center	12	100	N/A	188.5	Private	China's largest privately owned bookstore
Guangzhou Book Shopping Center	18	145	250	1,900	Equity	Guangzhou Xinhua Bookstore Group
Hubei Publishing Culture City Book Shopping Center	24	190	N/A	N/A	N/A	Hubei Book Distribution Group

[1] Thousand square meters
[2] Thousands of titles
[3] Millions of RMB
[4] Thousands of RMB

Figure 5.4 (Cont'd)

Store Name	Size[1]	Stock[2]	Annual Sales[3]	Highest Daily Annual Sales[4]	Ownership	Primary Investors
Knowledge Book Square	10	160	N/A	N/A	Equity	Xinhua Alliance and Beijing Xiuzheng Culture Development Co., Ltd.
Nanjing Book City	12	150	50	60	Equity	Private enterprise
North Book City	18	300	120	1,000	Equity	Liaoning Publishing Group
Shanghai Book City	10	200	199	1,280	Sole	Shanghai Press and Publications Administration
Shenzhen Book City	13	149	220	1,050	Sole	Shenzhen Xinhua Bookstore
Tianjin Book City	20	180	N/A	48	Sole	Tianjin Press and Publication Administration
Xi'an Book City	10	130	N/A	440	Equity	Xi'an Xinhua Bookstore
Zhejiang Book City	10	170	180	N/A	Sole	Zhejing Provincial Xinhua Distribution Group

[1] *Thousand square meters*
[2] *Thousands of titles*
[3] *Millions of RMB*
[4] *Thousands of RMB*

Source: *China Book Business Report*

In addition, several superstores are now under construction. Ten new superstores are planned to be opened in 2004. The most notable one is the Shenzhen Nanshan Book City, which will be 25,000 square meters, possibly the largest bookstore in the Chinese mainland in terms of physical size.

Professional bookstores are another kind of independent bookstore with unique features. At present, there are no statistics covering the number of professional bookstores in the Chinese mainland. Most professional bookstores specialize in social science books and are relatively well known to the public. In addition, there are professional bookstores specializing in medical, computer, legal, and architecture books. The best-known social science bookstores are the Beijing Taofen Book Center, Guo Lin Feng Bookstore, Feng Ru Song Bookstore, Wansheng Bookstore, Xueeryou Bookstore in Guangzhou, Xianfeng Bookstore in Nanjing, Scholar Bookstore in Changchun, Xiaofeng Bookstore in Fujian Province, Xi Xi Fu Bookstore in Guizhou Province, Jifeng Bookstore in Shanghai, and Hongwen Bookstore in Chengdu. Many are privately owned.

There is a relatively large number of computer and medical bookstores. According to industry experts there are over 100 professional medical bookstores. The most well-known are the Keyuan Book Co. in Changsha, Kexing Book Co. in Hangzhou, and Golden Camel Bookstore in Beijing. The well-known computer, science, and technology bookstores are Huangshun Bookstore in Xinjiang Autonomous Region, Dule Bookstore in Chengdu, Golden North Bookstore in Harbin, and Huiju Bookstore in Changsha. China Law Book Company is a famous legal bookstore. Many professional publishers also have their own professional bookstores. For example, the China Architecture & Building Press owns several bookstores. There are also foreign language bookstores in many big cities. These stores sell mainly English language books but they also carry books in other foreign languages such as Japanese, German, French, and Russian. The Beijing Foreign Language Bookstore and the Shanghai Foreign Language Bookstore are the largest foreign language bookstores.

2. *Bookstore Chains and Book Clubs*

If we exclude audio-video chains, there are dozens of bookstore chains, most of them regional. Very few of them operate across regions and a true national chain is non-existent. There are three kinds of bookstore chains: wholly owned, franchise, and hybrid. (See Figure 5.5.) A regional chain is normally formed by a provincial Xinhua bookstore and its subsidiary Xinhua bookstores at the prefecture and county levels. These Xinhua chain stores are wholly owned.

In addition, there are some privately owned chains such as the 21st Century Jinxiu Book Chain Co., Ltd., Jifeng Bookstore, Guanghe Bookstore, Xiaofeng Bookstore, and Lingyu Bookstore.

There are also quite a number of franchise chains such as the Modern Bookstore and the Xishu Bookstore. The Modern Bookstore is affiliated with the China National Publishing Industry Trading Corporation. It has opened more than 10 franchise stores in the Chinese mainland and also set up franchise outlets in Malaysia, Singapore, the United States, and Vietnam. Xishu Bookstore claims to have 500 franchise bookstores, most of which are small bookstores.

Some book "hybrid" chains consist of both wholly owned stores and franchise stores. The Joint Publishing Commercial Bookstore, Foreign Language Bookstores and bookstore chains formed by the Guangzhou Daily Publishing Group and Southern Daily are typical "hybrid" book chains. The Guangzhou Daily book chain not only set up two medium-sized book cities of 10,000 square meters in size, but also opened 100 bookstore chains, of which 30 stores are wholly owned while the rest are franchise operations.

In 2002, chain stores that were jointly invested and operated by Chinese and foreign partners were launched. In February 2002, Sony Music Entertainment Inc. (U.S.) formed a Shanghai Epic Music Entertainment Co., Ltd. (SEME) with Chinese partners. SEME is the first joint venture approved for audio-video distribution after China joined the WTO. Later, Bertelsmann purchased shares of the 21st Century Book Chain. The two sides

Figure 5.5
Major Bookstore Chains

Name	Owner	Number of Stores	Notes
Beijing Guo Lin Feng Bookstore	Beijing Guofeng Group	N/A	N/A
Beijing Jinhua Electric Power Bookstore	China Electric Power Publishing House	N/A	N/A
Beijing Rushiyuan Quality Bookstore	N/A	6	Shopping mall stores. 10 solely owned stores in Beijing and 20 franchises.
Changchun Scholar Bookstore	N/A	4	Stores in college community.
China Architecture Bookstore	China Building Industry Publishing House	300	Book chain consisting of distribution agents, bookstores, and outlets.
China Military Bookstore	People's Liberation Publishing House	N/A	Has branches in several provinces.
Dragon Media Advertising Bookstore	N/A	5	3 wholly owned stores and 2 franchises.
Fujian Xiaofeng Bookstore	N/A	9	N/A
Golden Camel Health Care Bookstore	Beijing Golden Camel Bookstore Co., Ltd.	N/A	N/A
Guangxi Nanguo Bookstore	N/A	3	Main store 3,000 sq. m. in size and two other professional bookstores.
Hangzhou Baitong Bookstore	N/A	N/A	N/A
Hunan Hongdao Culture Media Co., Ltd.,	N/A	13	N/A
Jifeng Bookstore	Jifeng Bookstore Co. Ltd.	5	Subway stores.
Jinxiu Bookstore	Beijing 21st Century Book Chain Co., Ltd.	30	Wholly owned stores and franchises.

Figure 5.5 (Cont'd)

Name	Owner	Number of Stores	Notes
Linyu Bookstore	Sichuan Feshan Linyu Book Co., Ltd.	9	6 wholly owned stores and 3 franchises.
Machine Industry Bookstore	China Machine Press	N/A	N/A
Modern Bookstore	China Publishing Industry Corp.	90	Has both solely owned stores, as well as franchise stores. Set up several franchise outlets in Southeast Asia.
National Art Book Specialty Stores	Arts Alliance Group	116	Member stores.
Ocean Book City	Guangzhou Daily Newspaper Group	100 stores and two superstores	30 wholly owned stores and 70 franchises stores.
Shenyang Dongyu Bookstore	Shenyang Dongyu Group	N/A	N/A
Shenyang Huiwen Bookstore	N/A	200	10 solely owned stores and 200 franchises.
South Daily Chain Bookstore	South Daily Group	40	Wholly owned stores and franchises.
The Commercial SDX Joint Publishing Bookstore	The Commercial Press and SDX Joint Publishing Co., Ltd.	13	Has both solely owned stores and franchises.
Tsinghua Bookstore	Tsinghua University Press	4	Direct management.
Xiamen Sunlight Bookstore	N/A	8	Community bookstores.
Xinhua Yizhan Chain	Xinhua General Bookstore and Chengcheng Culture Co., Ltd.	87	Franchises.
Xishu Bookstore	N/A	500	Franchises.
Yunan New Knowledge Bookstore	N/A	4	N/A

Figure 5.6
Book Clubs

Name	Establishment Date	Owner and Operator	Membership ('000s)	Notes
Atlas World Book Club	1998	China Cartographic Publishing House	N/A	N/A
Bertelsmann Book Club	1997	Shanghai Bertelsmann Culture Industry Co., Ltd.	1,500	A joint venture between German Bertelsmann AG and China Science and Technology Book Company.
China Book Club	1999	China National Publications Import & Export (Group) Corporation	350	N/A
China Legal Book Club	2003	China Legal Book Company, an affiliation of China Law Publishing House	N/A	Members are law professionals.
China Youth New Century Book Club	1998	The Central Committee of Chinese Communist Youth League	500	Built 1,000 branch clubs and stores all over China.
CNPITC Book Club	2002	China National Publishing Industry Corp.	N/A	Members are publishers. The club assists copyright cooperation between Chinese and foreign publishers.
East Tongfang Book Club	1998	The National Working Committee of People's Publishing Houses and *Wenhua Reading Weekly*	N/A	Equity controlled by Shanghai People's Publishing House.
Fashion Book Club	1997	Fashion Magazine	50	N/A
FLTRP Book Club	1998	Foreign Language Teaching and Research Press	50	Specialty Book Club.
Golden Camel Medical Book Club	N/A	Beijing Golden Camel Bookstore Co., Ltd.	N/A	N/A
Guo Lin Feng Book Club	N/A	Guofeng Group	N/A	N/A

Figure 5.6 (Cont'd)

Name	Establishment Date	Owner and Operator	Membership ('000)	Notes
Henan Provincial Xinhua Bookstore Reader's Book Club	2000	Henan Provincial Xinhua Bookstore	500	400 outlets in Henan Province.
Jiangsu Shuyuan Book Club	N/A	Jiangsu Provincial Xinhua Bookstore Group	N/A	N/A
Leaders' Book Club	2000	*Biweekly Forum* Magazine	N/A	As subscribers of *Biweekly Forum*, members are government officials and company managers.
Liaoning Book Lovers Club	1995	Liaoning Education Publishing House	30	N/A
SDX Joint Taofen Book Club	N/A	SDX Joint Publishing Co., Ltd.	N/A	N/A
"Magic Gourd" Young Readers Club	N/A	China Juvenile and Children's Publishing House	N/A	N/A
WPC Medical Book Club	1999	World Publishing Corporation	N/A	China's first specialty book club serving medical professionals.
Xishu Good Book Club	1997	Xishu Bookstore	220	Club member direct sales, book chain retail and online book sales.
Youth Digest Book Club	N/A	China Youth Press	N/A	A non-profit club.

will form a new joint-venture company, which is expected to be the first national book chain jointly owned by Chinese and foreign investors.

In addition, many firms such as the Xinhua Bookstores and the post offices in Beijing, Shanghai, and Guangzhou are making detailed plans to open city-wide book chains. New book chains continue to be set up but in general, the operation of book chains in the Chinese mainland is still at the start-up stage. the Chinese mainland still lacks the modern, national super book chains similar to Barnes & Noble or Borders in the West.

Book clubs have existed for less than 10 years in the Chinese mainland. The earliest book clubs include the Guangzhou Seven Star Book Club, Zhengzhou Reading Club, and Guangzhou Book Club. The number of book clubs gradually increased after the second half of 1998. Now, there are

Figure 5.7
Book Distribution and Fulfillment Centers in China

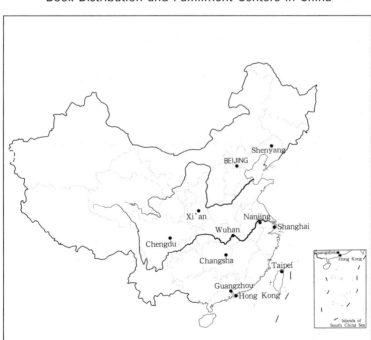

several dozen book clubs but only a dozen of them have any appreciable scale or influence. The main operators of book clubs in the Chinese mainland include publishers, state-owned bookstores, book import-export companies and privately-owned bookstores. (See Figure 5.6.) Bertelsmann, China National Publications Import & Export (Group) Corporation (CNPIEC), Book Lovers, Xishu, and Biweekly Forum are the most influential book clubs. Some book clubs have their own publications and websites. The Bertelsmann Book Club, jointly founded in Shanghai by the German Bertelsmann AG and China Science and Technology Book Company, is not only the first joint-venture book club approved by the government, but also the largest and most influential book club in China. At present, the book club has 1.5 million members, set up eight membership recruiting centers (six in Shanghai and two in Beijing), and has created an online media house (www.bolchina.com). Its annual revenues are over RMB100 million (US$12.05 million). (See Chapter 10-D.)

Online bookselling in the Chinese mainland also underwent fast growth in recent years. Today, there are more than 300 online bookstores in the Chinese mainland. Joyo.com, Dangdang.com and Bol.com.cn are a few of the leading examples.

3. *The Wholesale Market, Distribution Logistics, Book and Trade Fairs*

Wholesale markets and distribution logistics centers are the cornerstone of logistical support for bookstore sales. The publication wholesale markets underwent fast growth and now operate on large scales. Large wholesale markets serve as distribution centers for publications. They tend to be concentrated in urban areas that offer convenient transportation. Chinese cities capable of such large volume distribution are Beijing, Shenyang in Northeast China, Xi'an in Northwest China, Changsha and Wuhan in Central China, Nanjing and Shanghai in East China, Chengdu in Southwest China, and Guangzhou in the South.

The most well-known large book and magazine wholesale markets are the Sweet Water Garden Book Wholesale Mart in Beijing, Yangtze River Delta Book Wholesale Market in Nanjing, Book World in Wuhan, Ding Wang Dai Book Wholesale Market in Changsha, Wen Miao Book Wholesale Mart in Shanghai, Haiyin Book Mart in Guangzhou, and Shang Qin Lu Book Mart in Xi'an. Sweet Water Garden Book Wholesale Mart in Beijing is the largest and most influential wholesale market with the widest network of clients. It is 13,000 square meters in size and houses 400 booksellers. Its annual wholesale volume is RMB2 billion (almost US$241 million).

In contrast to large wholesale markets and superstores, distribution and fulfillment operations lag relatively behind. To keep up with new developments, Beijing, Jiangsu Province, Zhejiang Province, and Liaoning Province have all begun to build modern logistics centers to serve the trade and many new publication distribution centers have been put into operation. Logistics centers now in operation or under development are the distribution center of Jiangsu Xinhua Bookstore Group, the logistics center of Zhejiang Xinhua Bookstore Group, the book distribution center of Beijing Xinhua Bookstore General Store, and the fulfillment center of Jilin Xinhua Bookstore Group. (See Figure 5.8.) Taiwanese and foreign logistics companies have also entered into Chinese distribution logistics market through joint ventures. The Century/Qiuyu Distribution Co., Ltd., a joint investment between the Shanghai Century Publishing Group and Taiwan Qiuyu Fulfillment and Distribution Company, is already in operation. The Taiwan Elite Bookstore has entered into the market by providing logistics center development plans for Chinese book distributors such as the Xinhua Bookstore of Jiangxi Province.

By the end of 2004, several large logistics centers in the Northwest, East, and Central regions will be put into operation and will substantially modernize book distribution.

Each year many book fairs, book trade fairs, and book order fairs are held. These three kinds of events have different focuses. At book fairs, the display of new books is the priority while the

Figure 5.8
Major Book Distribution Centers

Name	Location	Size ('000 m²)	Status	Future Plans
Guangdong Xinhua Bookstore Group Logistics Center	Guangzhou	45	In use since 2001. Stocking 120,000 titles and shipping 100,000 tons annually.	Expanded by an additional thousand square meters. Complete in 2004.
Henan Provincial Xinhua Bookstore Fulfillment Center	Zhengzhou	30	In use since 1997.	Building a new distribution center of 87 thousand square meters.
Hubei Provincial Xinhua Bookstore Fulfillment Center	Wuhan	20	N/A	N/A
Jiangsu Xinhua Bookstore Group Logistics Company	Nanjing	80	30% capacity in use.	Completion in 2004.
Jiangxi Xinhua Bookstore United Co., Ltd. Distribution Center	Nanchang	40	In use since 2002.	N/A
Jilin Xinhua Bookstore Group Distribution Center	Changchun	47	N/A	N/A
Liaoning North Publications Logistics Co., Ltd.	Shenyang	74	In use since 2000. Guaranteed stock of 300,000 titles.	Matching commodity and distribution flows with information cash flows.
Sichuan Xinhua Bookstore Group Western Book Fulfillment Center	Chengdu	46	In use since 2002.	N/A
Xinhua General Bookstore Beijing Publications Distribution Center	Beijing	57	N/A	N/A
Zhejiang Xinhua Bookstore Group Fulfillment Center	Hangzhou	74	35% capacity in use with 145,300 titles in stock.	Completion in 2004.

Source: *CNPIEC*

book sales come second. International book trade fairs focus on copyright negotiation while standard book trade fairs are open to the public for retail sales. Wholesale transactions are also conducted at trade fairs. Book order fairs are mainly for wholesalers and new books are also on display. In recent years, the differences have gradually blurred.

Presently, the most important book fair, book trade fair, and book order fair are the Beijing International Book Fair (BIBF), the National Book Trade Fair and the Beijing Book Order Fair. The BIBF is the biggest event for Sino-foreign copyright and import/export trade. It is held in Beijing at the end of August or the beginning of September each year. BIBF is sponsored by GAPP, the Information Office of the State Council, the Beijing Municipal Government, and other government organizations. The book fair is organized by the China National Publications Import & Export (Group) Corporation. BIBF is the most important copyright trade fair among Chinese and foreign publishers. The exhibition is 26,400 square meters in size with 930–990 booths. Participants come from 40 countries, regions, and international organizations. More than 100,000 book titles and 10,000 audio/video publications are on display. The 11th Beijing International Book Fair will be held at Beijing Exhibition Hall from September 2 to 6, 2004.

The National Book Trade Fair is the Chinese mainland's largest book retail event. It is held in a different city each year over the last 10 days of May. The trade fair is mainly for retail sales and the transaction volume is huge. So far 13 such fairs have been held. There were 996 stands at the last National Book Trade Fair. Of these, there were 773 bookstands, 162 magazine stands and 101 stands for audio-video and electronic publications with more than 150,000 titles on display. The trade volume exceeded RMB16.7 million (US$2.01 million) at the main exhibition center and there were additional orders totaling RMB1 billion (US$120.48 million). The 14th National Book Trade Fair was held in Guilin in the Guangxi Autonomous Region in May 2004.

The Beijing Book Order Fair is held every January during which book publishers and wholesalers sign order agreements over four days. About 554 publishers, 100 magazines, 52 second-tier wholesalers and publishers' branches, and 78 publishing-related companies participated in the 2004 fair. In addition, 69 overseas Chinese bookstores also participated. There were 1,642 stands at the fair and orders totaled RMB2.59 billion (US$312.05 million).

In addition to the ongoing national book trade events, there are many other book fairs, trade fairs, and book order fairs every year. Most events are regional and, or category specific. Other major international book fairs in the Chinese mainland include the Beijing International Audio, Video and Electronic Book Fair and the Beijing International Children's Book Fair.

4. Publication Import and Export Trade

Engaging in the publication import and export trade requires a special business license. There are about 40 book import and export companies in the Chinese mainland. (See Appendix 5.) They are all state-owned and most are affiliated with provincial press and publications administrations or large publishing corporations.

For example, the China International Book Trading Corporation is affiliated with the China International Publishing Group. The Tianjin Publications Import and Export (Group) Corporation is affiliated with the Tianjin Municipal Press and Publications Administration. The China National Science-Technology Information Import and Export Corporation, Beijing Company is affiliated with the China Science Publishing Group. The largest book import and export companies with full services in the Chinese mainland are the China National Publications Import & Export (Group) Corporation, the China International Book Trading Corporation, the China National Publishing Industry Trading Corporation, the Beijing Publications Import and Export Corporation, and the Shanghai Book Traders. The latter two also own the Beijing Foreign Language Bookstore and the Shanghai Foreign Language Book Store.

The China National Publications Import & Export (Group) Corporation, affiliated with China Publishing Group, is the largest book importer and exporter. Its headquarters is in Beijing with branches in six cities including Shanghai, Xi'an, and Guangzhou. It also has overseas offices in the U.S. (New Jersey), U.K. (London), Germany (Frankfurt), Russia (Moscow), Japan (Tokyo), and Singapore. It has total assets of RMB2 billion (US$240.96 million) and employs 2,300 people and in 2002 its revenues totaled RMB1.4 billion (US$168.67 million).

In 2002, the total trade volume of publication imports and exports reached US$127 million. The publications import volume of all kinds of publications exceeded the export volume. The overall trade volume in book imports and exports is much smaller compared to that of developed countries, the main reason being insufficient purchasing power in foreign currency terms. An additional reason is that there have been substantial increases in the acquisition of foreign translation and reprint rights.

In 2002, exports of books, newspapers, periodicals, audio-video, and electronic publications totaled US$19.58 million while imports were US$107 million. The trade deficit was US$82.42 million. For books, exports totaled 3.21 million copies with a total value of US$136.3 million, and import ran to 2.58 million copies with a total value of US$26.22 million, a trade deficit of US$12.59 million. For magazines, exports totaled 2.06 million copies with a total value of US$3.03 million and imports totaled 5.12 million copies with a total value of US$61.2 million, a trade deficit of US$58.17 million. For newspapers, the Chinese mainland exports ran to 940,000 copies with a total value of US$740,000 and imports totaled 6.48 million copies with a total value of US$7.45 million, a trade deficit of US$6.71 million. For audio-video and electronic publications, imports totaled 885,000 copies with a total value of US$2.71 million and exports totaled 829,500 copies with a total value of US$12.23 million, leading to a US$10.06 million trade surplus.

The Publishing Industry of Taiwan

A. Overview

Taiwan, with a population of 23 million in an area of about 36,200 square kilometers, is the most developed region of the Chinese publishing industry, and its total publishing capacity ranks second among the three major Chinese publishing bases. In 2001, the GDP in Taiwan reached US$12,621 per capita, and people there spent an average of about US$74 yearly on books per capita.

Figure 6.1
Map of Taiwan

Chinese publishing in Taiwan began to develop in the late 1940s and made rapid progress shortly thereafter. Before the mid-1960s, there were less than 1,000 publishing houses but the 1,000 mark was broken in 1967. In the early 1980s, Taiwan had over 2,000 publishing houses and by 1988 the number surpassed 3,000. By the end of 2002, more than 8,000 book publishing houses had been registered in Taiwan, along with around 2,800 audio-video publishing companies, 7,800 magazine publishers, 450 newspaper publishers, and 270 news agencies.

A large number of books are published in Taiwan annually and in 2003 the total output reached 38,000 titles, of which 25,000 were new. In recent years, Taiwan's average annual book output reached 35,000 titles and in the late 1990s the average annual sales totaled NT$57 billion (US$1.67 billion).

Publishing companies in Taiwan are mainly located in the north of the island. Half of the entire industry is concentrated in the city and county of Taipei, with the rest scattered mostly in Taichung, Kaohisung, and Tainan. Taipei is home to 70% of the total number of book publishers, 80% of audio-video, 60% of magazine, 50% of newspaper, and 55% of news agencies. Most publishing houses are private companies, with the rest being public enterprises, or owned and operated by political parties or the military as "government publishers."

The publishing industry in Taiwan began to experience fierce competition from the 1980s. After 2000, factors like foreign investment and entry into the WTO have led to increased competition. As creative industries have become more important in the global economy, Taiwan has moved aggressively to promote intellectual property rights and foster creativity. By the end of 2003, experts from industry, the administrative sector, and the academic world worked together and formed the "Guiding Committee for Cultural and Creative Industries." The aim is to provide overall regulation and integration between the media, design, and arts sectors of the cultural and creative industries. Soon after, the First Taiwan Creative Design Exhibition was held, marking the first step toward regulating and integrating cultural and creative industries, including the publishing industry.

B. Book Publishing

1. *Overview*

About 7,000 to 8,000 book publishing houses are registered in Taiwan, but only 1,500 of them produce more than two titles annually and only 500 more than ten titles. According to statistics provided by the Taiwan Department of Commerce of the Ministry of Economic Affairs, 1,503 publishing companies paid taxes in 2002, with total sales of NT$20.92 billion (US$611.7 million).

A majority of Taiwan publishing houses do not have a long history. Throughout the entire industry, about 50% were established within the last five years and 20% are between 10 and 20 years old, 14% between 20 and 30 years, and only 0.03% have more than a 30-year history. The companies with a relatively long history are Eastern Publishing Co., Ltd., San Min Book Co., Ltd., Crown Publishing House, the Far East Book Co., Ltd. and those that moved to Taiwan from the Chinese mainland, such as The Commercial Press Ltd., Chung Hwa Book Co., World Book Co., Ltd., and Cheng Chung Book Co., Ltd.

The *2000 Taiwan Publishing Market Report* shows that 47% of the publishing houses have annual sales less than NT$10 million, 23% between NT$10 and 60 million, 2.5% between NT$60 and 100 million and 7.7% over NT$100 million. The average annual sales for book publishing companies is around NT$34.5 million (US$1.01 million).

In terms of capital assets, over half of the publishing houses have less than NT$500,000, 20% more than NT$5 million, and the rest between NT$500,000 and 5 million. By business structure, 34% (a different reference suggests 50%) are limited liability companies, 27% are incorporated companies, and 23% sole proprietorships. In addition, about 6% are operated by corporate agents.

In terms of personnel, about 56% employ less than 10 people, 11% between 11 and 20, 12% 21–100, 6% 101–500, and 0.55% more than 500 employees. Therefore, publishing houses in Taiwan are primarily small and medium-sized enterprises.

Prominent and comprehensive publishing houses include:

Cite Publishing Ltd., Yuan-Liou Publishing Co., Ltd., China Times Publishing Company, Linking Publishing Co., Ltd., the Crown Culture Corporation, Eurasian Press; The Commercial Press Ltd., Commonwealth Publishing Company, Wu-Nan Book Co., Ltd., San Min Book Co., Ltd., Cheng Chung Book, the Sitak Publishing Group, Chuan Hwa Science & Technology Book Co., Ltd., Unalis Publishing Company, Hsin-Yi Publications, Living Psychology Publishers, Locus Publishing Company, Kang Hsuan Educational Publishing Group, and the Ting Wen Book House.

In recent years, increased competition and a drive for growth has pushed publishers to form publishing groups. Three major methods have been explored and implemented. First, a publishing house spins off a number of subsidiary companies, that is how Crown Publishing House transformed into the Crown Culture Corporation. The second is to integrate several publishers, the method adopted by the Taiwan Mansion Books Group, which consists of Taiwan Mansion Books, Business Communication, Lifetime MENU, International Study Village, BMG Reading Society, Popular Book Study Room, and Visual Culture. The third way is restructuring by acquiring controling shares of other houses, as Cite Publishing Holding has done.

Cite Publishing Holding, controlled by Tom Group Ltd. in Hong Kong, is the largest publishing group in Taiwan. (See Figure 6.2.) It includes PC Home Group, Cite Publishing Group, Business Weekly Group, Sharp Point Group and Citta Bella Group. Overall, Cite owns about 30 publishing houses, 42 magazines and produces 25 million magazines and 10 million copies of books, with an annual income of NT$3.1 billion (US$90.64 million) and a net profit of NT$400 million (US$11.7 million) before taxes. Its Sharp Point Publishing, Rye Field Publishing, Owl Publishing House, Grimm Press, and Business Weekly Publications, Ltd., are all prominent publishing companies, and *Citta Bella*, *Business Weekly*, and *PC Home* are well-known magazines.

Publishing companies favor literature highly, followed by religion. Books on psychology, medicine, home economics, arts, and children's books also have considerable output. Of the total,

Figure 6.2
Organizational Structure of Cite Publishing Holding

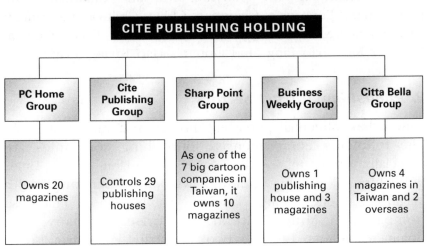

about 75% are in Chinese, 19% in English and 5.8% in Japanese. Literature always ranks first, followed by books on finance, industrial and business management, and comic books.

Book prices in Taiwan are higher compared with other Chinese book markets. According to the *2000 Taiwan Publishing Market Report*, the average price is around NT$222.40 (US$6.54), paperbacks at about NT$214.34 (US$6.27) and hardcovers at NT$291 (US$8.51).

There are many book awards in Taiwan. An important official award is the Golden Tripod Award, and the two most influential non-governmental awards, sponsored by the *United Daily News* and the *China Times*, are the Reader's Choice Award and the Opening-Book Award. The latter two awards offer annual prizes in three categories: non-fiction, fiction and children's books, with the winners announced at the beginning of the year. Some famous bookstore chains such as King Stone and Eslite also sponsor annual book awards.

Prominent figures in the Taiwan publishing industry include Cite's President Jan Hung Tze and General Manager Ho Fei Peng, Yuan-Liou's Chairman Wang Jung-Wen, Locus's Rex How, Common Wealth magazine's Charles H. C. Kao, Linking's distributor Liu Kuo-Jui, San Min's Chairman Liu Chen Chiang, Crown's Chairman Ping Shin-Tao, Wu-Nan's Chairman Yang Jung-Chuan, Eurasian's Chairman Chien Chih-Chong, Chuan Hwa Science & Technology's Jan I-Jeng, China Times' General Manager Mo Chao Ping, and Grimm's Hao Kuang Tsai.

2. Publishing Market Sectors

Taiwan has influential publishing houses in a variety of fields. The following comprehensive publishing companies are especially strong in social sciences: Yuan-Liou, China Times Publishing Company, Linking, Wu-Nan, Common Wealth Magazine, Cheng Chung, San Min, Youth Cultural Enterprise Company, Li Ming Cultural Enterprise Company, The Commercial Press, Laureate Book Company, Bookman Books Ltd., Literature, History, and Philosophy and Biographical Literature. Among them, Yuan-Liou, China Times Publishing, Linking, Wu-Nan, Common Wealth Magazine, and San Min are the most influential.

Established in 1975, Yuan-Liou is one of the largest publishing companies with over 170 employees and publishes more than 300 titles yearly with annual sales of over NT$600 million (approximately US$18 million). It produces books on psychology, literature, business and life management, children's books, and reference books. Its publications also cover foreign subjects, and it has published the *European Encyclopedia, Western Cultures Collection*, and *World Classic Biographical Works Series*. In addition, it publishes many magazines, including the popular American scientific magazine, *Scientific American*, in traditional Chinese.

China Times Publishing and Linking Publishing are affiliated with the two large newspaper groups in Taiwan, the China Times Group and the United Daily News Group. China Times Publishing has around 100 employees and publishes more than 300 titles yearly with annual sales of around NT$350 million (US$10.23 million). While upholding humanist ideals, it accommodates a variety of views, appreciates the development of new ideas and trends, and has established a strong brand name in the Taiwanese book market. So far, China Times has published books by the well-known comic writer Tsai Chih-Chung and influential writers such as Ha Jin, Yu Qiuyu and, thanks to the efforts of this company, Milan Kundera, Alvin Toffler, Italo Calvino, Günter Grass, Kenzaburo Oe, and Haruki Murakami have become household names in Taiwan. China Times also operates a reading website, www.readingtimes.com.tw. It is the first publishing company in Taiwan to be listed on the stock market.

Linking Publishing, founded in 1974, publishes high quality books on the humanities and social sciences. It produces more than 100 new titles annually and its publications include the imperial archives of the Ming and Qing dynasties; complete works by Chinese cultural masters such as Qian Mu, Ch'u Wanli, Xiao Gongquan (Hsiao Kung-chuan), and Mou Zongsan; and book series by Ray Huang and Gao Yang. It has published notable foreign literary works such as *In Search of Lost Time* and *The Lord of the Rings* among others. Of all the publishing companies in Taiwan, Linking has been awarded the greatest number of Golden Tripod Awards.

Common Wealth Magazine Co., Ltd. is a subsidiary of Commonwealth Publishing Company with about 80 employees and an annual output of 120 titles. It encourages its staff to "make work choices based on ideals and explore work methods with conscience," and has published many excellent social sciences titles. Its parent company, Common Wealth, produces the *Global Views Monthly* and operates a book club, Readers' Society, and a bookstore (93 Reader Space), as well as two websites, www.bookzone.com.tw and www.gvm.com.tw. Its founder, Charles H. C. Kao, is an internationally well-known economist.

Wu-Nan is strong in textbooks, reference books and books on law and test preparation. It produces more than 200 titles annually and owns several bookstores. San Min, boasting the longest history among the publishing companies in Taiwan, is a major publisher for reference books, humanities academic books, and textbooks for the higher education market.

Many publishers compete in publishing literature titles. Prominent names are Crown, Unitas Publishing Company, Eurasian Press, Rye Field Press, Sitak Publishing Group, Chiu Ko Publishing Co., Ltd., Elite Books, Hung-Fan Bookstore, Great Earth (Dadi) Publishing House, Chih Wen Publishing Co., Ltd., Morning Star Press, Hann Colour, Shui Yun Zhai, Vista Publishing, Avanguard Publishing Company, and Linbai, among others. Some new companies are also worthy of mention such as Locus Publishing Company, Aquarius Publishing Co., Ltd., and Ink Publishing Co., Ltd.

Crown, Eurasian and Sitak have a large share in the pop literature market. Crown Culture Corporation is a comprehensive publishing corporation and engages in a variety of activities including book publishing, audio-video production, film and TV production, as well as running an art gallery, theater, and dance troupe. In the publishing division, the Crown Culture Corporation has several subsidiary companies, including Crown Magazine, Crown Publishing Company, Ping's Publications, Ltd., Ping's Audio-Video Publications Limited and Ping's Paperback Book Publications Limited. In addition, Crown has also established a branch office in Hong Kong. Annually, Crown produces more than 250 titles. Eurasian, including Eurasian Press, Fine Press, and Athena Press, has set many records in literature publishing in Taiwan. For instance, it once issued 164 consecutive editions of *Wild Fire* by Long Yingtai, sold 200,000 units of Lin Qingxian's audio books, and had sales of NT$300 million (US$8.77 million) over just nine months. Sitak has 130 employees and produces more than 100 new titles annually. Over the 30 years since its establishment, Sitak has published many popular books such as *World Literature Classics Series, Aim High Psychology Series, The French Medal Literature Series, Discovery*, and *Shine.*

Among serious literature publishers, it is impossible to ignore the Unitas Publishing Company. Like Linking, Unitas is affiliated with the United Daily News Group and produces about 30 new titles annually. Most of its publications are works by contemporary Chinese writers. Beyond producing far-reaching books on literature and the arts, it also sponsors the most influential literature magazine in Taiwan, *Unitas*. The "Little Fives"—Chiu Ko Publishing, Elite Books, Hung-Fan Bookstore, Great Earth Publishing House, and Pure Literature Publishing House (now out of business)—are known for their dedication to serious literature. Founders of the "Little Fives" themselves were writers or poets and later became publishers. Elite and Chiu Ko have the honor of publishing annual anthologies of the best stories, poems and prose from Taiwan. Chiu Ko has published James Joyce's masterpiece *Ulysses*, a work notoriously difficult to translate, and has also founded the "Chiu Ko Culture and Educational Foundation."

There are not many art book publishing companies in Taiwan. At present the prominent ones include Lionart, Artist Publishing Company, and Art Book Co., Ltd. Lionart is the most well known art book publisher and has a history of 30 years. It has published art book series with more than 300 titles and issues the leading arts magazine, *Lionart Monthly*.

Taiwan has many children's book publishing houses with a large annual output. Major ones include Grimm Press, Hsin-Yi, Newton Publishing Co., Ltd., Lsiao Lu Publishing Company, Echo Publishing Co., Ltd., Formosan Magazine Press, Eastern Publishing Company, Children Publication Co., Ltd., Zhi Mao, Childhood, and Fuchun Culture. Grimm is a young company with over 300 well-received titles over seven years. The press often commissions first-class illustrators for its publications, and therefore it is not a surprise that several Grimm's books, such as *Modern Edition Classic Children's Stories*, *Classic Works Illustrated Edition* and *Shakespeare*, were selected for an exhibition at International Children's Book Illustrations Exhibition in Bologna, Italy. During the International Children's Book Illustrations Bangladesh Biennial, Grimm was picked as the best children's book publishing house in the world. Grimm's chief editor, Hao Kuang Tsai, was once invited to serve as a judge in the International Children's Book Illustrations Exhibition in Bologna.

Hsin-Yi was started in 1978 by the Hsin-Yi Foundation, the only foundation dedicated to pre-school education research. It specializes in picture books for young children. With the mission statement of "guarding childhood for children," Hsin-Yi publishes a variety of titles for children up to 12 years old, teachers, and parents. It also publishes many magazines including *Pre-School Education.*

Comic books have always held an important place in Taiwan's publishing industry. Such books have a large market share, and publishers have produced all variety of comic books. Well-known companies in this field include: Tongli Publishing Co., Sharp Point Publishing, Taiwan Tohan Co., Ltd., Youth Literary Book Store, Shang Deng, China Times Publishing, Ever Glory Publishing Co., Ltd., and Da Ran Culture Enterprise Co., Ltd. Together, they are known as the "Eight Bigs." Tongli, the largest among them, employs more than 100 people, publishes 1,400 titles annually, and owns 5 comic magazines, a film and TV media company, and operates a branch office in Hong Kong. In addition, Tongli has its own well-organized distribution network and eight direct sales centers in Taiwan. Its Hong Kong branch produces around 40 books every month. Tongli's comic books have entered into the international market with the copyrights of *The Little Monk* and *Wedding Peach* sold in Spain and Italy. Nevertheless, competition in this field is very fierce, and no publishing house is able to stay on top. Currently, Da Ran, one of the "Eight Bigs," already faces many difficulties.

In the science and technology publishing sector, prominent companies include Chuan Hwa Science & Technology Book Co., Ltd., Unalis Publishing Company, Scholars Publishing Company, XiaoYuan, and Jian Hong. Rapid development in information technology in recent years has led to the establishment of many e-book publishing companies. The well-known players are the TWP Corporation, Liwil, Flag Publishing, Team Strong Media Co., Ltd., Dr. Master Press Co., Ltd., Hudson Technology & Culture Company, Gotop Information, Inc., Informationist, and PCuSer Press Co., Ltd.

Chuan Hwa Science & Technology Book Co., Ltd. is a major science and technology publisher in Taiwan. In the 30 years since its establishment, it has published more than 5,000 titles specializing in information technology, mechanical manufacturing, civil engineering, industrial chemistry, and business management. It imports and markets books in Western languages and computer software. The company has more than 100 employees with annual sales of NT$300 million (US$8.77 million). It has made great contributions to Taiwan's scientific and technological education. Chuan Hwa controls several subsidiary companies: Quan You Book House, Song Gen Publishing House, Hua Li Publishing House, Electronic Book House, Mechanical Technology Magazine House, Electronic Technology Magazine House, and Yung Hwa Printmaking Plant.

Competition in educational publishing has always been fierce and has been even more so since 1989, when non-governmental publishing houses were allowed to publish textbooks. Leading companies with a considerable share in the textbook market are Kang Hsuan Education Group, Ting Wen Culture Group, Wu-Nan Culture Group, Chien-Hua Culture Group, and San Min Book. Kang Hsuan Education Group is the largest textbook publisher with over 600 employees and annual sales of NT$2.3 billion (US$67.25 million). Its major market is primary school textbooks and books used in bilingual schools. Over 50% of primary school students in Taiwan buy Kang Hsuan textbooks, and the company controls about 60% of the entire textbook market share. In addition, it operates bilingual education schools and has six education websites. Ting Wen Culture Group controls Ting Wen Book House and Dawa Fax Publishing in addition to several weekly test-preparation magazines, websites, printing houses, and tutorial centers.

Many influential publishing houses are also active in other areas. Publishers strong in finance and law books include Common Wealth Magazine Company, Wealth Group, Excellence Monthly Company, Harvard Management Services Inc., China Credit Information Services Ltd., Long River Publications, Wu-Nan, and Wei Li Law Office. Prominent linguistics publishers include Far East Books, Classic Communications Company, Bookman, Caves Books, Hall of Great Scholars, and Warmth Publications. Influential publishers of lifestyle books are Outdoor

Life Books Co., Ltd., Fine Press, Taiwan Tohan, Homer Publishing, Living Psychology Publishers, Shy Mau Publishing Company, Hilit Publishing Co., Ltd., and Yi Qun.

There are many religious publishing houses in Taiwan. Most are Christian and Buddhist, and some operate on a considerable scale. Large Christian publishing houses include Taosheng Publishing, Kuangchi Cultural Group, Christian Cosmic Light, and Logos Publishers Limited. Large Buddhist publishing houses include Dharma Drum Publishing Corp., Gandha Samudra Culture Company, Fo Kuang Culture Enterprise Co., Ltd., Heavenly Lotus Publishing Co., Ltd., Buddhist Publishing House, Foguang University Press, and Torch of Wisdom Publishing House.

C. Magazine Publishing

Like book publishers, magazine publishers in Taiwan also face a fiercely competitive environment. Around 7,800 magazine publishers are registered with about 1,500 magazines available on the market. Other than annual publications and quarterly magazines and journals, there are about 600 magazines. From official statistics, 835 magazine publishers paid a total of NT$18.35 billion in taxes in 2000. Chun Tsiao Yeh's *Taiwan Commercial Magazines Market Report 2000* shows that magazine sales range from NT$30 to 50 billion. This includes NT$10 billion from advertising revenue—accounting for 8% of Taiwan media advertising total NT$80 billion—NT$10 billion from retail sales, and NT$15 billion from subscriptions.

The *Taiwan Publishing Market Report 2000* recorded that the average capital of Taiwan magazine companies is around NT$33 million. 42% of these companies have capital less than NT$10 million, 14% between NT$10 and 50 million, 12% between NT$50 and 100 million and only 9% more than NT$100 million. Average annual sales of Taiwan magazine companies totals NT$65.7 million. The average staff number is around 58 and 38% have less than 20 employees, 20% between 20 and 50, 19% between 50 and 100, and 19% more than 100 staff. In terms of company structure, 50% are incorporated companies, 18% limited liability companies, and 16% are sole proprietorships. Fierce competition has led to high market entry costs. Presently, a monthly magazine needs starting capital of NT$20–30 million (US$584,795–877,193), and a weekly magazine requires about NT$50 million (US$1.46 million) to have a viable launch.

Taiwan magazine titles sell on average about 32,300 copies. 9% sell less than 4,000 copies, 15% between 4,000 and 10,000, 15% between 10,000 and 20,000, 24% between 20,000 and 50,000, 19% between 50,000 and 100,000, and only 5% more than 100,000 copies. In terms of distribution, 41% sell via their own distribution networks and sales agents, 38% rely totally on sales agents, and 15% distribute only largest via their own sales network.

Monthly magazines have the largest print runs, representing 40% of the total, followed in a descending order by quarterly, bimonthly, weekly, biweekly and magazines published every 10 days. According to an ACNielsen research, 28% of Taiwan readers prefer monthlies, and 16% favor weeklies. However, readers' need for timely information has forced many magazine publishers to change their strategy and increase frequency. It is common to see monthly magazines move to two issues per month. Magazines focusing on finance, economics, specific industries, and business are the greatest in number, accounting for 20% of total titles, followed by, in a descending order, magazines focusing on: education and culture, religion, society, communication, medicine and health, engineering technology, agricultural-forest-fishery products, and local news. Each of these categories has more than 200 magazines.

Magazines focusing on current affairs, entertainment, fashion, foreign language studies, and finance and economics enjoy large sales. In the entertainment and fashion sector, imported magazines are the old favorites, such as *Vogue*, *GQ*, *Marie Claire*, and *Elle*. Gradually, locally produced titles have gained market share, such as *Citta Bella*, *BEAUTY*, *Look*, *More Beautiful*, *My Birthday*, *Flea Market*, and *Taiwan Motor*. Other magazines with a sizable market include travel and leisure magazines, such as *Taipei Walker*, *Here!*, and *TO'GO*; foreign language studies magazines such as *Studio Classroom, Let's Talk In English, Time Express* and *Ivy League Analytical English*; financial and economic magazines such as *Wealth Magazine, Money,* and *Common Wealth Monthly.* Weekly magazines in Taiwan mainly focus on current affairs and news, and prominent ones include *China Times Weekly, Business Weekly, Next Magazine, The Journalist, Win Win Weekly, TVBS* and *4sight.*

Common Wealth Monthly is one of the most influential political-economic magazines in Taiwan. It provides in-depth reports on political and economic issues and attracts readers from politics and business including intellectuals and management professionals. It has won the Golden Tripod Awards and the Asian Financial News Awards sponsored by Citibank several times. It contains interviews with many famous world political and business leaders, such as Kenichi Ohmae, Peter Drucker, Peter M. Senge, Michael E. Porter, Bill Gates, Akio Morita, Mahathir Mohammed, Lee Kuan Yew, and Fidel Ramos. The *New York Times* highly recommends the magazine, calling it "the first complete economic magazine in Taiwan." This magazine's annual report on the top 1,000 manufactures in Taiwan has become the most authoritative survey of its kind. The Common Wealth Monthly Company also publishes *Common Health, Techvantage, Cheers,* as well as operating the Common Life Publishing website (www.cw.com.tw) and a bookstore (Book Garden.)

Citta Bella, a leading magazine on life and fashion, has a large readership primarily of young women and has sales of 20,000 copies. It has developed into a magazine group, publishing *Citta Bella, Mom Baby, Marie Claire,* and *Shape,* as well as establishing overseas operations.

Despite the fact that the number of literary magazines has fallen, some still have considerable influence such as *Unitas, Crown Magazine, Ink Literary Monthly, Fiction Star Monthly*, and *Yaputao Literary Magazine. Unitas*, sponsored by the *United Daily News*, is the most important serious literary magazine in Taiwan and is one of the most influential magazines in the Chinese literary world.

In recent years, magazine publishing has tended to become more internationalized as integrated magazine publishing groups have arisen. The local magazine groups include The Business Weekly Media Group, PCHome Corporation, and Common Wealth Magazine Publishing. The foreign joint-venture groups include China Times Magazines, Hachette Filipacchi, and Nong Nong Interculture Group. All have at least one well-known flagship magazine, which helps other group magazines with sales and distribution.

As foreign capital has flowed into Taiwan, entrepreneurs have begun to launch businesses abroad, investing in the Southeast Asian countries where Chinese is used, the Chinese mainland and Hong Kong. Nong Nong is a leader in international expansion and in cooperation with Singapore Press Holdings, has released *Citta Bella* in Singapore while its subsidiary company, MomBaby, has published *Ours* in Malaysia.

Well-known magazine publishing personalities include *China Times Weekly*'s Ralph C. S. Chien, *Common Wealth Monthly*'s Diane Ying, *Global Views Monthly*'s Wang Li-Hsing, *Business Weekly*'s James Jin, *Citta Bella*'s Lisa Wu, *Studio Classroom*'s Doris Brougham, *Vogue* (Taiwan)'s Bentham Liu, *Pursuing Righteousness*'s Lin Hsien-Chang, *Management Magazine*'s Frank L. Hung, and *Time Express*'s Richard C. C. Huang.

Despite the great number of magazines published, some fields are poorly covered or largely ignored. For instance, there are less than 10 popular science magazines. Translated editions of foreign magazines, such as *Newton Science Magazine, National Geographic*, and *Scientific American*, have strong sales, but the local magazines of this type can hardly make ends meet. Subscriptions to *Science* and *Nature* have dropped to between 3,000 and 4,000.

D. Distribution and Publishing Organizations

1. Distribution

Taiwan has a well-established distribution network with a variety of sales channels such as bookstores, direct, on-campus, and online. Bookstores sell the largest number of books, followed by mail order and online sales. Taiwan is full of bookstores. According to experts, there are more than 6,000 bookstores, and about 2,000 of them are over 33 square meters in size. The Taipei region is the largest publication sales market, accounting for 70% of total sales.

There are many bookstore chains in Taiwan. Since their initial development in the 1980s, the chains have spread all over the island. Prominent bookstore chains include King Stone, Eslite, Senseio Bookstore, Hess Bookstore, Caves Books, Q Books Center International, and Linking. (See Figure 6.4.) In addition, the 7-11 group also owns a chain with 48 outlets with 1,000 employees and annual sales of NT$6 billion (US$175.44 million). With a refined and elegant style, Eslite Bookstore has become a cultural landmark in Taiwan and Eslite's founder Robert C. Y. Wu is a leading figure in Taiwan's cultural arena.

King Stone, the first bookstore chain in Taiwan, has the greatest number of outlets at about 100, with two in Canada. Most of the stores are King Stone's direct sales outlets, while 20% are affiliated stores. It employs about 1,140 staff and has annual sales of NT$3 billion (US$87.72 million), ranking second

Figure 6.3
Picture of Eslite Bookstore

(Photo provided by Eslite Bookstore)

Figure 6.4

Major Bookstore Chains

Name	Number of Outlets	Annual Sales*	Number of Employees	Notes
Books Kinokuniya	6	N/A	N/A	All located in big department stores or shopping malls.
Caves Books	16	N/A	N/A	All direct outlets. Most are located near university campuses.
Eslite	45	1.76	1,000	All direct outlets. Has the largest sales among bookstores in Taiwan.
Hess Bookstore	7	N/A	N/A	All direct outlets.
King Stone	More than 100	N/A	1,140	With nearly 90 direct outlets and many affiliated stores. Two stores in Canada.
Nobel Bookstore	N/A	N/A	N/A	N/A
Q Books Center International	7	N/A	N/A	All direct outlets.
Senseio Bookstore	46	N/A	N/A	31 direct outlets and 15 affiliated stores.

* US$100 million

in terms of revenue among all Taiwan bookstores chains. King Stone stocks nearly 200,000 titles, and it usually places about 40,000–50,000 on its shelves at any given time. Every month, King Stone brings in 1,200 new titles and sells about 600,000 books. Besides books, King Stone sells over 500 different magazines and operates an online bookstore.

Book wholesalers in Taiwan, known as book and newspaper houses, distribute 50–70% of the total. The most influential companies include Nung Hsueh Co., Ltd., Chan's Book Syndicate, Li Ming, Red Ant, and Linking.

Nung Hsueh, the largest book wholesaler in Taiwan, represents more than 250 publishers, has many branches with over 660 employees, and annual sales of NT$1.3 billion (US$38.01 million). It has invested NT$400 million (US$11.7 million) to build a distribution center of 200,000 square meters. In addition to selling books, Nung Hsueh also provides warehousing for publishers and directly invests in publishing companies.

Direct sales contributed a considerable share when there were few bookstores and information spread slowly, and it has remained an important distribution channel. Many companies, such as Formosan Magazine Press, Chin Show Cultural Enterprise, Hwa I Book Co., Ltd., Newton Publishing, Han Sheng Company and Kwang Fu Enterprise Co. Group, all adopted this channel after their establishment and have expanded into large companies. Formosan Magazine Press starting with selling magazines like *Reader's Digest* and is now the biggest direct sales company. Other than Formosan Magazine Press there are two other sizable direct sales companies, Chan's Book and Tai Shiang Book. They both have about 900 employees and annual sales of NT$1.5 billion (US$43.86 million), sell about 630 magazines, 120 in Chinese and more than 500 in foreign languages. Their monthly distribution reaches 1.05 million total copies. Formosan Magazine Press has a very professional and highly effective sales division, with over 3.5 million customers in Taiwan. Over nearly 30 years, the company has sold 51 million magazines, i.e. 2.2 per person, or 7 per family.

In recent years, the increase of brick and mortar and online bookstores has led to a decline of direct sales. Direct sales are losing distribution share, and the number of such companies have gone under. Now only a few companies such as Formosan Magazine Press, Newton Publishing, and Taiwan Mac Educational Co., Ltd. continue to engage in direct sales exclusively.

A few publishing companies have also established distribution networks outside of Taiwan. These companies include Linking, Cheng Chung, Li Ming, and Cite. Among them, Linking possesses the strongest external distributing capacity. The *United Daily News* group owns more than 20 chain stores in North America and also has some business in Southeast Asia. Linking supplies books and magazines to these chain stores.

In addition to the above-mentioned sales channels, there are a large number of book clubs in Taiwan. Many publishing companies and bookstores have established their own clubs and some operate on a considerable scale, such as the ones sponsored by Yuan-Liou, Common Wealth Magazine, Cite, China Times Publishing, King Stone, Eslite, and www.books.com.tw.

Taiwan has several large foreign language bookstores, Caves Books, Bookman, and Art Land Book Co., Ltd. all sell a great number of foreign books. Stores such as Eslite and Senseio Bookstore also carry foreign language books. Caves Books, started by selling foreign language books 50 years ago and has now become the most well-known bookstore in this sector. It owns several subsidiary companies including: foreign publisher agencies, foreign book sale and publishing, and in English training. Dozens of Caves Books outlets are scattered throughout the island, and it owns an office building of 2,145 square meters.

In distribution, it is impossible to omit book rental stores. A great number of such stores always exist in densely packed areas around middle or primary schools. Previously, those stores mainly rented out comic books, but now they include romantic novels and books on life and fashion. Several rental stores have worked hard to improve their sales and service quality, and have transformed themselves into chain stores. Currently, Star Bookstore, an investment of Taiwan Cardtek Co., Ltd. is the most well known and the largest book rental chain. It owns more than 120 stores and has 200,000 regular customers. The company has pleasant and elegant stores, recognizes the importance of establishing and promoting its brand name, and has set up a website.

The existence of so many rental stores will definitely affect the business of publishing companies and bookstores. This already has become a frequently mentioned topic among publishers.

Every year many book exhibitions are held in Taiwan. The biggest one is the Taipei International Book Exhibition (TIBE), started in 1987, and includes both copyright and book sales. Since 1998, it has been held annually in the first or second month of the year. It held its 12th exhibition on January 28, 2004.

Taiwan imports and exports a large number of publications. In the late 1990s, Taiwan imported over 31 million books, 27 million magazines and more than 8.5 million audio-video items, while exporting more than 20 million books, 5.5 million magazines and over 9 million audio-video items.

2. Publishing Organizations, Media, and Research

Many non-governmental publishing organizations exist in Taiwan. In book publishing, there are the Publishers Association of Taiwan, Taipei Association of Publishers, and China Book Publishing Development Foundation. In magazine publishing, there are The Taiwan Magazine Publications Association and Taipei Association of Magazine Publishers. In the press, there are the Taipei Association of Newspaper Presses and the Association of Taiwan Journalists. In audio-video publishing, there are the Association of Taiwan Audio-Visual Recording Professionals and the Taipei IFPI. In the distribution sector, there is the Book Issuing Association of Taiwan. In addition, some organizations focus on copyrights such as Taiwan Audio-Visual Music Copyright Owners Association.

It is easy to find current publication information in Taiwan. With many newspapers dedicating a special section to books, such as the *China Times • Book Review*, the *United Daily News • Reader's Choice*, the *Min Sheng News • Book*, *Gongshangshibao • Dashufang*, and the *Central Daily News Reading*. Among them, the biweekly *China Times • Book Review* and the *United Daily News • Reader's Choice* are the most influential providers of publication information and news. The *Min Sheng News* also is known for its reports on culture and publications. (See Figure 6.5.)

Magazines focusing on providing publication information include *Publication Information*, *Publication Circulation*, *Publication Publishers*, *Publisher*, *Eslite Reader*, *Wen-hsun* and *New Book Information Monthly*. *Publication Information*, a monthly sponsored by King Stone Culture Square, a King Stone chain store, prints 40,000 copies each issue and is free for customers. Its annual special edition summarizes publication achievements of the past year and provides King Stone's list on popular books and sales information. It is a very important

Figure 6.5
Major Publishing Media

Name	Sponsor	Issue Frequency	Features
China Times • Book Review	China Times	Weekly	One of the two major players.
United Daily News • Reader's Choice	United Daily News	Weekly	One of the two major players.
Min Sheng News • Book	United Daily News	Daily	With daily reports on literature and publication news and weekly specials on various, current problems, writers, and publishers.
Central Daily News • Reading	Central Daily News	Weekly	N/A
Publication Publishers	Taipei Association of Publishers	Quarterly	Provides publication information.
Publisher	Taipei Association of Book Publishers	Quarterly	Provides publication information.
Publication Information	King Stone	Monthly	It is free of charge and provides book lists and sales statistics useful reference.
Publication Circulation	Nung Hsueh Co., Ltd.	Monthly	The only magazine focusing on publication distribution as well as publication news. Subscribers are mostly publishing houses and bookstores.
Wen-hsun (Literature Information)	Taiwan Literature Development Foundation	Monthly	An influential magazine providing cultural information focusing on literature.
Eslite Reader	Eslite Books	Monthly	An influential reading magazine, with readers mostly intellectuals and publishing professionals.
Net & Books	Net & Books Co., Ltd.	Bimonthly	Each issue focuses on a central topic and provides insightful reports.
Book Catalogue Quarterly	Student Book Co., Ltd.	Quarterly	Important information provider on the publication of ancient classics.
New Book Information Monthly	N/A	Monthly	Focuses on introducing books and providing publication information.
Bulletin of ISBN Taipei Center	N/A	Monthly	Provides information on the ISBN application received by the center.
Printer	N/A	Bimonthly	The most prestigious magazine in the Taiwan printing industry.

reference for the publishing market. *Publication Circulation*, a monthly sponsored by Nung Hsueh, provides book and magazine sales information for book sales outlets. *Eslite Reader* is sponsored by Eslite and offers both book and sales information. Its readers are mainly chain store members and it also attracts the attention of publishers and intellectuals. Previously, it was distributed to chain store members but in March 2004 it shifted to a formal subscription model. *Publication Publishers* and *Publisher* are organizational publications of the Taipei Association of Publishers and the Taiwan Association of Book Publishers, respectively. *Wen-hsun* focuses on providing information on art and literature, especially on Taiwanese contemporary culture, and is the most influential literary magazine. *New Book Information Monthly*, a comprehensive magazine on book information, introduces new books and publishes book reviews, as well as providing information on writers, their works and other related publication information. In addition, the Taiwan Information Office publishes *Publication Yearbook*.

Many TV and radio stations in Taiwan air reading programs with well-known programs including China Radio's *Book Fragrance Society*, News98's *Book Talk with Ca Chuen Chang*, and the Police Radio Station's *Making Friends with Books*. TV programs include PTS's *No TV Today* and CTITV's *Reading Room*. Some professional websites also provide publication information, such as www.tibe.org.tw, www.lib.ncl.edu.tw/isbn/ and online bookstores like www.books.com.tw.

Higher education specializing in publishing began to develop in the late 1990s in Taiwan. The Publishing Research Institute of Nanhua University was formed in 1997 and is the first higher education institution specializing in publishing research in Taiwan.

E. Audio-Visual Publishing and Online Bookstores

1. *Audio-Video Publishing*

There are about 2,360 registered audio-visual publishing houses (known as record companies in Taiwan), of which only about

200 are actually in operation. According to statistics from the International Federation of the Phonographic Industry (Taiwan IFPI), in 2001, 500,000 cassettes and 17.5 million CDs were sold in Taiwan, with total retail sales totaling NT$5.78 billion (US$169 million).

Prior to 1999, audio-visual sales in Taiwan had always been comparatively high, surpassing the Chinese mainland and Hong Kong, ranked top among Asian countries, second only to Japan. In recent years, however, the impact of piracy and the advent of MP3 technology has led to a considerable decline of the recording industry. Many companies went out of business and a majority of the surviving companies were forced to cut down their classical music projects to focus mostly on pop music with greatly reduced production volumes and personnel. Now annual sales of audio-visual products in Taiwan has dropped to NT$5 billion (US$146.2 million) from more than NT$10 billion, a decline of 50%.

Current prominent audio-visual publishing houses in Taiwan include Rock Records Co., Ltd., Forward Music Co., Ltd., Linfair Records Limited, What's Music Internationl Inc., Sunrise International Entertainment Corp., Magic Stone Music Co., Ltd., Avex Taiwan Inc., and Poem Culture. Well-known international records companies such as BMG Music, Sony Music Entertainment, Warner Music, EMI, and Universal Music have all set up branches in Taiwan, and these have become market leaders. The above international "Big Five" and Rock Records are known in Taiwan as the "Big Six."

Rock Records is the well-known record company started in Taiwan and was founded by Tuan Chung Tan in 1981 with only several employees. The company had rapid development and soon became the most influential recording company because of its good management, excellent talent recruitment, and originality in exploring new types of music. Today, Rock Records is the most well-known record company for Chinese music. Producing original songs and pursuing high quality music have been crucial for Rock Records' success. Prominent singers with Rock Records include Luo Da You, Chen Shu Hua, Lee Tsung Sheng, Chao Chuan, and Emil Chow. These singers have continuously released popular songs and have been great successes for the company. The originality of Rock Records enables the company to always be in front of the pack. Currently, Rock Records employs more than 100 people, has many branches and affiliated companies overseas, and it runs *Adm*, a famous advertising magazine in Taiwan.

Five main features of the audio-visual market in Taiwan have become apparent in recent years:

First, it is the most mature and active region in the Chinese market where professionalism prevails in both the production and distribution of audio-visual products. The recording companies benefit greatly from many excellent talents in the areas of production, planning, and distribution.

Second, the market is very diversified. While Chinese dominates the mainstream, foreign works also are able to take a sizeable share. Of the foreign titles, Japanese and Korean are the most popular, followed by European and American.

Third, in recent years, the market has begun to weaken and decline, especially over the last two years, reaching the lowest point of the past 10 years. In 1995, the Taiwanese bought two records per capita, spending US$15.90, and the audio-visual market totaled US$336 million, ranking 17th in the world. But in the last two years, this amount has been cut by half.

Fourth, it has close cooperation with the Chinese mainland, where Taiwan's audio-visual professionals and artistes go to seek new markets. In recent years, many Taiwan audio-visual professionals have gone to the Chinese mainland and have established close ties with their Chinese mainland counterparts that has never been reached before. For example, over the last two years no records of Taiwanese singers have sold more than 400,000 copies in Taiwan, but sales in the Chinese mainland have reached 700,000–800,000 copies on occasion.

Fifth, the copyright dispute between records companies and the media such as cable TV is basically over. With effort from the "Big Six" including Rock Records and BMG Music, and copyright organizations such as The Audio-Visual Music Copyright Owners Association, Taiwan cable TV companies have reached agreements with various audio-visual copyright organizations and have begun to remunerate the copyright owners.

2. Online Bookstores

The first online bookstore in Taiwan was www.books.com.tw, which opened in December 1995. The number of major online bookstores in Taiwan have since increased to about 30, including: www.books.com.tw, www.ylib.com.tw, www.readingtimes.com.tw, www.kingstone.com.tw, www.eslitebooks.com, www.soidea.com.tw, www.linkingbooks. com.tw, www.silkbook.net, www.bookzone.com.tw, www.cite.com.tw, www.chwa.com.tw, www.twpcorp.com.tw, www.hot.net.tw, www.booklife.com.tw, www.sanmin.com.tw, www.eztalk.tw, www.ebookclub.com, and www.jessb.com.

Most online bookstores in Taiwan are operated by publishing houses, bookstores, and IT companies. Of those mentioned above, Ylib.com.tw, Readingtimes.com.tw, Linkingbooks.com.tw, Chwa.com.tw, are managed by publishers; Kingstone.com.tw, Eslitebooks.com, and Jessb.com are run by bookstores, and a few such as Books.com.tw and Silkbook.net, are operated by IT companies. This shows that publishing professionals are highly interested in online book sales.

The management of these online bookstores is very similar. While some of the stores have developed their own style, Books.com.tw not only has the longest history but also has received comparatively the largest investment. In order to accelerate delivery, it has established cooperation with Taiwan's well-known 7-11 chain, which enables the buyer to pick up the book ordered at the nearest 7-11 two days after the purchase. The largest online bookstore, Ylib.com.tw, operated by a publisher contains many reviews with rich content and provides very good customer service. Yuan-Liou Publishing House is also one of the few publishers that has invested heavily in online sales. Bookzone.com.tw operated by Common Wealth Magazine Co., Ltd. sells mostly books published by the publisher itself and provides various book introductions, including content related to

Common Wealth Magazine. Silkbook.net was formed recently but is known for being the first to adopt POD (print-on-demand) technology in the Chinese book industry. All of the above online bookstores are managed in Taipei, except for Jessb.com, which is operated in southern Taiwan.

After experiencing the Internet bubble, online bookstores are slowly entering into a period of stable growth. In 2002, major online bookstores such as Books.com.tw, Ylib.com.tw, Bookzone.com.tw, and Kingstone.com.tw grew. Books.com.tw announced that its membership had surpassed 300,000, and Kingstone.com.tw stated that its annual sales reached NT$140 million (US$4.09 million). In order to attract more visitors, the online bookstores are consistently updating their content and adding more services. For example, Ylib.com.tw has *China Encyclopedia* and the *British Encyclopedia* online for readers to search for information, Kingstone.com.tw provides customized bookstore service, and Hot.net.tw attempts to make its book search service faster. However, it is worth noting that the regular bookstore with the highest number of book sales—Eslite, began to curtail its huge investment in online bookstores starting in May 2002 and has also reduced investment in advertising.

F. Outside Investment in Taiwan

Companies outside Taiwan began to invest in the publishing industry from the 1980s, and by the mid-1990s such investment reached a major scale. Foreign investment brings in experience that publishers can learn from, and also increases competition. Generally, there are two kinds of capital entering Taiwan, that from foreign countries, and investment from Hong Kong.

1. Foreign Investment

Before the 1980s only a few foreign publications were sold in Taiwan, typically *Reader's Digest* and book series from Time-Life Books. Taiwan's biggest direct sales company, Formosan

Magazine Press, started by representing foreign publishers and had rapid growth.

In the middle and late 1980s, foreign companies began to invest in Taiwan directly, establishing joint-venture bookstores and publishing companies. The first pioneers were Japanese companies, including Tohan Publishing Inc., Kinokuniya Company Ltd., and Nippan. European and Western companies arrived during the 1990s and, at present, there is Hachette Filipacchi Media from France; McGraw-Hill, Conde Nast, and Hearst Corporation from the United States; Longman Publishing Corporation from Britain; Popular Book Co., Page One, and Singapore Press Holdings from Singapore. In audio-video, large international companies such as the Universal Music Group, EMI Records Ltd., BMG Entertainment International Ltd., Warner, Sony, and MCA have all established branches in Taiwan.

Foreign investors can establish both independent companies and joint ventures in publishing and distribution. Three different models have been explored by foreign investors.

First, joint ventures have been formed to publish and distribute foreign publications. For instance, Hearst works with Hwa Ker Publishing Co., Ltd. to publish the Taiwan editions of *Bazaar*, *Cosmopolitan*, and *Esquire*; Hachette Filipacchi and its local partner produce Taiwan editions of *Ella* and *Car & Driver*; Japan's Kadokawa Shoten Publishing Co., Ltd. and Sumitomo Corporation works with Taiwan's Choice Group and have formed Taiwan Kadokawa Shoten, publishing *Taipei Walker* and other titles.

Ownership in these joint ventures varies. For Taiwan Kadokawa Shoten, 79% is held by the Japanese and 21% by the local company. Hachette Filipacchi Taiwan holds 51% shares, while the local company holds 49%.

All Taiwan editions generally contain local content. China Times, the original local producer for *Marie Claire* (Taiwan edition), buys 25% of the content for each issue from the French parent company. Taiwan companies pay high copyrights fees to their foreign parent firms and sometimes pay an extra 5–10% of profits. Local companies are responsible for advertising in the

Chinese edition and take full control of the advertising revenue. Nong Nong now publishes *Marie Claire* (Taiwan edition), which contains 30% local content.

The second business model is the establishment of a branch or subsidiary company in Taiwan. Many companies have followed this path, such as Tohan, Kinokuniya, Nippan and Benesse Corporation from Japan; Reader's Digest, McGraw-Hill, and Conde Nast from America; and Popular Holdings Ltd. from Singapore. The local companies publish Chinese editions of the magazines and books that their parent companies hold the copyright to, and occasionally produce publications by local writers or with local content.

In book publishing, Taiwan McGraw-Hill, formed in 1993 and with more than 30 employees, is typical. Its mission statement is "to make world wisdom known to China and Chinese wisdom known to the world." The first half indicates a short-term goal, translating foreign books into Chinese; and the second half reveals a long-term objective, translating Chinese books into foreign languages. This company does not invest large amounts in publishing as many books as possible and then promoting them with advertisements. Instead, it adopts a relatively conservative strategy, publishing only 20–30 titles annually. Its publications focus on series for management professionals and educational subjects. The first books were translations, including *Resumes Don't Get Jobs*, *Working with Americans*, *Top Dog: A Different Kind of Book About Becoming an Excellent Leader*, *How To Run A Small Business*, *Maximarketing For The Winner*, *I'll Get Back To You*, *Tips For Teams: A Ready Reference for Solving Common Team Problems*, and *The New Positioning*. It has now published over 300 titles in Chinese. Among them, *Adventures of A Bystander*, *The Greenspan Effect: Words That Move the World Markets*, and *The Coming Biotech Age: The Business of Bio-Materials* respectively won China Times' Top Ten Best Books Award, King Stone's Annual Most Influential Book Award, and Eslite's Annual Best Book Award. In addition, the company has published books by Chinese authors, such as *Chinese Economy: Understanding the*

World's Biggest Economic Entity, Catching Opportunities of the Chinese mainland Market Economy, written by the Chinese mainland's leading economists Cai Fang and Li Yifu. Also, it is worth noting that the company has already started to select Chinese books for English translation, the first one being *Stan Shih's Computer Legends*. Taiwan McGraw-Hill has set up a Chinese website, www.mcgraw-hill.com.tw.

The third business model is publishing local books and magazines through a joint effort of Taiwan and foreign publishers. For example, Lian Ya Century Publishing, established by Nong Nong, Singapore Press Holdings, Burda GmbH Co., Ltd., and Italy's Li Zuo Co., publishes *Living*, with circulation in both Taiwan and Singapore.

2. Investment From Other Areas of China

Hong Kong is a major investor in Taiwan with the two prominent companies being the Next Media Group and Tom Group. Next Media issues *Next Magazine* in Taiwan, which attracts reporters and editors with high salaries and mainly provides gossip news, dedicated to revealing secrets of politicians, industrial and business leaders, and famous entertainers. Each issue has up to 120,000–140,000 copies, ranking highly in the weekly distribution. It also issues the *Apple Daily* newspaper. World famous businessman Li Ka-shing's Tom Group spent about NT$3 billion (US$87.72 million) between 2001 and 2003 acquiring three publishing companies in Taiwan and restructured them into Cite, the largest publishing corporation on the island. In July 2003, the newly formed Cite group received loans of NT$1.88 billion (US$54.97 million) on different terms from five international financial organizations including DBS, Credit Lyonnais, United Overseas Bank, Bank SinoPac, and Scotiabank. This was the first time in the Taiwan region or even all of China that a publisher received a syndicated loan.

Failures exist with successes. Harlequin Enterprises Ltd. from Canada established a branch in Taiwan but it later had to withdraw due to poor management. Formed in 1982, Hong

Kong *Reader's Digest* Limited (Taiwan Branch) has cut down the number of employees from several dozens to six or seven. *People* (Taiwan edition), authorized distributor of its Chinese editions, stopped distribution in Taiwan after the contract expired.

The Publishing Industry of Hong Kong and Macau

A. The Hong Kong Publishing Industry

The Hong Kong Special Administrative Region (SAR), bordering the South China Sea and located at the eastern side of the Pearl River Delta, consists of Hong Kong Island, the Kowloon Peninsula, and the New Territories (including more than 230 islands). On the north, it is separated from the Shenzhen Special Economic Zone of Guangdong Province by the Shenzhen River, and to the west it is about 60 kilometers away by sea from Macau. Hong Kong has a total area of 1,092 square kilometers and a population of 6.6 million, 97% Chinese and 3% British and other foreigners. Both Chinese and English are commonly used, and the major religions are Buddhism and Christianity. After being ruled by the British for more than 100 years, Hong Kong returned to Chinese control in 1997.

As one of the three major Chinese publishing bases in the world, Hong Kong is third behind the Chinese mainland and Taiwan in terms of total book output and market size. However, as in Taiwan, the publishing industry in Hong Kong is highly market-oriented and competitive.

There are about 500 book publishing houses, 800 magazines, and more than 50 newspapers in Hong Kong. According to data from the Hong Kong authorities, about 40,000 people worked in 4,296 publishing and printing companies at the end of 2003.

Figure 7.1

Map of Hong Kong and Macau

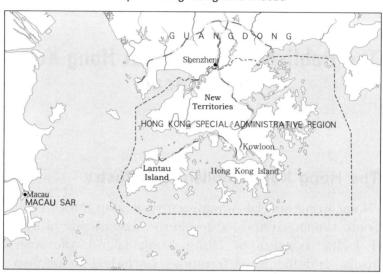

1. Book Publishing

Hong Kong has 500 book publishing houses with a total annual output averaging around 10,000 titles. In 2003, 13,075 new titles were registered and published.

The Hong Kong market favors books on management, personal finance, self-help, and practical applications. Comic books and popular novels are frequent bestsellers. In addition, books that have been adapted from films or TV shows and books related to current hot topics also have strong sales. Popular books in Hong Kong come from various regions and countries. Local books and books from the Chinese mainland and Taiwan are all well received and Chinese translations of foreign books also have the potential to become bestsellers.

Hong Kong book sales total about HK$5 billion (about US$641 million), of which HK$2.8 billion is from general books, HK$1.5 billion from textbooks, and HK$700 million from comic books. English books also enjoy strong sales.

Shen Peng Yin, an outstanding book dealer in Hong Kong and author of the book, *World Publishing Industry: Hong Kong and Macau*, divides the past 50 years of Hong Kong's publishing industry into four stages: the cultural desert period (prior to the early 1950s), the preliminary and formative period (the 1950s), the development and maturation period (the 1960s to the early 1970s), and the prosperous and thriving period (the early 1970s to the present).

Hong Kong has witnessed impressive development in the publishing industry in the past 20–30 years. Of the hundreds of publishing companies, about 100 have considerable production capacity. Prominent companies are The Commercial Press (Hong Kong) Ltd., Chung Hwa Book Co., (Hong Kong) Ltd., Joint Publishing (Hong Kong) Co., Ltd., Wan Li Book Co., Ltd., Cosmos Books Ltd., Ming Pao Publishing House, The Chinese University Press, Next Publications Ltd., Taosheng Publishing House, Sunbeam Publications (Hong Kong), Qin Jia Yuan Publishing Company, Sun Ya Publications (Hong Kong) Limited, and Juxian Guan Ltd.

There are also many publishing groups in Hong Kong, such as Sino United Publishing (Holdings) Ltd., SCMP Book Publishing Ltd., and Popular Holdings Ltd. Of these, Sino United is the largest in terms of both capacity and range.

Sino United Publishing (Holdings) Ltd. was formed in 1988 and is one of the most well known Chinese publishing corporations in the world with businesses in publishing, printing, and distribution. It owns 12 publishing houses such as the Joint Publishing (Hong Kong) Co., Ltd., Chuang Hwa Book Co. (Hong Kong), The Commercial Press (Hong Kong) Ltd., and Sino United Electronic Publishing Ltd., and more than 20 other subsidiary companies in the printing industry and media such as the C & C Joint Printing Co., (Hong Kong) Ltd. In addition to companies in Hong Kong, Macau, and the Chinese mainland, Sino United has branches or joint ventures in Southeast Asia, Japan, the U.S., and Canada. (See Figure 7.2.) Currently it employs 3,000 people and publishes 1,500 titles annually with sales of HK$2.8 billion (US$359 million). Besides achievements in publishing, printing, and distribution, Sino United has extended into other investments and real estate.

Figure 7.2

Organizational Structure of Sino United Publishing H.K. (Holdings) Ltd.

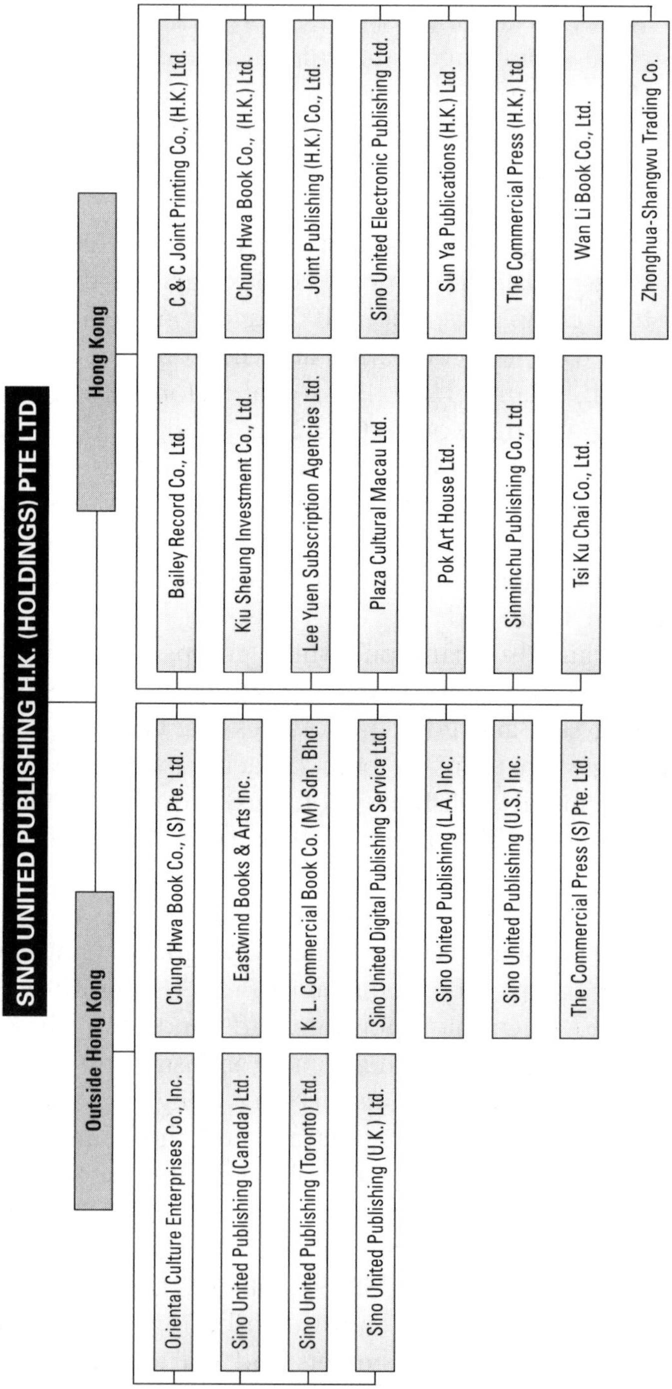

SINO UNITED PUBLISHING H.K. (HOLDINGS) PTE LTD

Hong Kong

- Bailey Record Co., Ltd.
- Kiu Sheung Investment Co., Ltd.
- Lee Yuen Subscription Agencies Ltd.
- Plaza Cultural Macau Ltd.
- Pok Art House Ltd.
- Sinminchu Publishing Co., Ltd.
- Tsi Ku Chai Co., Ltd.
- C & C Joint Printing Co., (H.K.) Ltd.
- Chung Hwa Book Co., (H.K.) Ltd.
- Joint Publishing (H.K.) Co., Ltd.
- Sino United Electronic Publishing Ltd.
- Sun Ya Publications (H.K.) Ltd.
- The Commercial Press (H.K.) Ltd.
- Wan Li Book Co., Ltd.
- Zhonghua-Shangwu Trading Co.

Outside Hong Kong

- Oriental Culture Enterprises Co., Inc.
- Sino United Publishing (Canada) Ltd.
- Sino United Publishing (Toronto) Ltd.
- Sino United Publishing (U.K.) Ltd.
- Chung Hwa Book Co., (S) Pte. Ltd.
- Eastwind Books & Arts Inc.
- K. L. Commercial Book Co. (M) Sdn. Bhd.
- Sino United Digital Publishing Service Ltd.
- Sino United Publishing (L.A.) Inc.
- Sino United Publishing (U.S.) Inc.
- The Commercial Press (S) Pte. Ltd.

Textbooks have a significant share of the market and in recent years competition in this sector has increasingly intensified. There are more than 20 publishers focusing on textbooks in Hong Kong such as Ling Kee Publishing Co., Ltd., Longman Hong Kong Education, Oxford University Press, Hong Kong Educational Publishing Ltd., Jing Kung Book Store-Educational Press, New Asia Publishing House Ltd., Zero to One Publishing Ltd., Aristo Educational Press Ltd., Learner Publishing House Ltd., and Keys Press Ltd. After Hong Kong's return to direct Chinese role, Chinese textbooks have become the new focus.

Many international publishers have branches in Hong Kong such as the Oxford University Press, Longman Publishing Company, Reader's Digest, Macmillan Publishers Ltd., Springer-Verlag Ltd., The Walt Disney Company, and Simon & Schuster Pte. Ltd., and a few have even established their regional headquarters in the territory. Popular Holdings Ltd., which started its business in Singapore and then expanded into Malaysia, Hong Kong, and Taiwan, now has its headquarters as well as many subsidiary companies in Hong Kong.

These Hong Kong companies serve as regional centers of their parent publishing companies and engage in business over the entire Asian-Pacific region, with publications tailored to the demands of the whole region. Some have also become functional centers for businesses in the Chinese mainland. Meanwhile, many companies participate in the local publishing industry. Many companies focus on educational publications, especially English language, and a few have even begun to produce Chinese publications. Strong performers in this field are Oxford University Press and Longman Hong Kong Education.

Longman Hong Kong Education (LHKE), a subsidiary of Pearson Education Asia Limited, publishes books on a variety of subjects for pre-school education, primary schools, middle schools, colleges, and universities. Besides book publishing, Longman also has various study-related products. It has published Chinese magazines such as *Chinese Bulletin Longman* in order to explore potential markets. LHKE is one of the largest foreign publishing companies in Hong Kong with over 300 employees. It also sells textbooks for Longman's other imprints such as Addison-Wesley, Prentice Hall, Penguin Readers, Ladybird, etc.

Oxford University Press has also achieved outstanding success in Hong Kong. The headquarters of Oxford University Press (China) Ltd. is located in Hong Kong, and it employs more than 200 people and publishes 500 new titles annually. Oxford focuses on textbooks in both Chinese and English and holds a significant share in the primary and middle school textbook market in English and Chinese, and the English study market. In addition, its publications on the natural and social sciences also have strong sales. In order to promote Chinese publications, it has established a Chinese publishing company, Keys Press, and has launched a Chinese website, www.keyschinese.com.hk.

Foreign companies in Hong Kong also serve as a stepping stone for their parent companies to enter the Chinese mainland and Taiwan. Longman, Oxford, Reader's Digest, and Popular Holding have all done this. For instance, Reader's Digest Asia Chinese Language Publishing Group manages its parent company's business in Taiwan and copyright trade with the Chinese mainland.

In recent years Taiwanese publishers have begun to enter Hong Kong. At present, publishers with Hong Kong branches include Crown, Cite, and Yuan-Liou. These companies started with promoting Taiwan books, but have since begun to enter the local publishing market more fully.

2. Newspaper and Magazine Publishing

In terms of population, Hong Kong publishes a large number of newspapers and magazines. There are about 864 magazines registered in Hong Kong, of which 523 are in Chinese, 129 in English, 17 in other languages, and 106 in both Chinese and English. In 2003, the total number of the registered periodicals was 13,427 (including publications imported into Hong Kong).

There are 52 newspapers registered in Hong Kong, of which 26 are in Chinese, 13 in English, 6 in other languages, and 7 in both Chinese and English.

Advertising is a major source of revenue for magazines and newspapers and the Hong Kong media industry's annual advertising expenditure totals HK$15 billion (US$1.92 billion), with the top five contributions being from TV, newspapers, magazines, broadcasting, and outdoor. The annual advertising sales of periodicals is about HK$1.8 billion (US$231 million) and accounts for 12% of media advertising income, and the annual advertising sales of newspapers is HK$4.4 billion (US$564 million), accounting for 29% of the total.

In addition to local newspapers and magazines, many prestigious international magazines and newspapers are also distributed in Hong Kong and some companies even issue localized editions of their publications. Statistics from the government states that about 106 international media companies have established offices in Hong Kong, and many internationally well-known newspapers and magazines choose Hong Kong as a distribution or printing center. For instance, Hong Kong is a regional distribution center for the *Far Eastern Economic Review* *Reader's Digest*, and *The Asian Wall Street Journal*. The *Financial Times*, *The Economist*, *USA Today* and *The International Herald Tribune* are printed in Hong Kong.

Hong Kong magazines are primarily divided into categories such as news, business, electronic information, academic research, and entertainment. Leading news magazines include *Asia Weekly*, *Ming Pao Weekly*, *Open Magazine*, and the *Mirror Monthly*. Influential business magazines are *Securities Journal*, *Capital*, and *Hang Seng Index*. Major computer magazines include *PC Home*, *Modern Electronics*, and *Electronic Technology*; and prominent academic magazines are *Ming Pao Monthly*, *Twenty-First Century*, *China Book Review*, and *Reader's Choice*. The serious magazine with the largest circulation is *Asia Weekly*.

A large number of Hong Kong magazines covering news, business and entertainment are weekly and biweekly magazines and entertainment magazines have the largest output. Well-known entertainment magazines are numerous and include *TVB Weekly*, *Ming Pao Monthly*, *East Week*, *East Touch*, *Next Magazine*, *Easy Finder*, *Sudden Weekly*, *Yes Weekly*, *Popular Lifestyle & Entertainment Magazine*, *Express Weekly*, *Monday*, and *Sisters*. These tabloid magazines attract readers by offering sensational news, love affairs, murder cases, and superstitious stories.

Backed by a world-renowned printing industry, Hong Kong printing magazines have superior print quality and are printed in large numbers. There are the *International Packaging News for China*, *Digital Printing Technology*, *Graphic Arts*, *Full Graphic*, *Graphic Arts Association Bulletin* and *Hong Kong Printing Resources Bulletin* and so on, and their presence reveals the strong capacity of the Hong Kong printing industry.

Many brand name international magazine publishers have entered the market, including Hachette Filipacchi which started publishing the Chinese edition of *Elle* 15 years ago, the first among the three Chinese editions. Today, many well-known international magazines continue to publish Chinese editions in Hong Kong, such as the recently launched French beauty magazine *Les Nouvelles Esthetiques*, American *Forbes* as well as many lifestyle magazines from Japan. The first even has two versions, one in simplified Chinese and another in the traditional form, distributing in the Chinese mainland, Hong Kong, and Taiwan.

The small population of Hong Kong has prevented its magazines from enjoying large distribution numbers. Most non-general interest magazines in Hong Kong circulate between 2,000 and 3,000 copies, with several of them surpassing 10,000, while a few tabloid magazines sell over 100,000 copies. Tough competition adds to the difficulties, and it is hard for magazines to sustain their existence. However, competition also leads to improvement of editorial quality and many Hong Kong magazines enjoy strong sales overseas.

Newspaper publishing is similar to the magazine sector. Chinese newspapers in Hong Kong can generally be divided into three categories: comprehensive coverage (with the largest number), business, and entertainment. Of the more than 20 newspapers, 70% focus on providing a variety of local and world news. Five newspapers specialize in reporting financial and economic news, and the rest cover mainly entertainment news.

Prominent comprehensive newspapers are the *Ming Pao Daily*, *Sing Tao Daily*, *Ta Kung Pao Daily*, and *Wenhui Daily*. Major financial and economic newspapers include the *Hong Kong Economic Journal*, *Hong Kong Economic Times*, and *Hong Kong Commercial Daily*. Among them, the *Ming Pao Daily*, *Economic Journal*, and *Economic Times* are the most influential, with regular distribution of between 50,000 and 100,000 copies.

The main entertainment newspapers are the *Oriental Daily*, *The Sun Daily*, *Apple Daily*, and *Sing Pao*. Such newspapers enjoy the strongest sales in Hong Kong. As with similar magazines, these newspapers focus on revealing the secrets and love affairs of celebrities, providing general entertainment news, erotic stories, and coverage of murder cases. Newspapers such as the *Oriental Daily* and *Apple Daily* have achieved a distribution of about 400,000 copies.

Prominent English newspapers are the *South China Morning Post* and *The Standard*. The former mainly covers comprehensive news and the latter focuses on financial and economic news. The *South China Morning Post* sells the most among the non-Chinese newspapers, with a circulation of around 100,000.

In recent years, Hong Kong newspapers have shifted focus towards entertainment coverage.

3. Electronic Publishing and the Internet

Hong Kong is always keen to take advantage of scientific and technological developments and follow the latest international trends. Electronic and Internet publishing have made impressive progress as the publishing industry began to enter the electronic age in the 1990s. More electronic publishing companies are emerging, along with an increasing number of electronic books. As for Internet publishing, several websites have started to provide book downloading services, such as www.cp1897.com.hk, www.ebooks.com, and www.chinesebooks.com.

Many Hong Kong readers choose electronic publications and according to a survey more than half of middle school students in Hong Kong own an electronic dictionary, increasing to 60% among junior high students. The extensive market demand maintains electronic publishers' enthusiasm.

Hong Kong is where Chinese Internet books first started. During the mid-90s, Internet publishing and online bookstores were launched. Major cyber-bookstores are www.cp1897.com, www.commercialpress.com.hk, www.jointpublishing.com, www.silkbook.com, www.oupchina.com.hk, www.longman.com.hk, www.wanlibk.com, www.chunghwabook.com.hk, www.eurekabookshop.com, www.bookworld.com.hk, and www.hkchinesebooks.com. These websites are managed both by publishers and non-publishers.

The bookstore www.cp1897.com was formed by The Commercial Press and a subsidiary of Sun Hung Kai & Co., Ltd. and is the largest Internet bookstore in Hong Kong with the greatest number of books and fast delivery services. Many Hong Kong publishers have established websites to promote publications. For example, Longman set up a Chinese website to promote its textbooks and it also runs a website for its SOS project, www.gssos.ilongman.com, which invites education experts to answer questions and provides teaching or learning material.

In order to provide better service and promote adoption of information technology in the region, the Hong Kong government and Hutchison Whampoa Ltd. worked together to launch a municipal online bookstore, www.esdlife.com, allowing residents to buy merchandise including government publications through the internet. In addition, the Hong Kong Education and Manpower Bureau has posted various textbook lists online to help schools choose textbooks. The biggest source of publishing information is www.publishing.com.hk of Joint Publishing (Hong Kong) Co., Ltd.

4. Distribution, Printing, and Professional Associations

Before the 1980's, specialized book distributors dominated book distribution, but with the development of the publishing industry, many publishing companies opened their own bookstores and established their own distributional networks. Accordingly, the number of specialized distributors in Hong Kong has dropped.

Major distributors in Hong Kong are Li Tung Books Ltd., Arts & Literature Books Co., Ltd, You Cheng Books, Lee Yuen Subscription Agencies Limited, and Challenge Books. These companies not only distribute locally produced books but also engage in exporting Hong Kong books overseas and importing books from Taiwan and the Chinese mainland. Joint Publishing (Hong Kong) Co., Ltd. is a major distributor of books from the Chinese mainland. Sin Min Chu Publishing Ltd., a subsidiary of Sino United, serves as a major supplier of Hong Kong and Taiwan books to the Chinese mainland market as well as an agent for inviting exhibitors to the Beijing International Book Fair.

At present, Hong Kong has nearly 1,000 bookstores, of which about 50 of the largest sell mainly Chinese books. The two largest ones are managed by The Commercial Press and Cosmos Books. The Seng Kwong (Star Light) Book Center, the 10th outlet of The Commercial Press, has about 2,000 square meters of space in an elegantly designed hall and is located at central Tsimshatsui. From its window, you can see Victoria Harbor and Hong Kong Island.

Currently, the Chinese and foreign language book trade in Hong Kong generates about HK$4–5 billion (about US$512–641 million) in revenue, of which HK$1.5 billion comes from textbooks, study, and teaching materials; while the other sectors sell about HK$2.5–3.5 billion (about US$321–449 million).

Annually, about 20,000 new titles enter the Chinese book market each year, with most from the Chinese mainland and Taiwan. Of the total new titles, 50% are from the Chinese mainland, 30–40% from Taiwan, and less than 20% from Hong Kong. In terms of sales, however, Hong Kong books garner 50% of total sales, while Taiwanese books take 40% and Chinese mainland books account for only 10% (Shen 1998). In recent years, sales of books from the Chinese mainland have begun to rise rapidly, and bookstores with a second floor specializing in selling these books have started to appear.

The most important book fair in Hong Kong is the Hong Kong Book Fair, held annually in July and organized by the Hong Kong Trade Development Council. The fair focuses on book sales, supplemented by copyright trade. Most books sold are Chinese books and exhibitors are mainly local publishers and international companies with offices in Hong Kong. Publishers from the Chinese mainland and Taiwan also participate in the event, as well as some Chinese book publishers from Singapore and Malaysia and a few other foreign publishers. In 2003, 325 publishing companies were represented at the fair, of which 82% were from Hong Kong, 13% from the Chinese mainland, and 4% from Taiwan. About 6,000 new titles were displayed during the fair, accounting for 60% of the total

Figure 7.3
View from Seng Kwong Bookstore of The Commercial Press (Hong Kong)

annual new title output in Hong Kong. More than 420,000 people attended the fair.

Hong Kong is a world-famous printing base and the print center of Asia. Printing and publishing employ the largest number of people among all manufacturing industries in Hong Kong. In 2002, exports of printing and publishing products reached HK$3.95 billion (about US$506 million), accounting for 3% of manufacturing exports.

The printing industry consists of about 4,700 printing companies. Advanced printing equipment ensures superior quality and C & C Joint Printing Co., (Hong Kong) Ltd. has received the Asian Printing Industry High Awards and the American Benny Awards several times.

Hong Kong has many professional publishing organizations including the Hong Kong Publishing Federation, The Anglo-Chinese Textbook Publishers Organization, Hong Kong Publishing Professionals Society, Hong Kong Book & Stationery Industry Association, Hong Kong Publishers & Distributors Association, The Hong Kong Printers Association, and Hong Kong Record Merchants Association, with the Hong Kong Publishing Federation being the largest. (See Figure 7.4.) For periodical publishers, there is the Newspaper Society of Hong Kong and Hong Kong Journalists Association. The journalists association has a membership of 600 and is the largest reporter organization and the most active of all trade unions.

The most prominent awards in the publishing industry are the Hong Kong Print Awards organized by the Graphic Arts Association of Hong Kong, the Hong Kong Publishing Professionals Society, and the Hong Kong Trade Development Council. The awards aim to reward outstanding achievements in publishing, distribution, design, and printing. Fifteen people have received awards, including Chan Man Hung, Henry Steiner, Lan Chuan, Lee Cho Jat, and Louis L. Y. Cha (Jin Yong). The Hong Kong government also awards honorary medals to outstanding professionals in the publishing industry, such as Lee Cho Jat and Shen Peng Ying. Other prominent publishers in Hong Kong include the Chairman of Sino United's Zhao Bin,

Figure 7.4

Major Publishing Associations in the Hong Kong Special Administrative Region

Name	Current Leader	Notes
Anglo-Chinese Textbook Publishers Organization	Mr. Chan Man Hung	An organization of local education publishers and local representatives of overseas education publishers.
Composers and Authors Society of Hong Kong	Mr. Leslie Ching	N/A
Educational Booksellers' Association	Mr. Hui Chiu-ming	N/A
Graphic Arts Association of Hong Kong	Mr. W. C. Yip	Formed by a group of young talents in graphic arts.
Hong Kong Book & Magazine Trade Association	Mr. Chan Chung Ling	A trade organization formed by members in the publishing, distribution and retail areas.
Hong Kong Book & Stationery Industry Association	Mr. Shen Peng Yin	N/A
Hong Kong Educational Publishers Association	Mr. Wong Wai Man	N/A
Hong Kong Institute of Chinese Painting, Calligraphy & Cultural Relics	Mr. Jao Tsung-I	Aims to promote Chinese culture, protect cultural relics, and foster close contacts among professionals.
Hong Kong Printing Industry Workers Union	Mr. Lau Kut Leung	Aims to protect labor rights and interest and to mediate the relationship between workers and business owners. It has nearly 10,000 members.
Hong Kong Publishers & Distributors Association	Mr. Yuen Ming Hung	N/A
Hong Kong Publishing Federation	Mr. Lee Cho Jat	The most authoritative publishing organization with related trade organizations and publishing companies.
Hong Kong Publishing Professionals Society	Mr. Steven K. Luk	N/A
Hong Kong Record Merchants Association	Mr. David Cheung	A trade organization for record distributor and retailers.
Hong Kong Reprographic Rights Licensing Society	Mr. A. F. D. Scott	Member of International Federation of Reproduction Rights Organizations (IFRRO).
International Federation of the Photographic Industry (H.K. group)	Mr. Ricky Fung	N/A
The Hong Kong Printers Association	Mr. James T. W. Lee	N/A
The Society of Hong Kong Publishers	Mr. Michael Wilson	An organization formed by local publishers and local representatives of overseas publishing establishments.

Chairman of Cosmos Books' Chan Chung Ling, Director of Press of the Chinese University of Hong Kong's Steven K. Luk, and Chief Editor of Oxford University Press (China) Ltd.'s Simon Li, General Manager of Ming Pao Monthly and Ming Pao Publications Ltd.'s Poon Yiu Ming, and Editor-in-Chief of Yazhou Zhoukan Ltd.'s Yau Lop Poon.

B. The Macau Publishing Industry

Macau is a frontier city bordering the South China Sea and is the smallest SAR of China with an area of just 27 square kilometers and a population of 444,000, of which 96% speak Chinese and the rest mainly Portuguese and English. Portuguese settlers arrived in Macau in the 16th century and later turned the port into a Portuguese colony. In December 1999, Macau returned to Chinese control. Macau's revenue comes mainly from gambling and tourism and each year it receives about 10 million visitors, of whom 700,000 are Western tourists. Though small, Macau is a well-known international city.

The Chinese publishing industry in Macau operates on a small scale and plays no important role in the Macau economy. Except for a few companies such as the *Macau Daily News*, most of the rest can hardly break even, and newspaper publishing in general is in a better position than magazine and book publishing. The publishing industry as a whole consists mainly of three types of publishers; the government which carries the most weight along, business groups, and a few individuals. Macau's unique cultural heritage places the city in an important position in terms of Portuguese culture and in interacting with other Portuguese-speaking countries.

There are eight Chinese daily newspapers in Macau including the *Macau Daily News*, *Journal Va Kio*, and *Tai Chung*. The *Macau Daily News* is the most prominent and influential with a distribution of 100,000 copies, accounting for 90% of Macau's total newspaper distribution. Besides newspapers, the publisher of *Macau Daily News* also engages in book publishing and distribution. In addition to Chinese newspapers, there are four Portuguese newspapers in Macau, of which three are daily newspapers and one weekly.

Macau publishes about 100 magazines in total, of which 60 are registered in the government's Information Bureau as regular periodicals. Most of the magazines are weekly, quarterly, and bimonthly and the most prominent are *Macau Magazine, Macau Monthly, China Macau, Mastv Magazine, Macau Image, RC: Review of Culture, Macau Law Journal,* and *Meng Ya (Sprouts).*

Macau magazines can be divided by subject categories into current affairs, finance and economics, social sciences, medicine, sports, leisure, culture, social organizations, and government information and guidance. Major current affairs magazines are the *Macau Monthly, China Macau,* and *Mastv Magazine. Macau Magazine* is a bimonthly sponsored by the Information Bureau with the largest circulation, and *Mastv Magazine,* sponsored by Macau Asian TV, has established liaison offices in Hong Kong, Taipei, Malaysia, and some other Southeast Asian cities.

The *Macau Image, Macau Manager,* and *Macau Economy* are finance and economics magazines. Leading magazines in the social sciences include *RC: Review of Culture, Macau Studies* and *Study of Sino-Western Culture.* The *RC: Review of Culture,* sponsored by the Cultural Institute of the Macau government, is the most authoritative social sciences magazine in Macau and is published in Chinese, Portuguese, and English. There are few cultural magazines and the only prominent one is the *Poesia Sino-Ocidental,* which is sponsored jointly by the Sino-Western Culture Study Institute of the Macau Polytechnic Institute and the Guangdong Writers Association.

Annually, about 100 Chinese titles are issued in Macau with financial support from the government. The Macau Foundation, established by the Macau SAR government, serves as a major book publisher and sponsor. Each year it receives 1.6% of Macau's tax revenue, (about Ptc400 million) and sponsors book series in Chinese, Portuguese, and English. Its prominent publications include *Macau Series, Macau Translations Series, Macau Law Series, Series on Comparative Studies of Laws in Four Regions, Macau Views, Macau Discussions,* and *New Macau*

Discussions, covering a variety of subjects including politics, law, finance and economics, history, and culture. Dr. Wu Zhiliang of the Macau Foundation is a major supporter.

The *Macau Daily News* publishes a large number of books. Other major publishing establishments are Macau Publishing House, Plaza Cultural Macau Ltd., University of Macau Publications Center, and the First Bookstore.

In terms of content, most books published in Macau focus on Macau and Portugal. Yet, in recent years, books with a focus on the Chinese mainland began to appear, such as the book by Wu Shaohong, *The Consumption Mode of Chinese Youth— Shopping Style and Moral Values.*

Publication and distribution volume of Chinese titles is not high in Macau. A majority of the titles issue between 1,000–2,000 copies for the first edition, and a title is considered popular if it achieves sales of more than 2,000 copies. In recent years, popular books in Macau have been *The Golden House* and the *Harry Potter* books. *The Golden House* traces the redemption of four young prodigals. It was published in May 2003 and sold 2,000 copies within a week, with total sales of 3,000.

Textbooks used in Macau are mainly provided by Hong Kong publishers such as Hong Kong Longman and the Hong Kong Educational Publishing Co. Only a few Macau publishers engage in textbook editing and publishing, for example the Plaza Cultural Macau edited and published *Moral Education for Citizens.*

In 2002, Macau's total publication output reached 350 titles. Macau holds many book exhibitions annually and engages in various book promotion activities. There are six to seven small to medium-sized bookstores in the city, including Plaza Culture Square, Seng Kwong Bookstore, Portuguese Bookshop, the First Bookstore, and Wan Tat Bookstore. Established in 1988 by the *Macau Daily News* and Hong Kong's Sino United, Plaza Culture Square is the largest bookstore with an area of 1,000 square meters. It employs about 50 people and owns four outlets with annual sales of Ptc50 million and a profit of Ptc3 million.

Most of the books sold in Macau are from Taiwan and Hong Kong, with a small number from local publishers and the

Chinese mainland. Many factors have led to such a situation. First, Taiwanese and Hong Kong books are published in traditional Chinese characters and are more similar in culture to Macau. Second, Taiwanese and Hong Kong books bring attractive profits. The sale price of Taiwanese and Hong Kong books in Macau is always listed at about one-third of the original price, but the price of books from the Chinese mainland is always similar to that listed there. For instance, *Hillary's Memoirs*, a 558-page book published by Taiwan China Times, is priced at NT$400, and is sold in Macau for Ptc133. While the same book, published by the Chinese mainland's Yilin Publishing House, is priced at RMB29 in the Chinese mainland and sells also for Ptc29 in Macau. Books from Taiwan and Hong Kong can generate two to three times more sales revenue than those from the Chinese mainland.

The governing copyright law currently applied in Macau was enacted in 1990.

Despite the fact that Macau's Chinese publishing industry has only a limited size within the global Chinese publishing industry, it has made rapid development in recent years. Within the four years after 1999, more than 1,000 titles were published, and professionals in the Chinese publishing industry call the period a "little bright spring."

Copyright Trade after China Joined the Berne Convention

A. Overview

China promulgated its current copyright law in 1990 which became effective on June 1, 1991. The first amendment to the copyright law was made in 2002.

China joined the Berne Convention for the Protection of Literacy and Artistic Works on October 15, 1992, and the Universal Copyright Convention 15 days later. In November 2001, it became a member of the World Trade Organization (WTO).

There are no copyright trade statistics available before 1990. In 1995, China began an official survey of its book copyright trade. (The author of this book is an advocate and designer of the initial copyright survey). In February 1996, the National Copyright Administration of China published the first statistics of the book copyright trade for the 1995 fiscal year, marking the beginning of annual data-collecting of copyright trade with other countries. The systematic survey laid the groundwork for an overview of the country's book copyright trade. In addition, the Chinese mainland conducted four surveys of the book copyright trade in different categories from 1990 to 2000.

According to incomplete statistics, 51,500 book copyright deals were made with overseas publishers from 1990 to 2002. Of these, 44,300 were deals that licensed works from overseas publishers, and 7,200 were deals that licensed works to overseas publishers. The deals include those with Taiwan and Hong Kong.

The inbound rights licenses far exceeded the outbound rights licenses over the past 13 years. The ratio of inbound to outbound rights licenses is about 7 to 1. Since 1995, rights acquisitions have increased by a large margin, and the ratio of inbound to outbound rights licenses was about 10 to 1.

Most foreign rights deals were negotiated through Chinese or foreign copyright agencies. Some big Chinese publishers obtained rights directly from overseas publishers. There are now about 30 copyright agencies, located in Beijing, Shanghai, Guangxi, Shaanxi, Guangdong, Anhui, and Shenzhen. The Copyright Agency of China (CAC) was the first rights agency established and other rights agents in the Chinese mainland are the Shanghai Copyright Agency, the Guangxi Wanda Copyright Agency, and the Beijing Copyright Co., Ltd. These state-owned rights agencies mostly handle book rights and a few of them also engage in TV programs and the audio-visual rights business.

In addition, rights agents in Taiwan and Hong Kong also do licensing rights deals with or on behalf of Chinese mainland firms. The most active agents are the Big Apple Tuttle-Mori Agency, Inc., Bardon-Chinese Media Agency, and Arts & Licensing International, Inc—all major players. These agents have also set up offices in the Chinese mainland. (See Appendix 4 on Copyright Agencies in China.)

There are three major international book fairs in China: the Beijing International Book Fair (BIBF), the Hong Kong Book Fair, and the Taipei International Book Exhibition; all of which have international participants. To Chinese mainland publishers, the BIBF is the most important event in the book rights business. (See Chapter 5-B-3 on BIBF.) In addition to the BIBF, there are also a number of regional book rights fairs. The Shanghai Copyrights Rights Salon is the second most important book fair after the BIBF.

In addition to book fairs in China, Chinese mainland publishers have also actively taken part in various international book fairs. Each year, a large number of publishing professionals are sent to the Frankfurt Book Fair, the Bologna Children's Book Fair, and to BookExpo America. In the past few years, it has sent some 500 to 600 publishing professionals to the annual Frankfurt Book Fair. In addition, Chinese publishers have also attended the London Book Fair, Salon du Livre Paris, São Paulo Internatinal Book Fair, Buenos Aires International Book Fair, Montréal Salon du Livre, Warsaw International Book Fair, Moscow International Book Fair, Budapest International Book Festival, International Book Fair – Barcelona, the New Delhi World Book Fair, Cairo International Book Fair, Tokyo International Book Fair, Seoul International Book Fair, Australian Book Fair, Asia International Book Fair (Singapore), Kuala Lumpur International Book Fair, and Philippine Book Fair.

The State Department has set up a National Copyright Administration and all provincial and local governments also have copyright bureaus at their respective levels. In addition to fighting piracy and advising on copyright issues, the government copyright bureaus mainly facilitate international copyright negotiations, conduct copyright trade statistics surveys, exchange copyright trade experiences, and award establishments that have done a fantastic job in trading copyrights. In addition, the local copyright bureaus are also responsible for registering rights contracts to safeguard the legal rights of Chinese and foreign authors and the copyrights holders.

B. Analysis of Book Rights Acquisition

In the 10 years since China joined the Berne Convention, it has acquired 40,000 foreign rights licenses. The rights acquisitions have the following key features:

1. Rapid Increase of Rights Acquisition

A few years before China became a member of the Berne Convention, the number of rights acquired increased by an average annual rate of 29%, which is considered moderate growth. Since 1995, the growth rate has accelerated. In 1995, the Chinese mainland acquired 1,664 titles from overseas. In contrast, 6,459 titles were acquired in 1999. By 2002, the number of foreign titles acquired increased to 10,235 titles. The annual growth rate of rights acquisition averaged 57%. (See Figure 8.1.) That is to say one out of every ten new books published each year is foreign, not taking into account the foreign books already in the public domain. The facts indicate that Chinese publishers got over the initial pain after China joined the two international copyright conventions and quickly adapted to the rules of the international copyright trade.

It also indicates that many Chinese publishers are well capable of engaging in active rights trading.

2. Major Copyright Trade Partners

China has translation rights trade with 40 countries. The most active trading partners are the U.S., U.K., Japan, Germany, France, Russia, South Korea, Canada, and a number of other European countries. These countries have become the main rights sources for the Chinese mainland. Taking 1998 and 2002 for example, the top eight licensors in 1998 were the U.S., U.K., Japan, Russia, Germany, France, South Korea, and Australia. The

Figure 8.1
Foreign Titles Acquired, 1995–2002

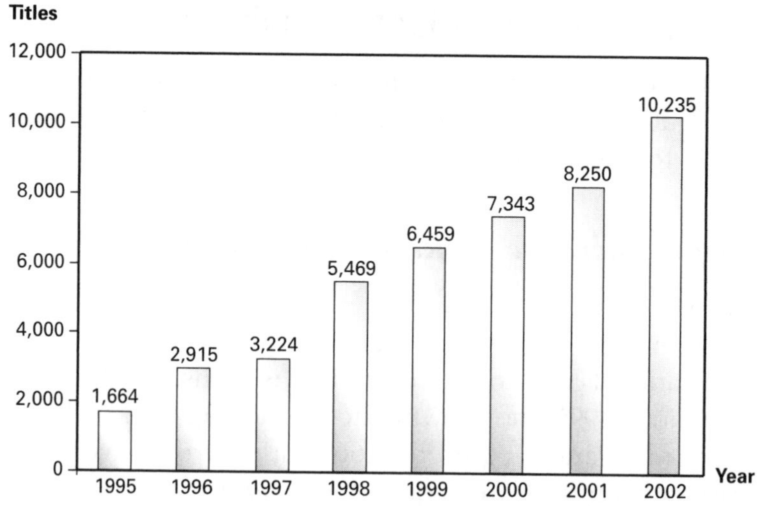

Titles

Year	Titles
1995	1,664
1996	2,915
1997	3,224
1998	5,469
1999	6,459
2000	7,343
2001	8,250
2002	10,235

Source: *National Copyright Administration of China*

number of titles acquired from these eight countries was 4,220, accounting for 77% of that year's total acquisitions. The top six in 2002 were the U.S., U.K., Japan, Germany, South Korea, and France. The Chinese mainland acquired a total of 8,146 titles from those six countries, representing 80% of that year's total acquired foreign titles. (See Figure 8.2.)

In the past 10 years, the U.S., U.K., and Japan have been the top three rights sources and the U.S., U.K., Japan, Germany, France, South Korea, and Russia have become the seven most important rights licensors.

3. Variety of Acquired Books

In the first few years after China joined the Berne Convention, rights acquisitions concentrated heavily on foreign language, literature, and children's books. The selection was quite narrow. This situation began to change in the mid-1990s when Chinese publishers began to expand their acquisitions into many fields

Figure 8.2
Major Copyright Trade Partners by Titles Licensed, 2002

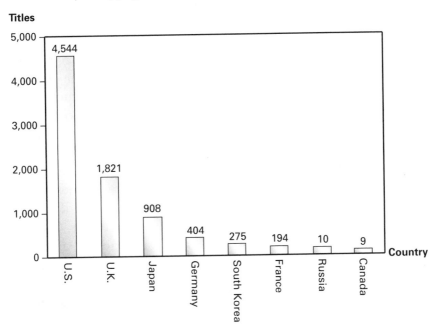

and acquired a wider variety of books. Books on electronics, business, science and technology, academic works, self-help, and inspirational books began to take important positions in the rights trade. Computer and business book fever, and self-help and inspirational book fads all drove the rights trade growth.

According to the statistics provided by the Beijing Copyright Bureau, science and technology books account for 40% of all foreign books acquired over the past five years. Computer books, economics and management books, language books, and children's books were the four pillars of rights acquisitions from overseas. The number of titles acquired in these four categories continues to grow. By acquiring a large number of business, law, science, technology, electronics and academic works, the book copyright trade has played an increasingly important role in the Chinese mainland's movement toward "building the country through science and technology," and in the country's legal reforms.

To take the acquisition of foreign law books as an example, the Encyclopedia of China Publishing House (ECPH), China's authority in encyclopedia publishing, published the *Foreign Legal Library*, the most comprehensive legal book series available in translation. Since its launch in 1991, ECPH has acquired several dozen world-famous legal works and now has published 30 titles. Its acquisitions range from *Law, Legislation and Liberty* by British author F. A. Hayek, *Einfubrung in Die Rechtswissenschaft* by German author Gustav Radbruch, and *Law's Empire* by American author Ronald Dworkin to *Criminology* by Italian author Baron Raffaele Garofalo, *General Theory of Law and State* by Austrian author Hans Kelsen, and *Civil Code of the Russian Federation* (which went into effect in 1995). *The Law Library* editorial board was led by Chinese legal expert Jiang Ping. Invited to sit on the consultant board of *The Law Library* were Xavier Blanc-Jouvan, Professor of Law Emeritus in the Law Faculty of the Université Paris I Panthéon-Sorbonne and President of the Société de Législation Comparée; Paul-André Crépeau, Emeritus Law Professor of McGill University (Canada); and President of the International Academy of Comparative Law; Whitmore Gray, a Professor Emeritus of Law at The University of Michigan Law School; and Hein Kotz, a Law Professor of University Hamburg and former Director of Max Planck Institute for Foreign and International Private Law, in Hamburg, Germany. *The Law Library* provides an invaluable reference in the construction of China's legal system and has become essential reading for Chinese legal experts, law professors, and attorneys.

More and more Chinese are now functional in a foreign language. The language ability of college students has increased to a higher level as the government encourages study. As a result, the number of people reading foreign original works and using foreign textbooks has grown very rapidly. Chinese publishers began to acquire more and more reprint rights of foreign textbooks and other related books and have published more and more books in foreign languages. Chinese publishers who have acquired a large number of original works in foreign languages include the Foreign Language Teaching and Research Press, Tsinghua University Press, Dongbei University of Finance and Economics Press, and the Higher Education Press.

4. Prominence of Acquired Children's and Cartoon Books

As most children's and comic books contain pictures with simple and direct stories and as all children share common characteristics, the market demand for children's books is strong. They have become a major category for rights acquisition by Chinese publishers. For some children's book publishers, the acquired titles of foreign origin represent more than one-third of their annual title output and have generated nearly half of their annual sales.

Tomorrow Publishing House of Jinan in Shandong Province aggressively acquired foreign titles over the past few years, which have helped double its sales and profits. Through a large volume of acquisitions, Tomorrow translated and published children's encyclopedias for different age groups, causing quite a stir in the market. It has won the title of the King of Children's Encyclopedias in the book trade. One of its editors specializing in foreign rights acquired 93 titles in one year, generating sales of RMB23 million (US$3 million) with profits of RMB5 million (US$606,000).

Another publisher, Hope Publishing House of Xi'an in Shaanxi Province, spent RMB4 million (US$481,928) in 2002 to acquire foreign titles, including *The Complete Collection of Snoopy* in 20 volumes which in turn generated sales of RMB25 million (US$3 million) and RMB2 million (US$240,964) in profits for the publisher.

Some children's book publishers launched many foreign children's titles that have become bestsellers thanks to extensive marketing efforts. Recently, foreign titles outnumbered local titles on the Chinese mainland's bestseller lists for children's books. The top bestsellers are *Wally's World* published by Shanghai Pictorials, *Harry Potter* by People's Literature Publishing House, *The Goosebumps Series* by Jieli Publishing House, *Tiger Team* by Zhejiang Juvenile and Children's Publishing House, *The Complete Collection of Snoopy* by Hope Publishing House, and *Mickey Mouse* by Children's Fun Publishing Co., Ltd.

Chinese publishers that have done a remarkable job in acquiring rights of foreign titles are Jieli Publishing House, Tomorrow Publishing House, Hope Publishing House, Children's Fun Publishing Co., Ltd., and Jilin Fine Arts Publishing House.

The strong sales of foreign children's titles have helped boost the market share of children's and young adult books. According to research conducted by the Beijing OpenBook Market Consulting Center, the retail market share of children's books increased by 6.7% in 2002. Foreign children's books contributed 81.8% to this growth, while books by local authors contributed only 1.6% to this increase.

5. Emerging Bestsellers with Higher Prices

The prices of licensed foreign books are generally a bit higher than that of local books. The average sales prices for various licensed foreign books are as follows:

- RMB20 (about US$2.41) for literature books;
- RMB13 (about US$1.57) for children's books;
- RMB30 (about US$3.61) for business books;
- RMB45 (about US$5.42) for computer books; and
- RMB40–100 (about US$4.82–12.05) for architectural and medical books.

In the retail market, translated foreign books in the areas of language learning, business, children's, fiction, electronics, and self-help, all sell well and have relatively large market shares. In the past two years, foreign self-help and inspirational books have had impressive sales and have become the new favorites according to many bestsellers lists. CITIC Publishing House, Jieli Publishing House, Tomorrow Publishing House, and Yilin Press have become strong performers specializing in foreign licensed books with CITIC Publishing House the strongest at present. Among CITIC's Top 10 bestsellers with sales totaling over 100,000 copies, there is only one title written by a Chinese author while the rest of the nine titles all are foreign. The number one bestseller published by CITIC *Who Moved My Cheese?*, licensed from the U.S., sold 2 million copies and has also set the new sales record surpassing all other bestsellers published in recent years.

6. Prominent Publishers in the International Copyright Trade

The substantial acquisition of foreign rights intensified competition in the book market and also stimulated market development. The bestseller statistics of the retail market indicated that in recent years foreign books dominated bestseller lists in the categories of English, children's, computers, business, and inspirational books. By comparison, local-themed books

Figure 8.3

Top Foreign Bestsellers (Chinese Editions) by Copies Sold in Recent Years

Rank	Title	Country of Origin	Publisher	Copies Sold[1]	Sales Revenue[2]
1	Who Moved My Cheese?	U.S.	CITIC Publishing House	2,000	33,600
2	Wally's World (8 volumes)	U.S.	Shanghai Pictorial Publishing House	1,600	15,680
3	Pokemon's Big Search (2 volumes)	Japan	Jilin Fine Arts Publishing House	1,290	11,310
4	Oxford Advanced Learner's English-Chinese Dictionary	U.K.	The Commercial Press	1,250	96,780
5	Harry Potter and the Goblet of Fire (Book 4)	U.K.	People's Literature Publishing House	1,250	42,290
6	Harry Potter and the Sorcerer's Stone (Book 1)	U.K.	People's Literature Publishing House	1,130	20,700
7	Harry Potter and the Chamber of Secrets (Book 2)	U.K.	People's Literature Publishing House	1,000	22,470
8	The Adventures of Tintin (22 volumes)	Belgium	China Children's Press and Publishing Group	980	15,080
9	Harry Potter and the Prisoner of Azkaban (Book 3)	U.K.	People's Literature Publishing House	930	25,210
10	Doraemon-Maze Manual (45 volumes)	Japan	Jilin Fine Arts Publishing House	900	5,400
11	Norwegian Wood (Paperback)	U.S.	Shanghai Translation Publishing House	870	16,356
12	Rich Dad, Poor Dad	U.S.	Publishing House of Electronics Industry	822	14,272
13	The Old Man and the Sea	U.S.	Shanghai Translation Publishing House	770	6,300
14	Robinson Crusoe	U.S.	People's Literature Publishing House	500	6,120
15	Cashflow Quadrant: Rich Dad's Guide to Financial Freedom	U.S.	Publishing House of Electronics Industry	440	9,920
16	Magic Pokemon TV Painting Series	Japan	Jilin Fine Arts Publishing House	300	2,380
17	The Blue Day Book	U.S.	CITIC Publishing House	280	5,530
18	Harry Potter (4 volumes)	U.K.	People's Literature Publishing House	270	41,440
19	Detective CONAN (45 volumes)	Japan	Changchun Publishing House	270	18,390
20	The Unbearable Lightness of Being	Czech	Shanghai Translation Publishing House	250	6,250
21	Eugenie Grandet	France	People's Literature Publishing House	250	2,330

[1] '000s
[2] '000s RMB

Figure 8.3 (Cont'd)

Rank	Title	Country of Origin	Publisher	Copies Sold[1]	Sales Revenue[2]
22	Pokemon Origami (2)	Japan	Jilin Fine Arts Publishing House	230	6,730
23	Pokemon Fun Maze Painting (1)	Japan	Jilin Fine Arts Publishing House	230	3,450
24	Pokemon Origami (1)	Japan	Jilin Fine Arts Publishing House	220	6,700
25	Pokemon Origami (3)	Japan	Jilin Fine Arts Publishing House	220	6,670
26	The Lord of the Rings: The Fellowship of the Ring (Hardcover)	U.K.	Yilin Press	210	4,746
27	The Lord of the Rings: The Return of the King (Hardcover)	U.K.	Yilin Press	210	4,452
28	The Lord of the Rings: The Two Towers (Hardcover)	U.K.	Yilin Press	210	3,948
29	Pokemon's Number Book (2)	Japan	Jilin Fine Arts Publishing House	210	3,690
30	Leadership and National Cultures on Business	U.S.	The Enterprise Management Publishing House	210	3,600
31	Hamlet	U.K.	People's Literature Publishing House	210	1,430
32	Fragrant Chrysanthemum	South Korea	Hainan Publishing Company	200	3,960
33	The Lord of the Rings: The Two Towers (Paperback)	U.K.	Yilin Press	200	3,440
34	Dr. Slump – Arale Chan (4 volumes)	Japan	Changchun Publishing House	200	2,400
35	The Lord of the Rings: The Fellowship of the Ring (Paperback)	U.K.	Yilin Press	190	4,047
36	The Lord of the Rings: The Return of the King (Paperback)	U.K.	Yilin Press	190	3,591
37	Not Study, But Learn	South Korea	World Publishing Corporation	190	3,420
38	The Story of My Life	U.S.	Huawen Publishing House	170	3,706
39	Oxford Advanced Learner's English-Chinese Dictionary (Extensive 4th hardcover ed.)	U.K.	The Commercial Press	160	14,880
40	A Brief History of Time	U.K.	Hunan Science & Technology Press	160	7,290

[1] '000s
[2] '000s RMB

Figure 8.3 (Cont'd)

Rank	Title	Country of Origin	Publisher	Copies Sold[1]	Sales Revenue[2]
41	First, Break All the Rules	U.S.	China Youth Press	160	3,808
42	Welcome to Dead House: Stay Out of the Basement (Goosebumps 1)	U.S.	Jieli Publishing House	160	2,600
43	The Curse of the Mummy's Tomb – Let's Get Invisible (Goosebumps 3)	U.S.	Jieli Publishing House	160	2,570
44	Digital Communication (3rd ed.)	U.S.	Publishing House of Electronics Industry	150	5,140
45	Might and Magic	Japan	International Culture Publishing Corporation	150	2,250
46	The Universe in a Nutshell	U.K.	Hunan Science & Technology Press	140	5,790
47	Where Women Have No Doctor: A Health Guide for Women	U.S.	Yilin Press	140	2,800
48	Fish! A Remarkable Way to Boost Morale and Improve Results	U.S.	CITIC Publishing House	132	2,376
49	Good to Great	U.S.	CITIC Publishing House	130	3,887
50	Professional JSP	U.S.	Publishing House of Electronics Industry	130	3,790

[1] '000s
[2] '000s RMB

have had mediocre performances. Foreign books have propelled the growth of these book categories in the retail market.

In the last 10 years, many publishers capable of international copyright trade emerged from many different sectors and they have done a remarkable job in acquiring and publishing foreign works.

The star performers in acquiring foreign rights of non-fiction trade titles are SDX Joint Publishing Co., Ltd. Peking University Press, Xinhua Publishing House, World Affairs Press, Hainan Publishing House, Liaoning Educational Publishing House, Encyclopedia of China Publishing House, and the Beijing Publishing House. SDX Joint Publishing Co., Ltd. earned a great reputation among Chinese intellectuals for its quality translations and publications of foreign social sciences works. Xinhua Publishing House, affiliated with Xinhua News Agency, China's largest news company, and World Affairs Press, affiliated with the Ministry of Foreign Affairs, both have multiple channels of information sources and excellent books.

Publishers specializing in foreign literature and fiction are Yilin Press, Shanghai Translation Publishing House, Writers' Publishing House, Lijiang Publishing House, Hebei Education Press, People's Literature Publishing House, and the Yunnan People's Publishing House. Of these, the first four are regarded as the "four powerhouses" of foreign literature. Yilin and Shanghai Translation acquire a large number of foreign fiction titles each year. They are the most important publishers of contemporary foreign literature. The Hebei Education Press is known for publishing the largest number of selected works as well as the complete works of foreign literary masters. For example, Hebei Education Press licensed *The Complete Works of Albert Camus* in four volumes from Gallima. The Chinese edition has been praised by Gallima as the most beautifully designed and bound edition among all the different language editions around the world. It also won the National Book Award, the highest book award in China.

Publishers that have done an outstanding job with foreign books on electronics, science, and technology are the Publishing

House of the Electronics Industry, China Machine Press, Tsinghua University Press, People's Posts and Telecommunications Publishing House, Hope Electronics Press, China Youth Press, Science Press, China Railroad Publishing House, and Beijing Aviation and Aerospace University Press. Of these, the first four are regarded as the "four powerhouses" of computer books. Each of the four powerhouses has acquired hundreds of titles annually. To take the Publishing House of Electronics Industry and China Machine Press as examples, they obtained licenses for 400 foreign computer books in 2002 alone. The licensed editions of the four power houses represented an impressive market share of 70% in this category.

The top performers in publishing foreign language books are the Foreign Language Teaching and Research Press, Shanghai Foreign Language Educational Press, The Commercial Press, Foreign Language Press, World Publishing Corporation, Anhui Science and Technology Press, and Higher Education Press. Publishers specializing in foreign inspirational books are CITIC Publishing House, World Publishing Corporation, Enterprise Management Press, Hainan Publishing House, China Youth Press, and the China Machine Press.

More and more foreign business books have entered the market, exerting an increasing influence every year. Publishers with excellent records with foreign business books are the China Renmin University Press, China Machine Press, Huaxia Publishing House, Hainan Publishing House, CITIC Publishing House, Economic Science Press, Peking University Press, China Financial & Economic Publishing House, Enterprise Management Press, Shanghai Financial & Economic University Press, World Publishing Corporation, Dongbei University of Finance and Economics Press, and the China Commerce Press.

Nonetheless, publishers big enough to acquire foreign rights are a small minority. In Beijing for example, 126 publishers acquired foreign rights in 2002, representing 56% of the total number of Beijing publishers. But the foreign titles acquired by the top 10 publishers accounted for 51% of the total foreign rights licenses.

Figure 8.4

Top 20 Publishers in Foreign Rights Acquisition, 2001–2002

Rank	Publisher	Title Quantity*	English	Japanese	German	French	Italian	Russian	Spanish	Korean
1	China Machine Press	790	784	1	5	0	0	0	0	0
2	Publishing House of Electronics Industry	782	782	0	0	0	0	0	0	0
3	Foreign Language Teaching and Research Press	435	407	10	15	2	0	0	0	0
4	Tsinghua University	433	426	0	6	0	0	1	0	0
5	People's Posts and Telecommunications Publishing House	302	302	0	0	0	0	0	0	0
6	Science Press	271	156	108	7	0	0	0	0	0
7	China Light Industry Press	269	142	126	1	0	0	0	0	0
8	Tianjin Science Translation Publishing Co.	175	147	28	0	0	0	0	0	0
9	Hainan Publishing House	158	145	0	5	2	3	1	0	0
10	Shanghai People's Publishing House	156	122	20	9	5	0	0	0	0
11	China Electric Power Publishing House	150	150	0	0	0	0	0	0	0
12	Liaoning Educational Publishing House	143	143	0	0	0	0	0	0	0
13	World Publishing Corporation	128	102	23	1	0	0	0	1	1
14	China Architecture & Building Press	122	92	26	0	0	0	0	0	0
15	People's Literature Publishing House	122	66	7	31	2	8	4	2	2
16	Yilin Press	117	90	4	12	0	3	3	4	0
17	Hunan Arts and Literature Publishing House	113	5	0	102	6	0	0	0	0
18	Shanghai Financial & Economic University Press	104	103	0	0	0	0	0	1	0
19	China Youth Press	92	58	23	0	0	0	5	0	0
20	Dalian University of Technology	91	33	42	4	0	1	0	5	6

* Figure includes other languages not listed here.

Source: *National Copyright Administration of China*

Of the 30 provinces and regions in the Chinese mainland, book companies strong in foreign books were mainly concentrated in seven areas. Beijing is the most concentrated, accounting for 60% of the Chinese mainland's total rights publishers. In addition to Beijing, Jiangsu, Shanghai, Guangxi, Liaoning, Guangdong, Zhejiang, Shandong, and Hunan also have had decent numbers of foreign rights publishers. The foreign rights volume of these regions represents an overwhelming majority of the entire country's output. There are another 10 provinces and regions which have never, or rarely, engaged in foreign rights licensing.

C. Chinese Rights Licensed Overseas

The Chinese mainland has not had much success in licensing Chinese rights overseas. In the past ten years, there were only 1,300 Chinese books that were licensed overseas, representing a mere 4% of the foreign titles acquired by the Chinese mainland. (See Figure 8.5.)

There are about 30 countries that have acquired book rights from the Chinese mainland. Those countries are primarily concentrated in Asia with some in Europe and North America.

In Asia, Singapore, Malaysia (often for reprint rights), Japan, and South Korea were the major acquirers of Chinese book rights. In the West, Germany, the U.S., and U.K. were the primary acquirers of book rights. Italy, France, Spain, Holland, Russia, Finland, Poland, Sweden and Denmark also acquired Chinese rights in small quantities. Europe as a whole acquired more Chinese rights than the U.S.

In terms of content, Chinese books licensed overseas are generally related to traditional Chinese culture, arts, and language. Many books acquired by Japanese and Korean publishers fall under these categories. Some examples are *An Outline History of Chinese Philosophy, The History of Chinese Martial Arts, Life of Chinese Hermits, Fables about Twelve Animal Signs of the Chinese Zodiac, Secret Sects of China, The History of Chinese Buddhism, The Dictionary of Chinese Herbal Food Remedies, Traditional Chinese Medicine Prescriptions in Ten Major Categories, Dialectics of Traditional Chinese Medicine*, and *Chinese Folk Remedies and Therapies.*

Figure 8.5
Chinese Titles Licensed Overseas, 1995–2002

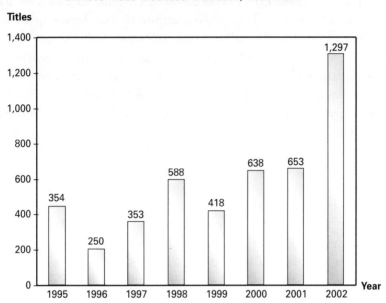

The same is true with Chinese rights licensing in the U.S. and European countries. Books include *Life and Landscape of Tibet, Traditional Chinese Internal Medicine, Chinese Herbal Medicine* and *The Illustrated Chinese Health Massages* to Germany; *The Art of Chinese Pottery Illustrations* and *The Myth of Longevity* to Italy; *Circular Qigong,* and *Chinese Tea* to Spain; *Chinese Healing Medicine* to Sweden; *The Collection of Documents on DungHuang Grottoes and Turpan* to France; *Chinese Natural Full Vitality Qigong, Essence of Qigong,* and *San Song Tang* to the U.S.; and *The Fundamental Theories of Traditional Chinese Medicine, 500 Cases of Treating Febrile Diseases,* and *Chinese Food Remedies* to Brazil.

A small number of countries are quite interested in the annual statistical studies of certain Chinese industries in addition to books on trends and development in China. Both Japan and the U.K. acquired the *White Paper on Chinese Economy: Trend and Outlook, Reports on China's National Strength, Reports on China's Agricultural Development* and *Reports on China's National Economy and Social Development.*

Singapore and Malaysia are primarily interested in Chinese language and children's books and their rights acquisitions focus on these categories. They have acquired *The Series of Chinese Children's Stories, The Illustrated Chinese Folk Tales* in large format, *The Illustrated Edition of Chinese Classical Literature, The Color Illustrated Tales of Gods and Ghosts, The Series of The Magic Gourd, Banana Grandma, Color Illustrated Children's Treasure in Chinese Phonetic Spelling, The Full Color Dictionary of Proverbs for Elementary School Students,* and *The High-School English and Chinese Dictionary.* Unlike other countries which acquire translation rights, Singapore and Malaysia mainly acquire the Chinese reprint rights because there are many Chinese speakers in these countries.

China is still a developing country and its global influence is still limited. Therefore, foreign publishers have only limited interest in acquiring Chinese books. This explains why there is such a big deficit in China's book copyright trade.

Sino-Foreign Book Copyright Trade

A. Sino-U.S. Book Copyright Trade

1. *Overview*

In the 40 years between 1949 and 1988, the majority of books translated into Chinese were Russian books published by the former U.S.S.R. However, from 1989 to the present, American works translated and published have surpassed Russian works both in book titles and print volume. In 1989, the Chinese mainland translated and published 3,472 foreign titles including reprints from 48 countries, of which 1,146 titles were from the U.S., representing 33% of the total. In the same year, the Chinese mainland printed 130 million copies of foreign books, of which 102 million copies were books from the U.S., representing 83% of the total. (See Figure 9.1.)

In 1992, China signed a bilateral intellectual property protection memorandum with the U.S. Later, the former agreed to adhere to the two main international copyright conventions. In the following two to three years, the number of acquired and translated works from the U.S. declined due to unfamiliarity with the rights licensing procedure by many Chinese publishers. Despite that fact, the total number of translation rights from the U.S. still ranks first among those from all other countries.

After 1995 the rate of acquisition of foreign rights by Chinese publishers began to accelerate. Rights acquired from the U.S. also increased by a large margin and in 1995, 423 titles were licensed from there. American works acquired by Chinese publishers increased to 2,920 titles in 1999 and to 4,544 titles in 2002. The total number of American titles licensed increased eleven-fold in seven years. (See Figure 9.2.)

Figure 9.1
Number of Foreign Books Translated into Chinese, 1989

Country	Title Quantity	% of Total	Copies Printed ('000)	% of Total
U.S.	1,146	33.0	101,915	83.0
Japan	629	18.1	7,500	6.1
Former U.S.S.R.	387	11.1	2,272	1.9
U.K.	353	10.2	2,915	2.4
France	165	4.8	1,603	1.3
Former East & West Germany	149	4.3	1,431	1.2
Italy	30	0.9	294	0.2
Canada	28	0.8	204	0.2
Denmark	27	0.8	606	0.5
Austria	21	0.6	198	0.2
Poland	19	0.5	162	0.1
Other Countries	518	14.9	3,649	2.9

Source: *National Copyright Administration of China*

Figure 9.2
American Books Licensed, 1995–2002

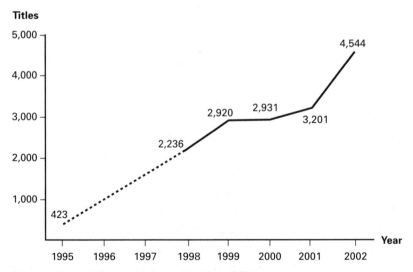

Source: *National Copyright Administration of China*

Figure 9.3

Top 10 U.S. Rights Licensors to Beijing in Recent Years

Rank	Publisher	Titles
1	McGraw-Hill	1,451
2	John Wiley & Sons Inc.	700
3	Pearson Education	496
4	Thomson Learning	486
5	Prentice Hall	448
6	Microsoft	283
7	Addison-Wesley	235
8	Sage Publications, Inc.	168
9	Aspen Publishers, Inc.	147
10	SYBEX Inc.	139

Source: *Beijing Municipal Bureau of Copyright*

In the past five years, the number of titles acquired from the U.S. each year on average accounted for 45% of the total number of rights acquired from all other parts of the world, and twice as many as the number of titles acquired from the U.K., which ranked second.

Of published titles each year, titles of U.S. origin account for 5% if we factor out titles already in the public domain. The U.S. is the most important trading partner for book copyrights since China joined the Berne Convention. With rapid economic growth in China and the increasing Sino-U.S. exchange, the number of translation rights acquired from the U.S. each year is expected to continue to grow.

2. *Details of American Books*

What kind of American books have publishers acquired in the past 10 years?

Chinese readers have a wide range of interests when it comes to American books and acquired titles span a wide spectrum, from current affairs, business, culture, science & technology to lifestyle. The most popular categories of U.S. books are business, fiction, computer science, language, inspirational, and children's.

For the fiction category, despite the fact that English, French, and Russian literature all have a long history and far-reaching impact in China, American Literature has been gaining popularity among Chinese readers. Chinese readers admire Walt Whitman's poetic imagery and boundless exuberance; Mark Twain's humor and sarcasm; and Ernest Hemingway's courage, valor and fortitude. They also love William Faulkner's *The Sound and the Fury* and Arthur Miller's *Death of a Salesman*. They pay attention to the Beat Generation and also read Pearl S. Buck. Works by all above-mentioned American writers have been translated and published in China. But Ernest Hemingway is the most popular. *The Old Man and the Sea* published by the Shanghai Translation Publishing House has sold over 700,000 copies.

In the past decade, American novels such as *The Band of Brothers, The Bridges of Madison County, The Horse Whisperer, The Silence of the Lambs, Catch-22, The Catcher in the Rye,* and *How Stella Got her Groove Back* have all been successes. Of these, *The Bridges of Madison County* and *The Horse Whisperer* have sold over 700,000 copies. More and more American popular writers have been introduced into China. For example, Yilin Press has acquired and published many popular novels by famous commercial American writers such as Sidney Sheldon, Michael Crichton, John Grisham, and Mario Puzo.

Chinese readers also follow with great interest, different movements of American works. For example, *On the Road* by Jack Kerouac, a representative work of the Beat Movement, was first published in the Chinese mainland in 1962, subsequently released by Shanghai Literature and Art Publishing House in 1984, and then by the Writers Publishing House in 1990. After China joined the Berne Convention, Lijiang Publishing House obtained the rights and published the authorized new edition.

The authorized Chinese edition of *On the Road* has 365 pages and is priced at RMB20 retail (US$2.41), which is one-fifth of Penguin U.S.A.'s 1997 trade paperback edition priced at US$12. *On the Road* had three print runs of 30,000 copies over eight months after its relaunch.

In recent years, Ralph Waldo Emerson and Henry David Thoreau have become popular, and all their major works have been published. *Walden* has been published in an elegant beautifully illustrated edition which has been very well received.

American and the Western non-fiction on current affairs, law, history, culture, and other subjects has always held an important position among foreign licensed books. In the past decade, the Chinese mainland has published *The Americans: The Colonial Experience, The National Experience* and *The Democratic Experience* by Daniel Boorstin; *Founding Brothers: the Revolutionary Generation* by Joseph J. Ellis; *A History of Western Political Thought* by J. S. McClelland; *The Clash of Civilizations and the Remaking of World Order* by Samuel P. Huntington; *World Civilizations* by Philip Lee Ralph, et al.; *From Dawn to Decadence, 500 Years of Western Cultural Life* by Jacques Barzun; *The Press and America: An Interpretive History of the Mass Media* and *The New Lifetime Reading Plan* by Clifton Fadiman; *The New York Times Scientists at Work* edited by Laura Chang; *John Adams* by David McCullough; *Steven Spielberg* by John Baxter; *Generation of Giants: the Story of the Jesuits in the Last Decades of the Ming Dynasty* by George H. Dunne; and *Journey to the Ants: A Story of Scientific Exploration* by Bert Holldobler and Edward Osborne Wilson.

Other popular American books are the *Encyclopedia Americana* and *The Complete Works of Albert Einstein.* The Chinese mainland has also published collections of famous articles in American history: *Words that Make America Great* by Jerome Agel (Random House) and *The American Reader* by Diane Ravitch (HarperCollins).

These books have a stable readership in the Chinese mainland. Though not instant bestsellers, they are backlist titles that consistently sell, year in and year out. For example, *A History of Western Political Thought* is published in Chinese in the trade paperback with 870 pages and is priced at RMB68 (US$8.19). *The New York Times Scientists at Work* is 510 pages long and is priced at RMB48 (US$5.78). Both Chinese editions had an initial print run of 5,000 copies, but now they have sold 14,000 copies each in total, with revenues of RMB952,000 each (US$114,699). The Chinese editions of *The New Lifetime Reading Plan,* a 610-page-long trade paperback priced at RMB35 (US$4.22), has sold 18,000 copies with total revenues of RMB630,000 (US$75,904). *Albert Einstein: Out of My Later Years* has also sold 18,000 copies.

In recent years, American books on personal finance, management and self-help have gained an impressive market share with more and more Chinese publishers acquiring rights to these kinds of books. The number of titles published under these categories has increased rapidly. The favorites are *The Power of Collaborative Leadership: Lessons for the Learning Organization, The Truth about Managing People...and Nothing but the Truth, Seven Habits of Highly Effective People, Forbes' Picks of Management Concepts,* and *Sales Management.* The Chinese mainland has published dozens of management books by the Harvard Business School Press. China Renmin University Press has published *The Harvard Business Review on Managing People* (translation) and *The Harvard Business School Cases* (English reprint). The Machine Press published *Managing Operational Control,* which contains articles by Harvard Business School professors. CITIC Publishing House has published four titles including *The Tipping Point,* one of the 20 most influential business books of the 20th century as selected by *Forbes* magazine.

Perhaps because people in China have begun to pay close attention to self-improvement, inspirational books and those on motivation, emotional help, and human interaction have become very popular in recent years. American books on these subjects have all done very well. On the non-fiction bestseller lists, these books dominated. Such American books with impressive sales in China are *Who Moved My Cheese?, Jack: Straight from the Guts, Good to Great: Why Some Companies Make the Leap...and Others Don't, The Five Faces of Genius: the Skills to Master Ideas at Work, Only the Paranoid Survive* by Andrew S. Grove, *Swimming Across: A Memoir* by Andrew S. Grove, and *Moving*

Forward by Henry Ford. Some of these titles have become blockbusters and have reached number one on bestseller lists. *Who Moved My Cheese?* sold 2 million copies, *Jack: Straight from the Guts* sold 800,000 copies and *Rich Dad, Poor Dad* sold 822,000 copies.

American children's books, especially cartoons, also hold a good market share in the Chinese mainland. Famous comics such as *Mickey Mouse, Garfield, Superman, Batman, Spiderman, Tom & Jerry,* and *Tarzan* are all very popular. Disney's *Mickey Mouse,* a biweekly Chinese version, sells 700,000 copies each month.

In recent years, American children's literature has also caught the attention of Chinese publishers. The New Buds Publishing House in Tianjin published *The International Children's Book Award Series,* which includes *Ella Enchanted* by Gail Carson Levine, *King of the Wind* by Marguerite Henry (author) & Wesley Dennis (illustrator), *The Cricket in Times Square* by George Selden (author) with drawings by Garth Williams, and *My Louisiana Sky* by Kimberly Willis Holt. The Jieli Publishing House acquired the American author R. L. Stine's, *Goosebumps Series,* and launched the series onto the children's bestseller list, selling 2.6 million copies in China to date.

The electronics and information technology industries are growing rapidly and the U.S. is the world's leader in these fields. Naturally, Chinese publishers have acquired many translation rights to American computer science books. The print runs of these books are large and the Chinese editions come out within two or three months of the American edition's release. The majority of computer science books acquired by the Chinese mainland's four computer book powerhouses are from the U.S.

For English language learning books, the majority of titles acquired or co-published have in the past come from the U.K. In recent years, the influence of American English has been increasing and publishers have begun to bring in more American-English learning books through rights licensing and co-publishing. Foreign Language Teaching and Research Press published *Family Album USA* and the *Webster's Dictionary of*

American English. The Commercial Press published *Random House Webster's College Dictionary* and University Press of Science and Technology of China published *The World of American Spoken English.* Anhui Science and Technology Publishing House published the *Chicken Soup for the Soul* series. Shanghai Far East Publishers published *Side by Side* for English language learning courses.

In sharp contrast to China's substantial rights acquisitions from the U.S., America's licensing from China is pathetically minimal. In the past 10 years, the U.S. acquired about a dozen books such as *Ancient Chinese Architecture* and *Soliton Theory and Its Application.* Most of these books were acquired by U.S. university presses and by scientific research institutions including the University of Hawaii Press, Yale University Press, University of California Press, and the American Mathematical Society. Some trade publishers have acquired a few controversial novels such as *Shanghai Baby* and *Beijing Doll.*

B. Sino-U.K. Book Copyright Trade

There is a long history of exchange and cooperation between British and Chinese publishers. According to Ms. Ou Hong's research (Ou 2003), the Oxford University Press was in Shanghai as early as 1916. In 1982, the British Publishers Association and the British Cultural Council formed the first Western publishers' delegation to visit China since its opening to the outside world in the late 1970s. Today, the U.K. is the second largest trading partner in book copyrights.

Before the 1990s, most of the copyright business between the U.K. and the Chinese mainland was conducted through Hong Kong intermediaries including the U.K. publishers' Hong Kong offices. Since 1997, British publishers have begun to seek business in China proper on a larger scale. British publishers, booksellers and literary agents who do business directly include the Oxford University Press, Cambridge University Press, Pearson (including Longman), Hodder Headline, BBC, Macmillan U.K., Reed Elsevier, Random House U.K., Dorling Kindersley

Ltd., HarperCollins, Hodder & Stoughton, The Continuum International Publishing Group Ltd., Blackwell, Octopus Publishers Group, A&C Black Publishers Ltd., Chrysalis Books Ltd., and Andrew Nurnberg Associates. The Oxford University Press, Cambridge University Press, Longman, Pearson, and DK have made great strides in the copyright trade and all of these publishers have established branches in the Chinese mainland. Some have even set up branch offices in several cities including Beijing, Shanghai, and Guangzhou.

Copyright trade is the most common business between British and Chinese publishers. Before China joined the Berne Convention, British books already accounted for a large percentage of foreign books published. In 1989, the Chinese mainland translated and published over 353 British books, which ranked fourth of all foreign books published. In 1995, the Chinese mainland acquired 208 U.K. titles, making U.K. second in rights licensing. The U.K. has kept the number two position in copyright trade among all countries. Between 1998 and 2002, U.K. rights licenses tripled from 594 to 1,821 titles.

In addition to copyright trade, progress has also been made in other areas of the book business. According to statistics obtained by researchers through different channels, some U.K. publishers have achieved initial successes in areas of the book trade outside rights licensing. Pearson has achieved 35%–50% growth in book exports and rights licensing to the Chinese mainland. In 2002, Pearson's total business volume with the Chinese mainland was US$7 million. The Oxford University Press' export sales to China have surpassed the US$2 million

Figure 9.4

Top Four U.K. Rights Licensors to Beijing in Recent Years

Rank	Publisher	Titles
1	Pearson Education Ltd.	916
2	Cambridge University Press	448
3	Wrox Press	102
4	Hodder & Stoughton	90

Source: *Beijing Municipal Bureau of Copyright*

mark and Blackwell's book trade with the Chinese mainland increased by 40% in the 2001–2002 fiscal year. Its annual sales of books and periodicals is estimated at £2 million. *The Design Magazine* of China's Electronic Industry launched by Reed Business Information has reached a circulation volume of 25,000 copies with an annual revenue of US$2 million (Ou 2003).

Foreign Language Teaching and Research Press, The Commercial Press, Peking University Press, Higher Education Press, Shanghai Foreign Language Educational Press, World Publishing Corporation, and the Liaoning Education Publishing House have all established very close ties with U.K. publishers. Foreign Language Teaching and Research Press (FLTRP) is a typical example of the cooperation between a Chinese and British publisher. FLTRP obtained authorization from the Oxford University Press to publish a reprint of *The World Classics Series*, which had 80% market share of English language books between 1993 and 1995. FLTRP also launched the *Longman Dictionary of Contemporary English, The Concise Oxford Dictionary of English, The Cambridge English Grammar Guide, Longman English Grammar,* and *The Oxford Guide to English* that have become the most famous English language reference books in China. FLTRP collaborated with Longman to revise *New Concept English*, of which they shared copyright ownership and profits. Since 1997, the revised edition of *New Concept English* has sold 2 million copies and 500,000 cassettes. FLTRP also has a copper statue of Louise George Alexander, the author of *New Concept English*, in front of the FLTRP office building.

The U.K. is the leader for licensing and co-publishing English learning books. Among all English learning books acquired from abroad, the overwhelming majority of them originate from the U.K. English language books took almost all the top spots on the bestseller lists of licensed foreign titles.

In addition to English language learning, U.K. books on politics, economics, law, history, and literature are also popular. U.K. books hold an important position both in title variety and sales volume among all licensed foreign books.

Figure 9.5
Statue of Louis G. Alexander

Statue of Louis George Alexander in front of the FLTRP office building. People standing behind, from left to right: Mrs. Alexander, Beijing Foreign Studies University official Yang Xueyi, U.K. Ambassador to China Sir Christopher Hum, and President of Pearson Education Will Ethridge.
(Photo provided by the FLTRP)

In recent years, the Chinese mainland has acquired U.K. titles on politics, law, and history such as The *World War Two Series, Contemporary Thinker Series, The Cambridge Illustrated History Series, Politics by Principle, Not Interest: Towards Nondiscrimination, Politics in the Ancient World, On Civil Procedure, Form and Substance in Anglo-American Law, Introduction to Politics, The Future of International Relations, International Systems in World History, Barbarians and Civilization in International Relations,* and *Losing Control: Global Security in the 21st Century.*

Some important U.K. academic works also made surprising showings in the Chinese mainland. For example, Shanghai People's Publishing House acquired *A Study of History Illustrated* (one-volume edition) from the Oxford University Press. This book is in large format, 470 pages long, and priced at RMB88 (US$10.60). The Chinese edition went back to print twice in the first 16 months of its publication run with a total of 30,000 copies produced. Shanghai People's issued another of Arnold Joseph Toynbee's works, *Mankind and Mother Earth*, which is also in large format, 580 pages long and priced at RMB60 (US$7.23). It had three print runs totaling 20,000 copies within one year.

For business books, the following have been released in recent years: *The Essence of Management Creativity, The Essence of Business Economics, Career, Aptitude and Selection Tests, The Murdoch Mission, Business Principles and Management, Game Theory and Economic Modeling, First Steps in Economic Indicators, Globalization,* and *E-Trends: Making Sense of the Electronic Communications Revolution.*

In recent years, U.K. books of arts and popular sciences have also become popular. *Sister Wendy's Odyssey* by BBC, and *A Brief History of Time* by Stephen Hawking have both had excellent sales with the latter selling 150,000 copies.

For U.K. children's books, the Chinese mainland recently published *The Blue Planet, Walking with Dinosaurs, Walking with Beasts, Eye Wonder, Rescue Vehicles, Ships, Cars, Jets, Planes Record Breakers, Space Tanks Trains,* and *A-Z of Dinosaurs.* In general, U.K. children's books, except for *Harry Potter*, garner a moderate share of the market.

Similar to the U.S., the U.K. acquired very few titles from the Chinese mainland. In 1999, the U.K. acquired just 20 titles, which was a record year. This is only one-fiftieth of the number of titles acquired from the U.K. in the same year.

C. Sino-Japanese Book Copyright Trade

Japan is China's third largest trading partner in book copyrights and is an important country both as a rights licensor and a rights acquirer. Since China joined the Berne Convention, Japan has occupied the third most important position in foreign book rights trade and is also among the top three buyers of Chinese books.

According to statistics from the National Copyright Administration of China (NCAC), Japan was ranked second in

1989 and third in 1995 in terms of total number of books that Chinese firms acquired from other countries. In 1989, 629 titles were acquired from Japan with 7.5 million copies printed, this accounted for 18% of total foreign book volume. By 1995, the Chinese mainland acquired 207 titles from Japan and printed 1.06 million copies, which represented 7% of total copies of foreign books printed. In the past five years, titles acquired from Japan doubled from 454 titles in 1998 to 908 titles in 2002.

The Sino-Japanese copyright exchange started quite early and remains vibrant. Many years ago, some well-known Japanese publishers such as Kodansha and Shogakukan helped train Chinese editors. Currently, Japanese publishers active in China are Kodansha, Shogakukan, Poplar Publishing Co., Ltd., Shueisha, Gakken Co., Ltd., Iwanamisyoten, Bungei Shunju, Shufunotomo Co., Kadokawa Shoten, Shinchosha Co., Obunsha Co., Ltd., and Ohmsha Ltd. Many Japanese copyright agents such as Japan UNI Agency, Japan Foreign Rights Center, and Tohan Co., Ltd. have engaged in major copyright trade and some Japanese publishers have set up offices in China such as

Figure 9.6
Japanese Titles Licensed, 1995–2002

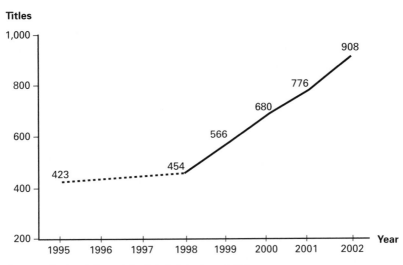

Source: *National Copyright Administration of China*

Shogakukan, Shueisha, Poplar Publishing Co., Ltd., and Dai Nippon Printing Co., Ltd. Kodansha and Shogakukan are among the most active rights licensors with Kadansha licensing 200 titles to Chinese publishers in 2003.

In 1997, NCAC hosted a Sino-Japanese copyright conference. Representatives of several dozen Chinese and Japanese publishers chartered a luxurious cruise ship on the Yangtze River. They negotiated copyright deals while enjoying the beautiful scenery of the Three Gorges.

Chinese publishers not only acquire many titles from Japan, but also acquire books in a wide variety of subjects. Among all the Japanese titles licensed to China, literature and cartoon books accounted for the largest percentage and also enjoy the largest market share. Japanese literature has a great influence and a wide readership in China. Modern Japanese writers attract much attention and Yasunari Kawabata, Inoue Yasushi, Yukio Mishima, Kenzaburo Oe, Haruki Murakami, and Banana Yoshimoto are all familiar to Chinese readers. In recent years, writers such as Kenzaburo Oe, Haruki Murakami, Junichi Watanabe have developed great followings. A majority of their works have been translated and published by Chinese publishers and have sold a large number of copies with Haruki Murakami being the most popular with almost all his works enjoying brisk sales in China. In order to promote a new book, Shanghai Translation Publishing House, the authorized Chinese publisher of Haruki Murakami, used such phrases in their ads such as "Dazzling Rendezvous with ...". His seminal work *Norwegian Wood* sold 700,000 copies. If we include the number of copies sold before China joined the Berne Convention, total sales of *Norwegian Wood* in China have surpassed one million copies. In the past two years, works by Junichi Watanabe and Koji Suzuki also have become popular. *The Complete Works of Junichi Watanabe* published by the Culture and Arts Publishing House and South Sea Publishing House also had good sales. According to the survey by Beijing OpenBook Market Consulting Center, books by these three Japanese writers account for more than half of all Japanese novels sold.

Japan is the country of cartoons and Japanese manga is very popular in China in all its formats. *Astro Boy, Elfin, RoboCat, Dragon Ball, City Hunter, Ninja Turtles, Slam Dunk, Crayon Shin Chan*, and *Pokemon's Big Search* have all enjoyed huge sales numbers. *Pokemon's Big Search* is the latest craze and has sold more than several million copies among all its formats. (See Figure 9.7.)

Figure 9.7

Japanese Bestsellers in the Chinese Mainland in Recent Years

Rank	Title	Chinese Publisher	Unit[1] Sales	Retail[2] Sales
1	*Pokemon's Big Search (Volume I and II)*	Jilin Fine Arts Publishing House	1,290 sets	11,310
2	*Doraemon-Maze Manual*	Jilin Fine Arts Publishing House	900 sets	5,400
3	*Norwegian Wood*	Shanghai Translation Publishing House	700	17,110
4	*Card Captor (12 volumes)*	Jieli Publishing House	720 sets	N/A
5	*Magic Pokemon TV Painting Series (14 volumes)*	Jilin Fine Arts Publishing House	300 sets	2,380
6	*Detective CONAN (45 volumes)*	Changchun Publishing House	270 sets	18,390
7	*Kafka on the Shore*	Shanghai Translation Publishing House	270	N/A
8	*Pokemon Fun Maze Painting (1)*	Jilin Fine Arts Publishing House	230	3,450
9	*Pokemon Origami (2)*	Jilin Fine Arts Publishing House	230	6,730
10	*Pokemon Origami (1)*	Jilin Fine Arts Publishing House	220	6,700
11	*Pokemon Origami (3)*	Jilin Fine Arts Publishing House	220	6,670
12	*Pokemon Number Book (2)*	Jilin Fine Arts Publishing House	210	3,690
13	*Dr. Slump–Arale Chan (4 volumes)*	Changchun Publishing House	200 sets	2,400
14	*Might and Magic*	International Culture Publishing House	150	2,250
15	*Bye Kelu*	Hainan Publishing House	90	N/A

[1] '000s
[2] '000s of RMB

Source: *National Copyright Administration of China*

According to the International Director of Kodansha, there are two new trends in China's acquisition of Japanese copyrights. One is the acquisition of "mega" books For example, the Hebei Education Press licensed *The Complete Art Works of Hirayama Ikuo* in seven volumes. Each volume is priced at 8,000 yen (US$70). Petrel Press acquired *UNESCOS World Heritage* in 13 volumes. The other trend is the systematic acquisition of serial titles. For example, China Textile Press and China Light Industry Press have systematically acquired book series, each of which have more than 10 volumes (Jiang 2003).

In recent years, Chinese publishers active in acquiring Japanese rights include the Shanghai Translation Publishing House, Jilin Fine Arts Publishing House, China Light Industry Press, China Textile Press, Jieli Publishing House, South Sea Publishing House Culture and Arts Press, Peking University Press, China Youth Press, and Shandong Fine Arts Publishing House. Each year, the Shanghai Translation Publishing House acquires about 50–60 Japanese titles.

Unlike other countries that are pure licensors, Japan is also a major licensee of Chinese book copyrights. According to statistics by the NCAC, Japan acquired 74 Chinese titles from 1991 to 1996, representing 19% of all Chinese titles licensed overseas. Japan is the second largest acquirer of Chinese titles and if the Chinese language rights obtained by Singapore are not factored into the calculation, Japan is the largest acquirer of Chinese titles. Since 1996, Japan has always been among the top four countries in terms of acquisition of Chinese books. In the past decade, the Japanese acquisition of Chinese titles averaged 14 titles per year.

Japanese publishers are mainly interested in four major categories of Chinese books: traditional culture (including literature, history, philosophy, and traditional Chinese medicine), current politics and economics, arts (including comics), and Chinese language.

Japanese publishers acquire the most books on traditional Chinese culture, literature, history, philosophy and medicine. The licensed books on culture include *Chinese Ghost Culture*,

Figure 9.8
Chinese Titles Licensed to Japan, 1991–2002

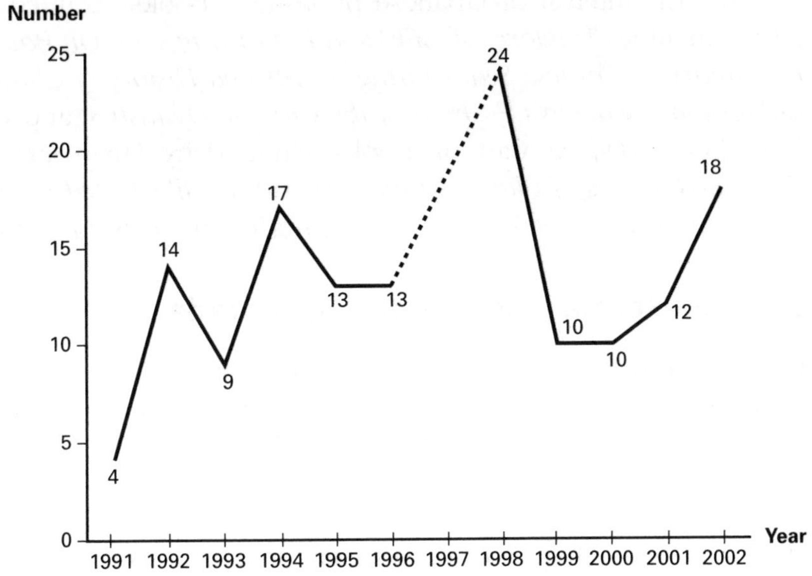

Number

Source: *National Copyright Administration of China*

Eunuchs—Slaves on the Top of Power Tower, Forbidden Books in China, Playing Cao Cao—the Collected Works of Wu Huan, and *The Suspense Cases in Three Kingdoms.* The acquired Chinese books on philosophy and religion include *History of Chinese Buddhism, The Series of Religious Stories—Taoism,* and *Chinese Secret Sects.* Books on traditional Chinese health and medicine acquired by Japan include *Encyclopedia of Chinese Herbal Cuisine, Chinese Folk Remedies, Introduction to San Shou,* and *Basic Taijiquan.*

The second largest category are books on modern Chinese politics and economics, which included *the Selected Works of Deng Xiaoping, Deng Xiaoping's Path, Before She was Called Jiang Qing (Madam Mao), Historical Stories of the People's Republic of China, What is the Socialist Market Economy, Economics White Paper: China's Economic Situation and Outlook (1994–1995), Yearbook of the China Petroleum and Chemical Corporation (1994),* and *Reports on China's National Economy and Social Development (1996).*

247

Chinese books on traditional Chinese arts such as calligraphy, paintings, fashion, and ethnic groups have also attracted the interest of Japanese publishers. Books acquired by Japan include *Folklore of Silk Road, Paintings of Qi Baishi, Dictionary of Chinese Seal Cutting, Illustrated History of Chinese Calligraphy, Women's Fashion of the Chinese Dynasties*, and *Old Tianqiao of Beijing*. Cartoon books acquired by Japan include *Illustrated Stories of Classic Chinese Literature, Illustrated History of China, The Art of War*, and *Xiaoping on What is Socialism*.

D: Sino-German Book Copyright Trade

Despite the fact that Germany lags behind the U.S., the U.K. and Japan in rights licensing, German books and culture occupy an important position for the Chinese readers.

In China, Karl Marx and Frederick Engels are known in every household. Immanuel Kant, George Wilhelm Friedrich Hegel, Arthur Schopenhauer, and Friedrich Nietzsche are also becoming renowned. Very few Chinese literary intellectuals do not know Gotthold Ephraim Lessing's *Laocoon* and Brecht Bertolt. Young literature lovers may not be aware of the difference between Faust and Johann Wolfgang von Goethe, but they all know *The Sorrows of Young Werth,* Friedrich Schiller, and Heinrich Heine. Every Chinese publisher is familiar with Bertelsmann and Frankfurt, a center of book publishing.

Germany is one of the most important partners in book copyright trade. Before China joined the two international copyright conventions, the total number of titles translated from the former East and West Germany ranked sixth of all foreign titles. Since the 1990s, the number of titles acquired from Germany continues to grow. According to statistics provided by the German Book Information Center of Goethe-Institute-Peking, China translated 28 German titles in 1992 and 135 German titles in 1996, accounting for 3% of all German titles translated into other languages. China began to acquire German titles in large numbers in 1998. Since then, China (i.e. the Chinese mainland,

Taiwan and Hong Kong) has become the largest licensee market for German publishers.

According to Germany's *Report on Book and Book Trade* released in 2000, German publishers licensed 471 titles to the Chinese mainland in 1999, accounting for 8.7% of total German titles licensed in other languages (English rights licensing accounted for 7.4%, ranked second, and Dutch totaled 6.9%). Since 1999, China has become the fastest growing market for German books and since 1995, the volume of German titles has increased five-fold. (See Figure 9.9.)

The statistics from NCAC indicate that Germany is ranked fourth in rights licensing after the U.S., the U.K. and Japan.

In 1998, the Chinese mainland and Taiwan acquired 369 titles from Germany, accounting for 8.9% of all German rights licensed in other languages. Among the German titles acquired, 93 were books for children and young adults, 60 were fiction,

Figure 9.9
German Titles Licensed in China, 1992–2002

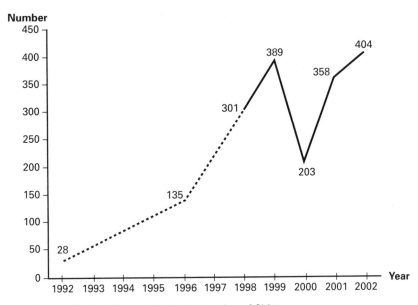

Source: *National Copyright Administration of China*

and 44 were history and art books. Children's books and books on philosophy, history, medicine, and information represented a large portion of the German books licensed, while fiction only accounted for a small part of the total.

Children's books represented a fast growing and large share of German books in recent years. China acquired 157 German children's titles in 1999 and 177 in 2001. According to the report on *German Children's Books in China* provided by Wang Xing of the German Book Information Center, 16 out of 18 of the main Chinese children's books publishers have published German children's books. The top three publishers are the 21st Century Publishing House, China Children Publishing House, and Zhejiang Juvenile and Children's Books Publishing House.

Tiger Team, published by Zhejiang Juvenile and Children's Books Publishing House, outsells all other German language children's titles. The series in 30 volumes have sold 2.6 million copies so far. Other titles with sales over 20,000 copies include *Alfred Hitchcock Die drei Fragezeichen* by China Children Publishing House, *Krabat*, *Momo*, and *4 1/2 Freunde* by 21st Century Publishing House. The 21st Century Publishing House has done an excellent job in promoting German children's books. When launching *4 1/2 Freunde*, it publicized the title in all the major news media and flew author Joachim Friedrich to Beijing from Germany for autograph and reading events.

Other influential German authors are the cartoonists Erich Schmitt, Hans Jurgen Press, and Bofinger, whose works are published under Yilin Press; and Geschichte der Wirtschaft Geschichte, whose *Money Produces Money* and *Economic History in Stories* are published under *Economics Daily Press*. The German children's classics, *The Complete Fairy Tales of Wilhelm Hauff* and *The Complete Fairy Tales of the Brothers Grimm*, are perennial bestsellers.

In general, there are comparatively few German art books published in China but some German books on performing arts are worthy of note. According to the article, "German Book Copyright Trade to China" by Tobias Voss of the International Department of the Frankfurt Book Fair, China acquired 37

German titles on performing arts in 2000 but the number in 2001 jumped to 158.

The most recently published German titles in China include business book such as *Die Welt der Boerse, Der Wachstums-code fur Siegermarken, Eiufuehrung in Projektmanagement,* and *Grundlagen und Probleme Der Betriebswirtschaft;* politics and law titles such as *Methodenlehre de Rechtswiss enschaft Rechtsphilosophie, Comparing Public Sector Reform in Britain and Germany, Das Unbehagen im Kapitalismus,* and *Grundkurs ZPO;* books on literature and biography such *as Kinderdetektiv-Buero Alina und Hung, Björn und die Autoknacker, Olli, Marco und Riesenbabys Bande, Hitler's Geheime Diplomantin,* and *Maerchen Monds Erben;* and science and technology books such as the *Injection Molding Handbook, Troubleshooting the Extrusion Process, Requirements Engineering, Overvoitage Protection of Low Voltage Systems 2nd Edition, Catalytic Membranes* and *Catalytic Membrane Reactors.*

Although Germany is ranked fourth in China's book copyright trade with foreign countries, the trade between Chinese and German publishers began very early and is extensive. German publishers have made achievements in some segments of the book market that are unparalleled by any other foreign country.

Research indicates that the first right acquisition contract that the Chinese mainland signed with a foreign country was with German publisher Springer-Verlag in 1980. Since then, Springer-Verlag has become the most important copyright trading partner with Chinese publishers. Rainer Justke, Rights Manager of Springer-Verlag, told the Chinese media that Springer-Verlag plans to sign 130 copyright contracts per year. Springer-Verlag's business is multidimensional. Its newest business is the online supply of academic periodicals and electronic books through SpringerLink.

Chinese subscribers have access to as many as 500 periodicals in electronic format that cover 12 disciplines: chemistry, computer science, economics, engineering, ecology, geology, law, biology, mathematics, medicine, physics, and astronomy. Many of the periodicals offered online are Springer-

Verlag's core journals. In May of 2002, the Documentary Information Center under the Chinese Academy of Sciences and the Library of China Medical Academy became the first Chinese subscriber to SpringerLink. Now many Chinese universities subscribe to SpringerLink including 60 institutes under the Chinese Academy of Sciences.

Bertelsmann is another German company with a large presence. Bertelsmann's China Book Club now has more than 1.5 million members and achieves annual sales of RMB100 million. By the end of 2003, Bertelsmann acquired 40% ownership of the 21st Century Book Chain, China's first private national bookstore chain with 18 outlets nationwide. Bertelsmann has become the second largest shareholder of the 21st Century Book Chain. This is the first major acquisition by a foreign company in the Chinese mainland's book trade. (See Chapter 10.)

At present, there are several dozen German publishers that have developed copyright businesses with Chinese publishers. They include Rowohlt Taschenbuch Verlag GmbH, Bärenreiter, Comelsen, Wiley-Vch Verlag, Ravensburger Buchverlag Otto Maier GmbH, Eichbom Verlag, Deutsche Taschenbuch Verlag, Lowe Verlag, Gerstenberg Verlag, and Schott Musik International. Most of these German publishers entered the market around 1998.

According to a survey by the Beijing Municipal Bureau of Copyright, Springer-Verlag, Rowohlt Taschenbuch Verlag GmbH, Bärenreiter, Wiley-Vch Verlag, and Anel have all licensed more than 30 titles to Beijing-based publishers in 2002.

In contrast to the acquisition of German books, there are very few Chinese books acquired by Germany. According to statistics, Chinese publishers have only managed to license 80 Chinese titles to Germany, which included literary works, general interest non-fiction, and science and technology books.

Interestingly, the introduction of Chinese works to Germany started very early. According to the author's research, German publisher Eugen Diederichs introduced Chinese writer Ku Hongming to Germany in 1911. Ku was a conservative and eccentric Chinese scholar who was fluent both in English and Chinese. Diederichs published a German language edition of Ku's English book *Oxford Movement*, which was translated by Richard Wilhelm. The initial print run was 5,000 copies. The book was available both in paperback (priced at 2.5 German Marks) and hardcover (priced at 3.5 German Marks). In 1924, Diederichs published another book of Ku's, *The Spirit of the Chinese People*, translated into German by Schmitz. Historical records indicate that the German edition was published under an agreement with Ku Hongming. This was perhaps the first Chinese book authorized by a Chinese author to be published by a foreign language publisher before China was a member of any international copyright conventions.

Although the scale of rights licensing between Germany and China is relatively small, the exchange between the two countries are expanding in other areas.

China and Germany maintain a relationship based on friendship and trust and feel the need for deeper understanding. According to Joachim-Groger, the German ambassador, there are 10,000 Chinese students enrolled in German universities alone. If visiting scientists and scholars and those in language schools are included, there are about 30,000 Chinese studying in Germany. In 2001, Chinese scientists won 165 research awards in Germany, ranking first among all nations in the outstanding foreign scientists program set up by Alexander von Humboldt Stiftung. More than 20 German universities offer Chinese language courses. In Berlin alone, more than 500 German students chose Chinese as their major. China plans to set up a Chinese Culture Center in Berlin, similar to the Goethe Institute.

It also needs to be pointed out is that the cooperation between Chinese and German publishers is becoming more active. Chinese publishers are the most active and the largest group of foreign participants in the Frankfurt Book Fair. By the same token, German publishers are also active participants of the Beijing International Book Fair. Since 2001, the *China Book Business Report*, the most important book trade publication in China, and the Goethe-Institute Beijing have jointly published

German Specials during the Beijing International Book Fair. This covers all aspects of German publishing: German publishers, new German titles, the current situation, and examples of successful cases of Sino-German copyright cooperation. The Chairman of the Frankfurt Book Fair and the German Ambassador to China contributed articles to these specials. The size of the publication is unmatched by those of any other country. The German Book Center of Goethe-Institute Beijing and Ms. Cladia Kaiser in particular have done remarkable jobs in promoting publishing exchanges between the two countries. Chinese scholar Cai Hongjun has set up the Hercules Business & Culture Development GmbH in Germany to promote and license German books to Chinese publishers. The agency has operated for seven years and has secured licenses 600 German books.

E. Sino-French Book Copyright Trade

The French may not know that the introduction of foreign literature in recent history started with French literature in 1898. What is more amazing is that Li Xu, who introduced the French masterpiece *La Dame Aux Camélias* to China was a Chinese scholar who did not know any foreign languages. Li Xu was a great master of the Chinese language and was also addicted to foreign literature. He relied on the collaboration with people who knew foreign languages to translate a large number of foreign works into Chinese.

French literature has had great influence and it is no exaggeration to claim that French literature has influenced several generations of writers and translation of French literature has produced a number of outstanding Chinese translators. The most famous Chinese translator in modern history is Fu Lei, who specialized in the translation and research of French literature.

Quite a number of French books have been translated into Chinese. There were 1,800 French titles (including re-translations) that were translated into Chinese from the end of the 19th century to March 1993. This is recorded in the *Index of Chinese Editions of French Books on Social Sciences and Humanities*, compiled by

Figure 9.10

Photo of Fu Lei

Fu Lei, a famous French literature expert, educator, and translator.
(Photo provided by Liaoning Education Press)

the Chinese–French Cultural Relations Research Institute of Peking University and the Reference & Research Department of Beijing Library. According to other statistics by Xu Jun, a well-known Chinese scholar on French literature, more than 500 French literature works have been translated into Chinese. However, after China joined the international copyright conventions, the number of French works introduced to the Chinese mainland has substantially declined.

According to statistics of the State Copyright Bureau, French books ranked fifth among all foreign books translated into Chinese both in 1989 and in 1995. In 1989, China published 128 French books, accounting for 7% of total foreign books published. In the same year, 1.276 million copies of books with French origin were in print, accounting for 8% of all foreign books. By 1995, 165 French titles were published, accounting for 4.7% of all foreign books, and 1.603 million copies of French books were printed, accounting for only 1.3% of all foreign books. From 1998 to 2002, China acquired an average of 200 French titles per year. France has remained in the fifth position in foreign rights licensing until 2002 when it was bumped to sixth by South Korea.

According to statistics from France, China is the seventh largest country in the world in acquiring French titles and the second largest country in Asia after South Korea. Although French literature is not selling as well as it did in the past, books on literature, arts, and humanities still constitute the majority of French books. According to the French Publishers Association, literature and humanities books accounted for 80% of all French titles licensed.

In recent years, some French books published are *Modern French Literature Series* published by the Shanghai Translation Publishing House, *Famous Modern French Novels Series* published by Yilin Press, *Modern French Philosophy and Culture Translation Series* published by The Commercial Press, *French Library* published by Guangxi Normal University Press, *Midnight Library* published by Hunan Arts and Literature Publishing House, *Duras Series* published by Lijiang Publishing House, and *The Completed Works of Albert Camus* published by the Hebei Educational Press. Translated French literature is still much sought after. For example, Shanghai Translation Publishing House acquired the French editions of 13 works by Czech writer Milan Kundera. Each of his 13 novels sold more than 100,000 copies. *The Unbearable Lightness of Being* sold 250,000 copies in just six months.

The new star publisher of French literature has been the Haitian Publishing House located in Shenzhen, a coastal city in Southern China. Haitian published almost all the French bestselling and award winning novels in recent years under its *Western Bestsellers Translation Series*. In addition, Haitian held a French Day two years in a row and invited French writers including a Prix Goncourt winner to China for French book events. Haitian's editor Hu Xiaoyue is the most active editor of French literature in China and is also a member of China's French Literature Research Association.

A few French books have had brisk sales in China. Thirty titles in the *French Library* of Guangxi Normal University Press

Figure 9.11

Top Five French Rights Licensors to Beijing in Recent Years

Rank	Publisher	Titles
1	Editions du Seuil	41
2	Presses Universitaires de France	15
3	Éditions Gallimard	13
4	Nathan	13
5	Bayard Presse	13

Source: *Beijing Municipal Bureau of Copyright*

have sold over 10,000 copies each. *Lover* and *Truismes* have also sold over 10,000 copies each. The Jieli Publishing House recently launched *Peggy Sue et les fantômes*, a French *Harry Potter* in three volumes. Jieli sold 40,000 sets and 120,000 single copies.

Some French publishers have done quite well in the copyright trade. Éditions Gallimard, for example, has signed 160 contracts with 30 Chinese publishers. The complete works of three famous writers and scholars Albert Camus, Jean-Paul Sartre, and Simone de Beauvoir have been translated and published in China. Gallimard is also active in translating and publishing Chinese works into French. Gallimard has published classics by Luo Guanzhong, Shi Naian, Cao Xueqin, and works by such modern Chinese writers as Ba Jin, Lao She, Han Shaogong, and Jia Pingwa.

In general, French books and movies have had a lukewarm response in the Chinese market. They simply cannot compete with American and British books. Hu Xiaoyue believes that this is because modern French literature does not suit the tastes of Chinese readers. General interest books are also not popular with Chinese readers because of the large differences between the two countries. French books on science and technology cannot compete with American and British books. Self-help and inspirational books, which sell very well , are not favored by the free-spirited French. The French language is far less popular than the English and this makes it difficult to promote French culture. Very few people know French, let alone are familiar with outstanding French translators. Nowadays, Chinese readers have too many choices and this is why French books seem to receive little notice from Chinese audiences.

Perhaps because of China's development, Chinese readers no longer restrict their interest to only French literature. They also want to experience French fashion and style. In contrast to the poor sales of French books in China, the Chinese language editions of French fashion magazines are very popular. Hachette Filipacchi has become an excellent magazine publishing partner in the Chinese mainland, Taiwan, and Hong Kong. Hachette's magazine joint ventures in the Chinese mainland such as *Elle*, *Car and Driver*, and *Marie Claire* have all become leaders in their respective categories. (See Chapter 10-B.)

Another interesting phenomenon is that some of the works written in French by some Chinese writers not only caused a sensation in France, but are also much sought after by Chinese publishers. Examples are the international bestseller *Balzac and the Little Chinese Seamstress* by Dai Shijie; *The Girl Who Played Go* by Shan Sa, winner of Prix Goncourt; and *Le Dit de Tianyi* by François Cheng, winner of Prix Femina and Grand Prix du Roman de l'Academie Francaise. These titles have all been published in Chinese and have received a warm response.

At present, both the Chinese and French publishing communities are pushing for greater exchange. In 2000, French publishers led by the French Publishers Association formed a 13-member delegation to attend the Beijing International Book Fair. They booked a 45-square-meter booth at the Beijing International Book Fair and exhibited 600 French titles. In 2002, the Culture and Science-Technology Cooperation Department of the French Embassy to China worked with the *China Book Business Report* to publish *French Specials*. Though not as rich and vivid as the *German Specials*, the *French Specials* contained much useful information.

As France and China are jointly holding a "Culture Year" in each other's countries from October 2003 to July 2005, this should enhance the interaction between the Chinese and French publishing communities. China was chosen as the theme country

Figure 9.12

Paris Book Fair, March 2004

French President Jacques Chirac (right), accompanied by Shi Zongyuan (left), Minister of the General Administration of Press and Publication and Zhao Jinjun (middle), China's Ambassador to France, visited the China Hall at the event. *(Photo provided by Syndicat National de L'Edition)*

at the French Book Fair in March 2004. It was the first time that China was chosen as a theme country at a large international book fair. The GAPP and the Information Office of the State Council jointly hosted various events at the book fair. Chinese publishers recommended 100 Chinese books to French publishers and will fund the translation and publication of these books in France. Presently, a few dozen titles have been published including modern Chinese literary works such as *Les Sourires du Sage* by Wang Meng, *La 12 Lune* and *La Fleur de Blé* by Tie Ning, *Officier* by Liu Zhenyun, and *Les Sources Chaudes* by A Lai.

F. Sino-Russian and Sino-Korean Book Copyright Trade

1. *Sino-Russian Book Copyright Trade*

China published numerous Russian works before the fall of the U.S.S.R. From 1949 to 1988, the U.S.S.R. was the single largest source of foreign works. The former Soviet Union also published many Chinese works. The commercial book copyright trade between China and Russia was formally started in 1993.

China joined the Berne Convention and the Universal Copyright Convention in October 1992 and Russia was a member of the Universal Copyright Convention and joined the Berne Convention in 1993. A legal foundation was thus laid for the Sino-Russian book copyright trade. In September 1992, the Copyright Agency of China signed a cooperation agreement with the Russian Copyright Association, Russia's largest copyright agency. From then on, the copyright business between the two countries has steadily grown. By 1996, the two countries had signed about 50 copyright contracts annually, which covered 300 titles. China's acquisition of Russian works comprises a large part of the total Sino-Russian copyright trade.

In 1989, Russia's dominant position in Chinese translation of foreign works was eclipsed by the U.S. and Chinese translation of Russian books declined year by year. In 1989, 387 Russian books were published, accounting for 11% of all foreign books published and Russia was the third largest rights-licensing country and more than 2.27 million copies of Russian books were printed, accounting for 13% of the total foreign works. In 1995, the number of Russian books published dwindled to 139 titles, accounting for 7.2% of all foreign books. (See Figure 9.11.) Russia moved down to fourth among the largest rights licensors to China. Over 1.130 million copies of Russian books were in print, accounting for 7.4% of the total copies of foreign books. Since 1996, acquisition of Russian books fell by another 50% and Russia slipped to seventh position. In 2002, only 10 books were acquired from Russia, which further slipped to eigth position.

The majority of Russian titles acquired are literature. Owing to historical reasons, the literary works of the Soviet Union have had a profound impact. In the mid-1980s, the influence of Russian works weakened but in the mid-1990s, some Russian works found new readers. The majority of influential Russian works were by Russian authors and a few works were by writers from other countries of the former U.S.S.R.

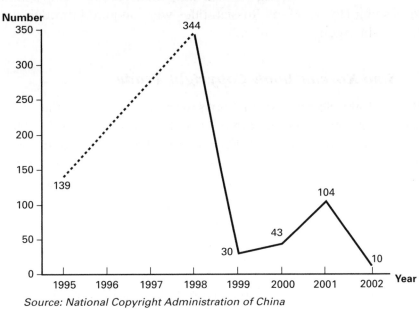

Figure 9.13
Russian Titles Acquired, 1995–2002

Source: National Copyright Administration of China

The Russian works published include *And Quiet Flows the Don* by Michail Sholokhov, *The Foundation Pit* by Platonov Andrey Platonovich, *The Master and Margarita* by Mikhail Afanasevich Bulgakov, *The Birth of the Amgunsky Regiment* and *The Rout* by Alexander Alexandrovich Fadeev, *The Iron Flood* by Alexander Seravimovich, *First Joy by* Konstantin Fedin, *Days and Nights*, and *War Triology* by Konstantin Simonov, *The Storm* and *The Thaw* by Ilya Ehrenburg, *The Dawns Here Are Quiet* by Boris Vasilyev, *Doctor Zhivago* by Boris Pasternak, and *Gulag Archipelago by* Alexsander Solzhenitsyn. Up to now, all famous Russian works that were under copyright protection have been introduced into the Chinese mainland.

A small number of Russian biographies and books on the humanities were also introduced. They include *Midnight Diaries—Boris Yeltsin's memoir*, and *Gorbachev: On my Country and the World.*

Chinese publishers active in publishing Russian books are the People's Literature Publishing House, Baihua Arts and

Literature Publishing House, Haiyan Publishing House, Yilin Press, Haitian Publishing House, and the Shanghai Translation Publishing House. Many Russian titles were acquired through the Copyright Agency of China.

2. Sino-Korean Book Copyright Trade

Before 1999, South Korean books were not really on the radar screens of China's book copyright trade researchers but in 1997, China acquired more South Korean than Russian titles and South Korea became the seventh largest partner in the copyright trade.

It was only recently that South Korean books caught the attention of Chinese readers. This happened when a movie tie-in book called *My Sassy Girl* entered the Chinese market along with the TV show of the same name. Soon afterwards, *Fragrant Chrysanthemum*, which had sold two million copies in South Korea, was introduced.

South Korean books have entered along with Korean movies and TV shows. In 2002, South Korean TV shows became popular in the Chinese mainland and Taiwan as never before. In many areas, entire families were glued to the TV screen watching South Korean dramas unfold. Suddenly "South Korean Fever" swept across China. The same happened with South Korean computer game software and South Korean products dominated the Chinese computer game market. Since teenagers are the primary consumers of computer games, adults did not follow with much interest. Therefore, South Korean computer

Figure 9.14

Top Five Korean Rights Licensors to Beijing in Recent Years

Rank	Publisher	Titles
1	Youngjin.com	40
2	Sisa Education	39
3	Jigyunsa Ltd., publisher	30
4	VITSAEM	26
5	Cyber Publishing Co.	11

Source: *Beijing Municipal Bureau of Copyright*

games did not achieve the same unprecedented attention in China as the South Korean TV shows.

Since 1998, the number of South Korean book rights licensed has continued to grow. The Chinese mainland acquired 82 South Korean titles in 2000, 97 titles in 2001, and an unprecedented 275 titles in 2002. South Korea has overtaken France to become China's fifth largest partner in the copyright trade. South Korean publishers that have entered into the Chinese market are YBM Sisa, Youngjin.com, Sisa Education, Jigyungsa Publishers, Woongjin Group, VISTAEM, Cyber Publishing Co., and Kyelim. The most active is YBM Sisa's branch in Beijing—Waisi Education and Culture Co., Ltd.

Chinese publishers active in acquiring South Korean titles are mainly concentrated in Beijing, Northeast China and North China—which are all geographically close to South Korea. Beijing, Jilin, Shandong, Liaoning, and Heilongjiang are the areas with the densest accumulation of South Korean copyright acquirers. The number of Chinese publishers acquiring South Korean books has grown very fast and has reached 40 in number.

South Korean books are becoming a new force in the Chinese fiction market. Its TV and movie tie-ins, best selling fiction and serious literature have begun to enter the market on a large scale. Many South Korean writers became instant celebrities. Kim Ha-In has become a new best selling writer of romance in the style of Qiong Yao (the Chinese romance queen) and Hai Yan. Some readers regard him as South Korea's Haruki Murakami. So far, *Fragrant Chrysanthemum* has sold 200,000 copies. Other influential South Korean novels are the *Winter Sonata, Autumn In My Heart,* and *A Portrait of Witch Picture.*

South Korean novels have won the hearts of Chinese readers not only because the two countries have close cultural and historical ties, but also because the young people of the two countries share similar lifestyles and values. According to Jin Chun Xian, a scholar on South Korean literature at the Central Nationalities University, the division of the Korean Peninsula led to thousands of broken families and deep hurt inspired tragic sentiments in South Korean literature but the younger generation does not share the same "sad feelings" as the older generation.

Economic development and the encroachment of Western culture have led some young South Koreans to value money over all other things. A common and current theme in literature and TV dramas is how money can come between family or love. People have also indulged themselves in watching soap operas about the life and loves of the middle class. Young South Koreans only had a faint memory of what traditional values are until suddenly, *Fragrant Chrysanthemum* gave them a shock. For a long time, people had not seen such pure and transcendent love and such solid family values. *Fragrant Chrysanthemum* awakened a national heritage buried deep in the hearts of young South Koreans. By the same token, the younger Chinese generation, who has never experienced any hardship since China's opening to the world, found that they identified with the young South Koreans.

The Chinese mainland has also acquired children's books, business books, design books, and computer books from South Korea. Other popular South Korean books include *Mashi Maro* and *Never Ever Study English*. The latter was launched by the World Publishing Corporation and has sold over 200,000 copies.

South Korean books recently published in China include children's books such as *Building Creativity for Children, 3D IMAGE of Solar System, 3D IMAGE of the Sea,* and *Searching for Seven Magic Seeds*; books on politics, law and business such as *Grasp the Golden Opportunity—South Korean Industry Culture and its Main Policies, The Relationship between Capital and Labor in South Korea, Economics in the Global, Intellectual and Commercial Era,* and *Korean Workers: The Culture and Politics of Class Formation;* design books such as *Hello, Remodeling, Can do!, Green House Design Book,* and *D.I.V.A-Digital Idol Visual Artwork;* and computer books such as *Flash MX Web Animation* and *Dreamweaver MX.*

South Korea is one of the few countries that has acquired many Chinese books. In 2002, South Korea acquired the rights to 103 books from Chinese publishers, setting a new record.

Foreign Investment in China's Publishing Industry

A. Overview

1. Market Entry

When you look at the front page of the China Book Business Report, the most influential trade newspaper in the Chinese publishing industry, you may see three advertisements on the bottom half of the page. On the right are two advertisements: "2004 Book Distribution Logistics Management Forum" and "2004 Open Book Franchise Bookstores." On the left is the prominent logo of John Wiley with its tagline "Publisher since 1807" on a job advertisement. The ad reads "John Wiley Beijing Branch has vacancies for three positions: copyright manager, copyright coordinator/executive, and account manager-subscription."

Foreign investment in the publishing industry started as early as one century ago. In 1903, a Japanese firm was allowed to invest in The Commercial Press on the basis of 50% Chinese ownership and 50% Japanese. Later, The Commercial Press became China's largest and most famous publishing house. (See also Chapter 2-D.)

In 1949, the People's Republic of China was founded and from 1966 to 1976, the country experienced 10 years of turmoil during the Cultural Revolution. In 1978, China started on its course of economic development, embarking on a new road to reform and opening to the outside world. On December 11, 2001, it became a member of the WTO.

In 1973, the Chinese government invited the German publisher, Springer-Verlag, to hold a mobile book exhibition across the country. This was perhaps the first cooperation between a Western publisher and the Chinese mainland. As a result, Chinese publishers signed the first copyright trade contract, acquiring foreign titles from Springer-Verlag.

On September 13, 1980, the International Data Group (U.S.) formed the China Computer World Publishing with a Chinese partner. *China Computerworld* became the first joint-venture periodical.

In 1982, the British Publishers' Association and the British Council jointly sent a delegation that was the first Western publishing delegation to visit since the country opened its doors to the outside world. In 1998, the China National Publications Import & Export (Group) Corporation formed the first publishing joint-venture with a U.K. publisher, Wanguo Academic Press.

However, focused and large-scale foreign investment did not happen until the late 1990s. In 1997, the German company, Bertelsmann AG, launched its book club in Shanghai. Around the same time, many foreign publishers began to set up offices in the Chinese mainland. In February 2002, Sony Music Entertainment Inc. (U.S.) set up the Shanghai Epic Music Entertainment Co., Ltd. (SEME) with Chinese partners. SEME became the first cooperative joint venture to obtain national distribution rights for audio/video products. In December 2003, Bertelsmann obtained partial ownership of the 21st Century Book Chain. This new joint venture is the first foreign-owned joint-venture national book chain.

2. Models of Foreign Investment in China's Publishing Industry

There are four models of foreign investment in the Chinese publishing industry: one-time cooperation, long-term cooperation, joint ventures, and sole ownership.

One-time cooperation often refers to cooperation between foreign investors and Chinese publishers on only one title or a set of books. A typical example of this is the collaboration between the Foreign Language Teaching and Research Press

(FLTRP) and Longman, a British publisher. Together, they co-published *New Concept English*. *New Concept English* is an English learning book that was written by the British for Germans learning English. In 1995, FLTRP and Longman Asia agreed to revise the book, and publish the new edition. The new edition was cowritten by the original British author, Louis George Alexander, and He Qixin, a Chinese author. FLTRP and Longman assigned their own editors to the project. The new edition took two years to finish and consisted of four volumes. Longman and FLTRP are joint copyright owners of the revised edition. The new edition sold two million copies, becoming the most famous English learning textbook in China. It also led to the publication of companion study guides, supplementary readings, a VCD, and other related multimedia products.

Go For It!, co-published by Thomson Learning and the People's Education Press, is another example of such success. The Chinese mainland's edition of *Go For It!* is based on Thomson Learning's English edition and is revised according to the *Curriculum Standard* issued by the Ministry of Education of China. This set of textbooks have been approved by the *All China ELHI Textbooks Review Board* and was adopted on a trial basis in selected schools in 24 provinces beginning in the fall semester of 2003. This set of textbooks consists of five volumes, covering three-year junior high school levels. Companions for the textbooks include student's books, workbooks, teacher's books, assessment books, audio tapes and classroom charts. Presently, *Go For It!* is in used by 7.28 million junior high students, representing 80% of the student population in the textbook trial schools throughout 24 provinces.

Long-term cooperation between foreign and Chinese publishers is common in magazine publishing. Shufu To Seikatsusha Co. of Japan, Hachette Filipacchi of France, Hearst Corporation of the U.S., and the Bauer Group of Germany have all forged long-term cooperative business relationships in China. The common feature of this kind of long-term cooperation is rights licensing. A foreign partner authorizes its Chinese partner to use their name and content for publication in the Chinese mainland on a long-term basis. In exchange, the Chinese partner will pay the foreign partner royalties.

The magazine *Rayli Fashion* is a typical example. In 1995, Shufu To Seikatsusha Co. of Japan and the China Light Industry Press agreed on a licensing deal to publish *Rayli Fashion Quarterly*. The magazine, originally priced at RMB13.80 (US$1.67), became an expensive and high-quality women's magazine. The magazine has won the favor of Chinese white-collar women who responded warmly. Consequently, the two sides launched a series of magazines: *Rayli Women's Glamor, Rayli Lovely Vanguards,* and *Rayli Home Decorating*, which all have become popular and now are published monthly. Rayli has hosted a number of events including a national competition for cover girls, which caused quite a sensation. The China Light Industry Press also published *Rayli Mini-series* and launched a website for Rayli (www.rayli.com.cn). *Rayli Fashion*, now priced at RMB20 (US$2.41), sells 250,000 copies per issue, generating monthly revenues of RMB5 million (US$602,410).

Publishing businesses under co-investment are mainly operated through a joint-venture company formed by Chinese and foreign partners. For example, the International Data Group (IDG), Bertelsmann AG, and the Singapore Pan Pacific Publications Co., Ltd. have all formed joint ventures with Chinese partners.

Foreign sole ownership is common in the printing industry. Additionally, some foreign companies set up solely owned offices in China, whose main businesses include marketing and promotion, information collection, copyright trade, direct sales, and public relations. At present, investors from foreign countries, Taiwan, and Hong Kong have set up 500 solely owned printing companies in the Chinese mainland.

B. Foreign Investment in the Magazine Market

Chinese-foreign cooperation in magazine publishing gets the most attention among all foreign investment in the publishing industry. Today, more than 50 foreign magazines have Chinese

Figure 10.1

Foreign Publishing and Media Establishments

Parent Foreign Company	Branch in China	City	Main Business	Notes
Andrew Nurnberg Associates (U.K.)	Office	Beijing	Book rights licensing	
Asia Pulp & Paper Co., Ltd. (Indonesia)	Factory	Shanghai	Paper	
Avery Dennison (U.S.)	Subsidiary company	Shanghai	Printing	
Bauer Group (Germany)	Office	N/A	Magazine publishing	
Bertelsmann AG (Germany)	Bertelsmann Directgroup China	Beijing and Shanghai	Book club, book/audio/video retail sales, online bookstore, entertainment and media consulting, and printing.	Please also see Bertelsmann Investment in China Chart in this chapter.
BMG (U.S. subsidiary of Bertelsmann)	Office Taiwan subsidiary	Beijing Taipei	Audio/Video	
Bobst Group (Switzerland)	Subsidiary company	Shanghai	Printing equipment	
Buchinformationszentrum (Germany)	Office	Beijing	Book export sales and marketing, and copyright licensing.	
Bureau of National Affairs & San Francisco Chronicle (U.S.)	Office	Beijing and Shanghai		
Cambridge University Press (U.K.)	Office	Beijing	Co-publishing	
CCH (Holland)	Beijing Veeco Business and Legal Publishing Consulting Co., Ltd.	Beijing	Information service	
Charlesworth Group (U.K.)	Beijing Charlesworth Software Development Co.	Beijing	Book export sales and marketing, co-publishing.	
Dai Nippon Printing Co., Ltd. (Japan)	Subsidiary company	Beijing	Printing	
Dorling Kindersley (U.K.)	Office	Beijing	Book export sales and marketing, packaging and printing.	

Figure 10.1 (Cont'd)

Parent Foreign Company	Branch in China	City	Main Business	Notes
Egmont (Denmark)	Children's Fun Publishing Co., Ltd. (joint venture)	Beijing	Book publishing and distribution	Publishing *Mickey Mouse Weekly*, and other foreign and Chinese books.
EMI (U.K.)	Office Taiwan subsidiary	Beijing Taipei	Music	
Goethe-Institut Inter Nationes e.V (Germany)	Goethe-Institut Inter Nationes e.V. Peking	Beijing	Publishing and copyright information service and culture exchange	
Gruner + Jahr (Germany)	G+J Consulting (Beijing) Co., Ltd.	Beijing	Magazine publishing	Publishing parents and car magazines.
Hachette Filipacchi Media (France)	Office subsidiary	Beijing	Consumer magazine publishing	Publishing Chinese editions of multiple consumer magazines.
Hearst Group (U.S.)	Office Branch	Beijing Taipei	Magazine publishing	Publishing *Good House-keeping*, *CosmoGIRL!* and *Harper's Bazaar.*
Heidelberger Druckmaschinen AG (Germany)	Subsidiary companies	Beijing, Shanghai, Shenzhen, Hong Kong	Printing	
Hercules Business & Culture Development GmbH	Rep. Office	Beijing	Rights licensing	
International Data Group (U.S.)	Rep. Office Subsidiary company	Beijing Taipei	Computer magazines, rights licensing, and electronic information services.	IDG has invested in 80 companies in China.
John Wiley & Sons Pte. Ltd. (U.S.)	Office	Beijing	Book export sales and marketing and public relations.	
LexisNexis (U.S.)	Rep. Office	Beijing	Internet, print, and CD-ROM information services.	

Figure 10.1 (Cont'd)

Parent Foreign Company	Branch in China	City	Main Business	Notes
LINTE (Japan)	LINTE	Tianjin	Printing equipment	
Macmillan U.S.	Office	Beijing	Co-publishing	
Madame Figaro (France)	Office	Beijing	Magazine publishing	
MAN Roland (Germany)	Subsidiary company and offices	Beijing Chengdu Guangzhou Shanghai and Shenzhen	Printing	Has seven offices.
McGraw-Hill Companies (U.S.)	Rep. Office Subsidiary company	Beijing Taipei	Book export sales and marketing, public relations, magazine investment, and online publishing.	McGraw-Hill publishes the Chinese language edition of *Business Week*.
National Geographic Society	Office	Beijing Taipei	Magazine publishing.	
New Century Succeed Development Co., Ltd. (U.S.)	Office	Beijing	Magazine publishing and electronic publishing.	Publishing China E-Commerce, China E-Market.
News Corporation (U.S.)	Rep. Office	Beijing Shanghai	Entertainment, media, and telecommunications.	Second foreign media company to obtain broad-casting rights in the Chinese mainland.
Oxford University Press (U.K.)	Oxford University Press China, Ltd.	Beijing Hong Kong, Shanghai	Co-publishing, rights licensing, export sales and marketing.	
Pan Pacific Publications Group (Singapore)	Yunan Book City (a joint venture with Yunan Provincial Xinhua Bookstore)	Kunming	Book distribution and venture investment.	

Figure 10.1 (Cont'd)

Parent Foreign Company	Branch in China	City	Main Business	Notes
Pearson Education Group (U.K.)	Office	Beijing Shanghai	Co-publishing, rights licensing, export sales and marketing.	
PIA Corporation (Japan)	Office	Beijing	Co-publishing and rights licensing.	
Poplar Publishing Co., Ltd. (Japan)	Office	Beijing	Co-publishing and rights licensing.	
Popular Holdings Limited (Singapore)	Office	Shenzhen Taipei	Publishing, distribution and rights licensing.	
RR Donnelley (U.S.)	RR Donnelley Shenzhen (joint venture) RR Donnelley Shanghai (joint venture)	Shenzhen Shanghai	Printing	
Shogakukan Inc., (Japan)	Office	Beijing	Co-publishing and rights licensing.	
Shueisha Inc., (Japan)	Office	Beijing	Co-publishing and rights licensing.	
Sony Music (U.S. Group)	Shanghai Epic Music Entertainment Company and Taiwan subsidiary	Shanghai Taipei	Audio/Video	First Sino-foreign joint venture in music distribution.
Springer Group (Germany)	Ref Office	Shanghai	Co-publishing, rights licensing, book export sales and marketing.	
Thomson Learning (Canada)	Rep Office	Beijing Shanghai	Book export sales and marketing, rights licensing, and information services.	
Time Warner (U.S.)	Office	Beijing Taipei	Entertainment and media	First foreign media company to obtain broadcasting rights in the Chinese mainland.

Figure 10.1 (Cont'd)

Parent Foreign Company	Branch in China	City	Main Business	Notes
Toppan Printing Co., Ltd. (Japan)	Factory	Shanghai	Printing equipment	
Universal Record Co., Ltd.	SUM Entertainment (joint venture)	Beijing	Music	
	Taiwan subsidiary	Taipei		
Vivendi Universal (France)	Office	Beijing	Entertainment, TV programming, telecommunication and environment protection.	
Vogel Burda Media (Germany)	Beijing Vogel Consulting Co., Ltd.	Beijing Shanghai	Magazine publishing and electronic information.	
Walters Kluwer (Holland)	Office	Shanghai	Legal information services	
Warner Music (U.S.)	Office	Beijing	Music	
	Office	Shanghai		
	Taiwan subsidiary	Taipei		
YBM Asia (South Korea)	Beijing Waisi Education and Culture Co., Ltd.	Beijing	Co-publishing and rights licensing.	

language editions. Co-published magazines concentrate on three major areas: technology, business, and fashion. Foreign publishers enter the market with their brand magazines and form cooperative ventures with Chinese partners, either through publishing the Chinese language edition of their brand magazine, or through licensing content and the brand to the Chinese counterparts. In addition to magazine licensing, these media companies also engage in publishing and non-publishing related businesses.

The McGraw-Hill Co. licenses the *Business Week* brand and content to the China Commerce and Trade Press to publish a Chinese edition. Harvard University collaborates with China Social Science Documentation Publishing House to publish the Chinese edition of *Harvard Business Review*. In some cases, Chinese publishers only purchase the editorial content of foreign magazines. For example, China Youth Press licenses content from French Figaro Publishing Group and uses the Chinese translation in its own magazine *Rainbow*. The Italian publisher of *Newton* and a Japanese publisher are the long-term content providers for *Science World*, published by the Science Press. Hachette Filipacchi and Shanghai Translation Publishing House jointly publish the Chinese Edition of *Elle* under both companies' logos. The Hearst Corporation and Fashion magazine collaborated in a similar way to publish a Chinese version of *Cosmopolitan*.

Foreign publishers develop different business models through both cooperation and joint investment. Some media companies publish Chinese language editions of their magazines. For example, Ziff Davis (U.S.) launched Chinese language editions of *PC Magazine, eWeek, Electronics and Computer*, and *Computer Products* and *Distribution*.

Foreign media firms that enjoy the greatest success in magazine publishing are the International Data Group, Vogel Burda Media, Hachette Filipacchi, and the Hearst Corporation.

1. *The International Data Group*

In September 1980, the International Data Group (IDG) co-founded China Computer World (CCW) with the Institute of

Scientific and Technical Information (ISTI) under the Ministry of Information Technology of China. *Computer World* became China's first weekly magazine published by a joint venture. According to the contract signed then, both sides invested US$250,000 into the joint venture with 49% owned by IDG and 51% by ISTI. The Board of Directors consisted of three Chinese and two American members with a Chinese chairman on the Board. Patrick J. McGovern, IDG Chairman, was Vice Chairman of the joint venture. The contract had a 10-year term. CCW was just the 18th joint venture in China at that time.

In the 1980s, *Computer World* became an immediate success. It earned US$150,000 in revenue within the first year and recouped the initial investment by the third year. In the 1990s, as computers were becoming popular, *Computer World* became the messenger for the IT industry and continued to grow. Soon it launched *Computer World Monthly*, among other magazines, and organized the "China Computer World Fair." In 1996, the *Computer World* website was launched, becoming one of the earliest media websites in China. In 1998, CCW established branches in Shanghai and Shenzhen. In 2002, it hosted the first "China IT Fortune Forum."

Today, CCW has become the most important IT and electronics media group in China. It publishes three newspapers, four magazines and employs 700 people. Since 2001, CCW maintained annual sales of over RMB400 million (US$48.19 million). Its flagship magazine, *Computer World*, boasts 260 pages per issue, carries 1,000 articles, and 20,000 pieces of commercial information. The Business Publication's audit confirmed that *Computer World* had 21,480 subscriptions in June 2003 and it prints 260,000 copies per issue and has a total of 1.8 million readers. The CCW Media Group now has one million subscribers and three million total readers, influencing decision-makers at all levels of the China IT industry.

In 2000, the Periodical Bureau of the GAPP hosted the "Symposium on the Computer World Phenomenon" to introduce the CCW experience to the Chinese media. In 2002, CITIC Publishing House issued the *New Media in War—the Legend of China's Computer World*, a biography chronicling the growth of

Figure 10.2

China *Computer World* Annual Revenues

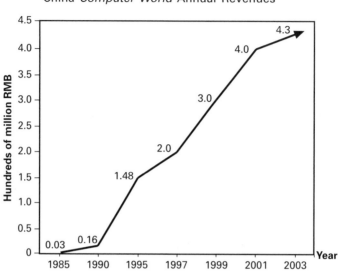

Source: *Jiang, Q. 2002, New Media in War, CITIC Publishing House, Beijing.*

CCW. In addition to China Computer World, IDG has since invested in 80 other Chinese companies.

In the past 22 years, IDG's US$250,000 investment has yielded US$51.2 million in profits and royalty payments, with an average 931% return on capital a year and a growth of 28% per year. On November 6, 2004, IDG president Patrick J. McGovern announced IDG's plans for China, including the launching of 10 new publications per year, launching four to five new expositions and conferences each year, greatly increasing websites, webcastings, e-newsletters, and e-commerce activities. IDG will also invest in periodical distribution, the creation of television programs, and TV advertising. He estimated that by 2020 IDG's business activities in China would reach US$7.2 billion a year, making IDG one of the largest media companies there, with China representing 18% of IDG's global revenue.

2. *Vogel Burda Media*

Vogel Burda Media also has had an impressive performance in the Chinese mainland. Unlike IDG, it maintains a low profile. Vogel Burda Media is a famous German technical publishing group consisting of Vogel Media and Burda Media. It entered the Chinese mainland in 1995 initially partnering with the Science-Technology Information & Publications Bureau under the Ministry of Machine Building Industry to publish technical magazines. In 1996, it set up an office in Beijing. In 1998, it formed a joint venture, the Beijing Vogel Consulting Co., Ltd. with its Chinese partner and opened an office in Shanghai.

Beijing Vogel Consulting focuses on the machinery and electronics industries. It engages in a wide range of businesses: publishing, distribution, trade fairs, and consulting. It publishes the Chinese editions of its various technical magazines and books and offers translation, editing, page layout, and printing services for product catalogs and brochures. It also provides direct mailing to its various specialized databases. It organizes various mechanical trade shows and promotes clients' brands at important industrial events. It also advises manufacturing companies on technical issues on doing business in China. Beijing Vogel Consulting has its own Chinese website (www.vogel.com.cn).

For its publishing joint venture, Vogel Burda Media licensed the name and content of its brand-name magazines to its Chinese partners. So far they have co-published the Chinese language editions of *Modern Manufacturing, Chip, Automobile Industry, Chemical Industrial Process, MM Plastics,* and *Beer and Beverage Production.*

Many of the these magazines have become the leading trade publications in their respective industries. For example, *Chip*, co-published with the Electronics Research Institute under the Ministry for the Information Industry, has achieved a circulation of 100,000. *Chip* has also set up Chip Online (www.chip.cn), Chip Book Club and the Chip CD. *Automobile Industry China,* published by Vogel Burda Media, has become a well-known trade magazine covering automobile making, automotive equipment, and products, with a circulation of 20,000 copies.

Vogel Burda Media is also involved in planning and publishing computer books and has achieved impressive results. For example, it assisted Electronics Industry Publishing Company in launching the *Easy Computing* series. *Easy Computing* is published every two weeks and a single issue can sell 200,000 copies.

Vogel Burda Media also sponsors many international trade shows and conferences. For example, it hosted a summit on "Advanced Manufacturing Technology and Automotive Making— IT for Auto Makers." It also acted on behalf of CeBIT Hannover to organize CeBIT Asia, Asia's largest information and communication technology show, and CeBIT CE, Asia's largest consumer electronics show. It also undertook the editing, interviewing, and publishing of *CeBIT Asia* and was directly involved in brand promotion and exhibition planning.

3. Hachette Filipacchi in China

Fashion magazines are generally more glamorous than technology magazines. Although Hachette Filipacchi (HF) entered much later than IDG, it enjoys more fame in China's magazine world and has almost become a name synonymous with prestigious foreign magazines. HF has been in the Chinese market for a decade and its operation extends across the Chinese mainland, Taiwan, and Hong Kong.

HF first started in Hong Kong. In 1987, it launched the earliest Chinese language edition of *Elle* before launching *Car and Driver,* and *Beauty.* In Taiwan, Hachette Filipacchi Taiwan, HF's wholly owned subsidiary, launched *Elle* (Taiwan) and *Orient Beauty.* In addition, HF Taiwan worked with Taiwanese partners to publish *Car and Driver* and *Marie Claire.* It has also compiled and published company magazines for famous brands such as BMW, Lancome, SK-II, Roaming, and Fidelity Securities.

HF expanded into the Chinese mainland in the mid-1990s. Presently, it publishes the Chinese language edition of *Elle* and *Car and Driver* through a licensing agreement with the Shanghai Translation Publishing House. It also publishes *Woman's Day,*

Bo, a sports magazine; and *Marie Claire*, through licensing with the China Sports Publishing Group. It was reported that HF also took a stake in *Air China* magazine.

HF's magazines in China have impressive sales. *Elle* and *Car and Driver* sell 200,000 copies and 120,000 copies per issue, respectively.

HF's Chinese partners in different regions often create alliances to co-market HF's publications. For example, HF's Shanghai partner, the Shanghai Translation Publishing House and HF's Beijing partner, the China Sports Publishing Group, launched a joint promotion of *Elle* and *Marie Claire*. Readers who subscribed to both magazines got a 25% discount and a free gift. Promotions like these are rare in the magazine industry.

Today, Hachette Filipacchi Media employs 700 people in Asia and publishes 40 magazines in nine countries, ranging from women's and men's fashion, beauty, lifestyle, automobile, movies, and sports.

Figure 10.3
Hachette Filipacchi's Investments in China

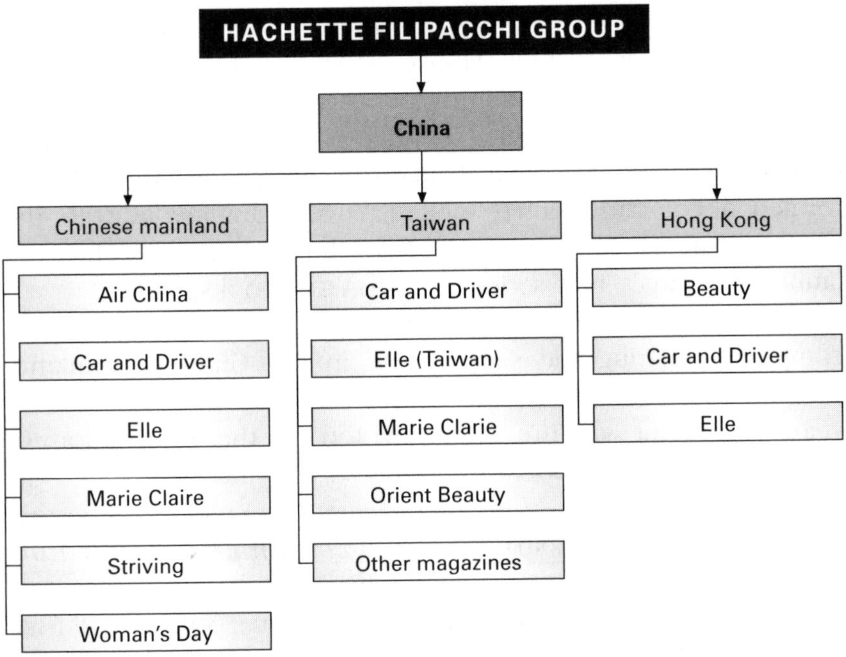

HACHETTE FILIPACCHI GROUP

China

Chinese mainland	Taiwan	Hong Kong
Air China	Car and Driver	Beauty
Car and Driver	Elle (Taiwan)	Car and Driver
Elle	Marie Clarie	Elle
Marie Claire	Orient Beauty	
Striving	Other magazines	
Woman's Day		

HF also cooperates with China's publishing industry in many other ways. The company provides training sessions to Chinese professionals, an initiative much talked about in the industry. It is eager to help Chinese publishers improve their skills in running a successful magazine. HF cosponsored a symposium on managing large-scale magazines with GAPP. It has since become the largest international magazine publishing event in the Chinese mainland. HF's chairman, president, CEO, deputy CEO, editor-in-chief, and other senior executives were invited to China and they all gave presentations to the editors-in-chief and publishers of 100 Chinese magazines from across the country. HF also arranged for many Chinese magazine publishing delegations to visit France for training and research.

C. Foreign Investment in Book Publishing, Electronic Publishing and Online Book Selling

At present, foreign cooperation with the Chinese mainland's book publishing industry is mostly confined to copyright trade and editorial initiatives. Presently, there are only two publishing joint ventures: The Commercial Press International and the Children's Fun Publishing House. However, foreign publishers are also entering the publishing industry through other avenues. For example, Springer-Velag jointly set up a Springer editorial department with Tsinghua University Press. McGraw-Hill has formed a company called Caijing Yiwen Multimedia with the China Financial and Economic Publishing House and has co-launched China's first series of EMBA textbooks.

The Commercial Press International (CPI) consists of five companies sharing the same name in the Chinese mainland, Taiwan, Hong Kong, Singapore, and Malaysia. Over the past 10 years, the joint venture was devoted to the publication of language, reference books, and books on the humanities. Its publications such as *Chinese and English Xinhua Dictionary* (with 360,000 copies sold), *Modern American English*, and *Tang Poetry on CD* are all popular. It now employs 30 people and published 80 new titles per year with annual sales of RMB20 million (US$2.41 million).

Children's Fun Publishing Co. Ltd. is another joint venture that is much more active than CPI. Children's Fun is the first joint venture in children's book publishing. Founded in October 1992 with the approval of GAPP, the original investors were UDI (U.S.), Egmont, and the People's Post and Telecom-munications Publishing House (PPTPH). Its main product is a simplified Chinese monthly edition of *Mickey Mouse Magazine*, the Chinese license of which UDI and Egmont obtained from Disney. On June 1, 1993, the Chinese edition of *Mickey Mouse Magazine* was officially launched.

Children's Fun is registered with US$500,000 in capital, with the Chinese side controlling ownership. Today, it employs 100 people. Its headquarters is in Beijing and it has an office in Shanghai along with sales representatives in 25 Chinese cities.

Children's Fun is considered a successful venture with sales of *Mickey Mouse Magazine* being very strong. *Mickey Mouse* has converted from a monthly to a biweekly and each issue sells 350,000 copies, for a total of 700,000 copies monthly. Along with the magazine, Children's Fun began to publish children's books and very soon became a leader in children's book publishing. Now, both its magazine and book publishing business are running smoothly. In 2002, Children's Fun published 424 new titles and had annual sales of RMB84 million (US$10.12 million) and the company has accumulated assets of RMB63 million (US$7.59 million). Children's Fun is set to become one of the top five children's book publishers by 2005.

Children's Fun publications consist of licensed and local work. Licensed publications include *Mickey Mouse Magazine*, those based on other Disney characters, English learning, picture books for toddlers, and children's world classics. Though a joint venture, Children's Fun has done remarkably well in publishing local cartoons. Local publications accounted for 15% of its total title output in 2002. *Lotus Lantern, Monkey King, Snow Child, Little Monk, I am Crazy with Songs, White Dove Island* and *3,000 Whys of Blue Cat* have made quite an impact (See Figure 10.4.) In 2003, sales of local cartoon books reached RMB20 million (US$2.41 million).

Figure 10.4

Top 10 Bestsellers of Children's Fun Publishing Co., Ltd.

Rank	Title	Retail Price (RMB)	Unit Sales ('000s)
1	3,000 Whys of Blue Cat (1–10)	58.00	2,650
2	Disney Classics (1–40)	664.00	2,100
3	I Am Crazy with Songs (1–26)	104.00	1,560
4	Natu legend (1–5)	49.00	1,300
5	Tiger Team (1–12)	108.00	1,294
6	Teletubbies (1–14)	95.20	1,232
7	My First WTP (1–6)	48.00	320
8	Lion King	30.00	300
9	Lotus Lantern	14.80	180
10	Witch Pocket Book (1–5)	60.00	170

Source: *Children's Fun Publishing Co., Ltd.*

Children's Fun sponsors and participates in many goodwill events that have had good results. For example, it cosponsored the "Creativity Cup" summer camp with the Central Children's Working Committee of China Communist Youth League and the China Children's Newspaper. It also hosted a "National Community Special Team Work" event, the "Election of Mickey Mouse Magazine Cup Best 10 Guardian Angels" in Harbin, the "Mickey Mouse Magazine Cup Good Youngster" event in Shenxiang, the election of "Mickey Mouse Magazine Cup Best 10 Youngsters" in Xi'an, and the election of "Children's Fun Cup Best Ten Young Pioneers" in Chengdu.

Recently Children's Fun launched two new magazines: *Winnie the Pooh*, a Chinese/English publication in collaboration with Movie Comics; and *Hercules*, a new Disney cartoon magazine. Both magazines have had good sales. It is reported that Children's Fun is planning to expand its operations into advertising, rights licensing, book wholesaling, retail sales, and mail order.

Sino-foreign cooperation is also present in electronic publishing and online bookselling. McGraw-Hill, China McGraw-Hill, and China Financial and Economic Publishing House (CFEPH) have jointly formed the Beijing Caijing Yiwen Electronics Co., Ltd. The new company combines the publishing and distribution strength of CFEPH and the content resources of McGraw-Hill to develop business books in electronic format. BTB Wireless (U.S.) and China Educational Electronics Company are collaborating to develop a mobile learning and reading platform.

Among online booksellers, some are joint ventures such as Dangdang.com while others are solely owned by foreign companies such as Bol.com.cn. Dangdang.com is China's largest online bookstore and is a joint venture of IDG (U.S.), Luxembourg Cambridge Group, Softbank (Japan), and Science and Culture Co. (China). The Bertelsmann Book Club's website (www.bol.com.cn) not only provides book order services to Chinese customers but is also linked to the Chinese home page of the German Bertelsmann AG (www.bertelsmann.com), making Bertelsmann the first foreign publishing company that has a Chinese home page of its parent company.

D. Foreign Investment in Distribution and Printing

1. *Foreign Investment in Distribution*

With the liberalization of book distribution, more and more foreign companies are expected to enter the market. The recent promulgation of the *Regulations on Foreign Investment in Distribution Channels of Books, Newspapers and Periodicals* will provide the legal framework for foreigners to seek business opportunities in publications distribution.

At present, foreign companies enter into distribution in two ways. One way is to set up bookstores, book clubs and online bookstores to sell local publications. The other is to engage in export sales of original English language books.

Foreign companies export books to the Chinese mainland mainly through their China offices or through Chinese book import and export companies. As the number of people who have a good command of English rapidly increases and the government advocates English learning, demands for original English books, especially textbooks, is expected to grow. This will provide a market opportunity for imported books.

Presently, foreign publishers that have direct export sales to the Chinese mainland are mainly educational publishers such as Pearson, McGraw-Hill, Thomson Learning, John Wiley, and Random House. Each has set up a representative office in Beijing which employ about 10 people. Their main responsibility is to promote and sell their original English books to Chinese National universities. Most of their books are imported through the China Import & Export (Group) Corporation. Random House is the foreign trade publisher that is most active in exporting to China.

Of course, export sales are only one business model for foreign publishers to enter the market. These companies listed above are also major licensors of rights to Chinese publishers. Some foreign publishers have a grander vision, however. For example, Pearson is developing many publishing-related education programs in addition to its rights and export sales business. It cofounded Pearson CCTV Media with China Central Television. This joint venture will develop English learning programs to be broadcast at the national level along with publishing a TV tie-in book series. It also provides English training courses. These activities will have great impact on the book industry.

Foreign investment in distribution actually started as early as the mid-1990s. In 1995, the Singapore Pan Pacific Public Co., Ltd. formed a joint venture with the Yunnan Province Xinhua Bookstore to build Yunnan Xinhua Book City. The superstore was opened in 1992 and began to earn profits in 2001. Operating profits have continued to grow in recent years.

In February 2002, Sony Music Entertainment Inc. (U.S.) formed the Shanghai Epic Music Entertainment Co., Ltd., (SEME) with Shanghai Xinhui Record Group and Shanghai Jingwen Investment Co., Ltd. SEME became the first cooperative joint venture to obtain national distribution rights for audio-video products. In December 2003, Bertelsmann took a large stake in the 21st Century Book Chain, which has become the first joint-venture national book chain.

2. Bertelsmann in China

Of all the foreign companies to enter the Chinese book distribution market, the German company Bertelsmann AG has made the most impact. In 1995, Bertelsmann jointly formed the Shanghai Bertelsmann Culture Industry Co., Ltd. with the China Science and Technology Book Company. In 1997, the joint venture invested US$15 million to set up the Bertelsmann Book Club and began the Bertelsmann book distribution business in China. By 2000, the book club had recruited 1.5 million members, becoming the largest Sino-foreign joint-venture book club. According to media reports, the club's annual sales are over RMB100 million (US$12.05 million).

Currently, the Bertelsmann Director Group manages the operations in China. Its subsidiaries, the Bertelsmann Book Club and Bertelsmann Online, are playing active roles in the book and audio-video retailing market, both on and offline. Bol.com.cn has also developed into one of the best e-commerce sites for media product distribution. To reinforce localization, Bertelsmann Director Group has forged a strategic alliance with Rongshuxia.com, a rising star among original Chinese literature e-publishing sites.

Figure 10.5
The Bertelsmann Office Building

(Photo provided by Bertelsmann China office)

Bertelsmann is also working on plans to build a modern distribution network in East China with Shanghai as its hub. The Bertelsmann Book Club offers door-to-door delivery in seven cities. This service allows book delivery and payment collection to be accomplished simultaneously. The club also offers express delivery in 70 cities. In 2002, Bertelsmann partnered with the Shanghai Branch of Commercial Bank, which is known for its electronic banking services, to issue the Commercial Bank/ Bertelsmann debit card. This card has all the functions of a bankcard but also allows holders to shop at Bertelsmann's website and at selected shopping centers. Bertelsmann has indeed become a trail blazer in China's online book sales market.

Bertelsmann has set up Bertelsmann Consulting (Shanghai), Bertelsmann Asia Publishing (Hong Kong), Gruner+Jahr-China Light Industry (Beijing) Publishing Consulting Co., Ltd., and BMG China Inc. (Beijing office) to provide media consulting services in the book, magazine, and music industries. (See Figure 10.6.)

In addition, Bertelsmann AG established Bertelsmann China Holding (Shanghai representative office), which is responsible for internal liaisons and communications with the company headquarters. It also handles all external government and media relations, including cultural exchanges between China and Germany, and is charged with the planning and organization of public events.

In December 2003, Bertelsmann purchased a 40% share of the 21st Century Book Chain, becoming its second largest owner. Sources disclosed that the new joint venture will be named "Bertelsmann-21st Century and will be the first joint-venture national book chain in China. It is also the first investment in a Chinese book distributor by a foreign company. A year ago, Sony Music Entertainment Inc. (U.S.) formed the Shanghai Epic Music Entertainment Co., Ltd. (SEME) with Chinese partners, which became the first joint venture in the distribution of audio-video products.

The three-year-old 21st Century Book Chain solely owns eight chain stores, each of which is 40,000 square meters in size. However, sales were not strong. Evidently, Bertelsmann hopes to venture into the book chain business through its investment in 21st Century.

Bertelsmann has worked out a three-in-one model (book club, online sales, and book chain) in the Chinese mainland. Industry experts point out that Bertelsmann has a first-mover advantage compared with other foreign book distributors. To some extent, the alliance with 21st Century is Bertelsmann's rehearsal to get to know the distribution sector of the industry.

Figure 10.6
Bertelsmann's Operations in the Chinese Mainland

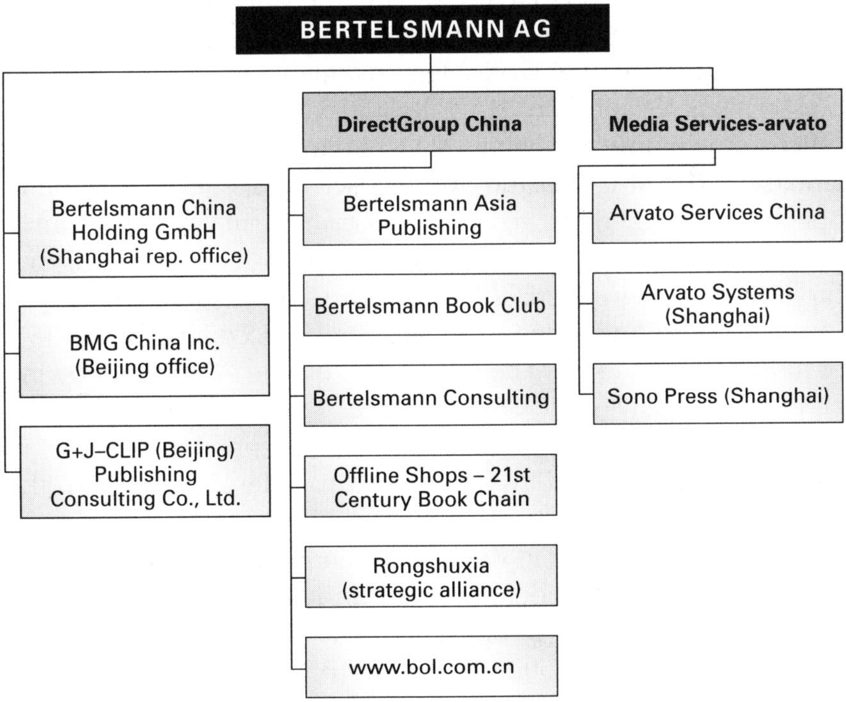

Source: *Bertelsmann China*

3. Foreign Investment in Printing

A great number of foreign investors have ventured into the printing industry. According to 2001 official statistics, there are 1,055 printing joint ventures, 473 wholly foreign-funded printing firms, and 267 printing firms serving foreign clients. Foreign investment comes mainly from Singapore, Japan, the U.S., Hong Kong, Taiwan, and Macau.

In 1994, RR Donnelley (U.S.) cofounded Shenzhen Donnelley Bright Sun Printing Co., with the Shenzhen Petrochemical Co., Ltd. The joint venture became the largest printing center for China's yellow pages. In 2002, RR Donnelley and the Shanghai Press and Publications Administration jointly invested US$30 million to set up the Shanghai-Donnelley Printing Co. This Shanghai joint venture is poised to become China's largest printing facility serving the Chinese market, along with Amercian and European clients.

MAN Roland, the world famous manufacturer of web-fed presses, has established MAN Roland (China) Ltd. with seven offices, including Shanghai MAN Roland (Shanghai) Ltd. In January 2004, MAN Roland (China) set up its seventh printing operation in Chengdu to serve customers in Western China. MAN Roland (China) pointed out that the average spending per capita in printing materials in Western China is only half of the national figure and printing in the region accounts for 10–15% of the national total. The economy of the West is growing rapidly especially under the Chinese government's "Go West" strategy. MAN Roland (China) believes the printing industry in the West has tremendous potential for development in the future.

Foreign investment in the printing industry is concentrated in Guangdong, Shanghai, Jiangsu, and Beijing. Guangdong Province is the largest printing center and is heavily funded by foreign capital. In 2002, about RMB552 million (US$66.51 million) of foreign investment flowed into Guangdong to fund printing facilities. Shenzhen's printing output value accounted for 20% of the national total. In Shanghai, the annual operating revenues of foreign-funded printing firms exceeded RMB4 billion (US$481.93 million). Many foreign printing firms perform well— Leefung-Asco Printers Ltd., a Japanese investment, has annual operating revenues of over RMB100 million (US$12.05 million).

Foreign investment is not limited to publishing. If we look further, we find that foreign companies have ventured into all areas of the Chinese media. Foreign firms similar to Hachette Filipacchi are operating all across the Chinese mainland, Taiwan, and Hong Kong. Typical examples are Time Warner and News Corporation. These two media giants were the first to obtain broadcasting rights in the Chinese mainland. Time Warner owns CETV, China Entertainment Television, *Time*, and *Fortune* (Chinese language edition). In Taiwan, Time Warner publishes *Time Express*, *Time* for students and *Popular Science* through rights licensing. In the Chinese mainland, Time Warner formed an alliance with FM365.com, a popular website operated by the Legend Group, Cthe Chinese mainland's largest IT corporation. Time Warner obtained permission from the Chinese government to broadcast its CETV, 24-hour Mandarin Chinese information and entertainment channel in Guangdong Province. Time Warner is the first foreign cable TV company to gain a foothold in the Chinese mainland's market.

News Corporation owns Star TV, Star Plus, Star Satellite TV, Vijay, and Phoenix TV in Hong Kong. It also owns a cable TV station in Taiwan. In 1999, representative offices were set up in Beijing and Shanghai. It was the first foreign media company that obtained permission to open an office in Shanghai. In December 2001, News Corporation's wholly owned subsidiary, Star Satellite TV, obtained permission to broadcast Mandarin Chinese programs in Guangdong. News Corporation also moved into the Chinese telecom market by buying a stake in the state-owned China Netcom. It hopes to provide channels, programming, and mobile services throughout China.

Market Entry and Survival Strategies

A. Sectors Open to Foreign Investment and Entry Methods

The publishing markets in the four regions of China (the Chinese mainland, Taiwan, Hong Kong, and Macau) vary in their openness to foreign investment.

In the Chinese mainland, the publishing industry is generally divided into three sectors. The first sector focuses on content editing (also called "publishing" in a narrow sense). The second specializes in printing, with the last sector covering distribution (including both wholesale and retail). The Chinese mainland has adopted a policy to gradually open the publishing industry.

According to Chinese law, the publishing industry sectors open to foreign investment are printing and distribution only. The publishing or content editing sector has not yet been totally opened. Only a few joint ventures or cooperation projects with special permission are allowed to operate and these include *New Concept English*, a product of Sino-foreign cooperation, and *Computer World* and *Mickey Mouse*, published by joint-venture publishers. Most of such operations serve as trials for the purpose of accumulating experience for the future promotion of such practices. Nevertheless, in the first sector there is no restriction on copyright cooperation and publishing planning.

The printing sector was the earliest to be opened to foreigners. According to Chinese law, foreign companies can conduct their business, through independent investment, joint ventures, and cooperation programs.

With the Chinese mainland's entry into the WTO, the distribution sector was also opened to foreign companies. In this area, the Chinese government has made the following pledges:

For the distribution of books, newspapers and magazines, the Chinese government gave the assurance that by December 11, 2003, all provincial capital cities, Chongqing, and Ningbo will be opened and foreign investment will be allowed in retail companies. Before December 11, 2004, all restrictions on foreign investment will be removed, with regards to access, location, investment amount, status of shareholding, and the company structure. The only restriction is on foreign shareholding in chain bookstores and until December 11, 2006, foreign investment may not control a chain bookstore with more than 30 outlets.

The Chinese government also assured that foreign businesses are allowed to establish cooperation with Chinese partners and engage in the distribution of the audio-video products and entertainment software, on the condition of recognizing Chinese authority in censoring the content of these products.

The government has adhered strictly to all of these commitments

In order to implement these reforms, the General Administration of Press and Publication (GAPP) and the Ministry of Commerce (once known as the Ministry of Foreign Trade and Economic Cooperation) jointly promulgated *The Measures on Management of the Foreign Invested Business in Book, Newspaper, and Periodical Distribution*, which came into effect on May 1, 2003.

Under these new measures, after May 1, 2003 the Chinese mainland allowed the establishment of foreign retail companies for books, newspapers, and periodicals. After December 1, 2004, the Chinese mainland will allow the establishment of foreign-invested wholesale companies for books, newspapers, and periodicals.

The Measures stipulated detailed regulations for foreign participation in the Chinese mainland's distribution market. For instance, "distribution" refers to both retail and wholesale. "The books, newspapers, and periodicals distributed by the company"

refers to the books, newspapers and periodicals published by authorized publishers and only limited liability and incorporated companies are allowed with the duration of operation limited to 30 years.

Compared to the Chinese mainland, Taiwan, Hong Kong, and Macau are more open and in all three regions, foreign companies are allowed to invest in all areas of publishing, printing, and distribution. Because of geographic and population factors, foreign investment has shown more interest in Taiwan and Hong Kong. Of the two, the latter's market is the more open one where foreigners can do business just as locals do.

B. How to Apply to Set Up a Distribution Business in the Chinese Mainland

1. *Applicant's Qualification*

To establish a distribution business in the Chinese mainland, the applicant should meet the following criteria:

a. The applicant must be independently responsible for civil liability, possesses the capability to do business in the distribution of books, newspapers, and periodicals, and shall have no record of violating any rules and laws in the last three years.

b. The legal representative or the general manager shall have a Publication Distributor Certificate above the intermediate level, and the distributors shall have a Publication Distributor Certificate of or above the elementary level.

c. To set up a retail company, registered capital shall not be less than RMB5 million (US$602,410), and the applicant must have a suitable fixed business location.

d. To set up a wholesale company, the applicant should have a suitable fixed business location, with a size of no less than 50 square meters, or no less than 500 square meters if the place is independently established, and registered capital shall not be less than RMB30 million (US$3.61 million).

2. Application Procedure

There are only a few steps in the process:

a. Submit the application to the provincial administrative department of press and publication (generally known as the Bureau of Press and Publication) in the province where the company is located.

b. After obtaining permission, submit required documents to the provincial administrative department of commerce (generally known as the Committee of Foreign Trade and Economic Cooperation) to apply for a Certificate of Approval for Foreign-Invested Company.

c. After obtaining the approval certificate, submit required documents to the provincial administrative department of press and publications to apply for a Publication Business Permit.

d. Next, submit the Publication Business Permit and the Certificate of Approval for Foreign-Invested Company to the local administrative department of industry and commerce to obtain a business license.

3. Time and Documentation Requirements

Chinese government departments in charge of applications must reply within 90 working days after the application is submitted. Within 90 days after receiving the Publication Business Permit and the Certificate of Approval for Foreign-Invested Company, the applicant must go to the provincial administrative department of press and publication to obtain a Publication Business Permit.

When submitting the application, the applicant must submit all required documents.

When the applicant first submits the application to the provincial administrative department of press and publication, the required documents include:

Figure 11.1

Application Procedure for Setting Up a Foreign-Invested Business in Book, Newspaper, and Periodical Distribution

a. Application for the establishment of foreign-invested distribution company for books, newspapers, and periodicals.

b. Project proposal and feasibility research report that is recognized by all investors, and signed by the legal representatives or general managers of all parties.

The project proposal should include the following contents:

i) Titles and addresses of all investing parties.

ii) Title, legal representative, address, commercial scope, registered capital, and total investment of the proposed foreign distribution business for books, newspapers, and periodicals.

iii) Form and amount of investment of all investors.

   c. Business licenses or registered certificates, financial credentials of all investing parties, and valid identification documents and professional certificates of the legal representatives.

   d. If the Chinese party of a Sino-foreign joint venture or a Sino-foreign cooperation has a stake in state-owned assets, it shall submit an evaluation report on these assets and a document (or record) recognizing the conclusion of the evaluation report.

C. How to Enter the Chinese Mainland Market

A company should engage in preparatory work in order to start a business in the Chinese mainland. This should begin with at least the following preparations:

1. *Knowing the Chinese Mainland's Laws*

First, a knowledge of the related laws and regulations governing the publishing industry sector into which the investor plans to enter is required.

Foreign companies generally shall abide by two kinds of laws and regulations. One governs the trade and industry that the foreign company is engaged in, and the other regulates foreign investment. The most important law in the publishing industry is *The Regulations on Publication Management*, promulgated by the State Council, while other important ones include *The Regulations on Audio-Video Publication Management, The Regulations on Management of the Printing Industry, The Regulations on Management of the Publication Market*, and *The Preparatory Measures on Choosing Important Topics of Books, Periodicals, Audio-Video Products and Electronic Publications*. (Refer to Appendix 1.)

The most important laws and regulations governing foreign investment are *The Measures on Management of Foreign Invested Businesses in Book, Newspaper and Periodical Distribution, The Provisional Regulations for Establishing Foreign-Invested*

Printing Enterprises, and *The Rules on Management of Sino-Foreign Cooperative Distribution Enterprises for Audio-Video Products*. In addition, the investor should know related laws and regulations governing the chosen business form. For instance, if the investor chooses to establish a joint venture, it should review *The Law of the People's Republic of China on Sino-Foreign Joint Ventures*. If the investor chooses to have cooperative operations, it should review *The Law of the People's Republic of China on Sino-Foreign Cooperation*; and if it chooses to establish an independent company, it should know *The Law of the People's Republic of China on Foreign Enterprises*.

Moreover, some other laws and regulations also should be reviewed, such as *The Income Tax Law of the People's Republic of China for Enterprises with Foreign Investment and Foreign Enterprises*, *The Provisional Regulations of the People's Republic of China on Business Tax*, and *The Decision of the Standing Committee of the National People's Congress Regarding the Application of Provisional Regulations on Taxes such as Value-Added Tax, Consumption Tax and Business Tax to Enterprises with Foreign Investment and Foreign Enterprises*.

2. Learning Trade Realities and Business Practices

There are similarities and differences between the publishing industry in the Chinese mainland and the publishing industries of Europe and the U.S., and the investor must know these before entering the market.

For instance, when promoting trade books, many Chinese publishing houses such as the China Writers Publishing House, Jieli Publishing House, CITIC Publishing House, Changjiang Literature and Art Publishing House, Foreign Language Teaching and Research Press have adopted similar promotion methods to those used by European and American publishers. These Chinese publishing houses have strong promotion capabilities similar to their European and American counterparts. The difference is that such publishing houses are not common and except for a few outstanding publishers, the majority are unable to promote their publications effectively.

Some special features and practices exist in the publishing, printing, and distribution sectors in the Chinese mainland. For example, in most cases, authors receive payment in the form of a basic remuneration plus payment based on number of copies printed. The rate of remuneration is generally negotiated by the concerned parties, and if the publisher and author have not signed a publishing contract or signed a contract without specific agreement regarding the rate of remuneration, the remuneration shall be paid in accordance with the rates stated by the *The Regulations on Remuneration for Publishing Wordage Works* promulgated by the National Copyright Administration. Also, the author can be paid royalties which start within several months after publication of the work. Only a few authors of popular works are able to obtain royalties upon signing of the contract.

As for distribution of books and periodicals, most books sold in bookstores are provided by publishers who will receive payment only after the bookstores have sold the books. Magazines are mostly distributed by the Post Office which controls subscriber lists and usually will not provide this information to magazine publishers.

In controlling book quality, the Chinese mainland has its own standards for proofreading, layout design and printing quality, and a publication that is unable to meet the standards will be banned from market distribution. A main standard for book quality is error ratio. The book is banned if the error ratio is more than 1 per 10,000 words.

3. Searching for the Right Agent or Partner

A partner is very important when doing business in the Chinese mainland. Having the right partner is half the battle won. Good partners may be different in many ways, but at the least they must be vigorous in implementing contracts, have the know-how to explore markets and be sincere in achieving a win-win situation. As publishing is a cultural enterprise, it is best to have a partner with high standards of cultural appreciation.

How does one find the right partner? There are several methods:

1) Consult research organizations and consulting services such as the Chinese Institute of Publishing Science, Beijing OpenBook Market Consulting Center, and Beijing Hui Cong Media Research Center, or consult various publishing companies and copyright agents;

2) Consult trade organizations such as The Publishers Association of China or the China Periodicals Association;

3) Obtain information through related printed media such as the *China Book Business Report* or the *China Press and Publishing Journal*;

4) Consult publishers and scholars to get their recommendations;

5) Consult government organizations for information on book and periodical publication and distribution, consult the Books and Publications Administration Department, the Newspaper and Periodicals Publication Administration Department, and the Publication Issuance Administration Department of GAPP. Consult provincial bureaus of press and publication.

When collecting information on partners, the investor should consult at least two organizations or experts in order to get the most accurate and complete information available.

Currently many foreign companies have established branches or offices in the Chinese mainland. Some of them have had impressive progress, while others fail to achieve their original expectations even though they have been operating for a long time. An important cause could be their choice of partners.

D. Problems and Solutions

There are undoubtedly many difficulties and problems in doing business in the Chinese mainland. Typical problems that might occur with the Chinese partner include the fact that there are breaches of contract or little feedbacks and reluctance to inform foreign partners when problems occur.

Many factors lead to these problems, of which three are prominent. First, the Chinese partner lacks professionalism in fulfilling the terms of the contract. Second, the Chinese partner lacks understanding of the cooperation and thinks his responsibility is over after paying royalties for the first print. Third, the Chinese partner lacks strong capacity to explore the market. For instance, after publishing the first print of a book with an imported copyright, the Chinese partner turns to something else without further efforts to expand the sales for the book, even though potential may exist. In fact, because of the lack of strong capacity for market exploration, many Chinese publishers make the same mistake with local books.

How can one avoid these problems and difficulties? How can one handle them if they do occur? The following are some suggestions:

1. *How to Avoid a Breach of Contract?*

When having less than full knowledge about the partner, the investor should first adopt some protective measures to avoid losses in the case of a breach of contract, such as demanding a deposit or stipulating compensation in case of contract breach. Both measures are allowed by Chinese law. Also, if the Chinese partner is authorized to publish a work, the foreign party may require the Chinese partner to print the book at an appointed printing factory in order to prevent the Chinese partner from printing more copies than agreed upon.

When the Chinese partner obtains the copyright from overseas, the foreign party can also request the Chinese publishing house to buy permanent translation rights instead of limited usage rights. Without the former, the Chinese publisher might face difficulties if the original translator does not agree with the continuous publication of the translated book.

2. *How Should One Deal with a Breach of Contract?*

First, be fully aware of what happened and request explanations from the Chinese party involved. If the Chinese party neglects the contract, then the foreign party must directly remind them to carry out what was agreed on as soon as possible. Many Chinese partners pay attention only to important parts of the contract and neglect certain details. For instance, some publishers honor the agreements on the amount of royalties and when the payment shall be made, but neglect when sample books should be sent and thus they pay royalties on time but are late in sending out the samples. Many foreign publishers have encountered this problem. In such cases, the foreign party must make it clear to the Chinese party that this will be considered as breach of contract and force the Chinese party to bear due liability if the samples cannot be delivered on time.

If the Chinese partner intentionally breaks the contract, then the foreign party should explicitly point out that they shall face serious penalties.

In accordance with laws such as *The General Principles of Civil Law of the People's Republic of China* and *The Contract Law of the People's Republic of China*, any party who fails to perform its contractual obligations, or performs them at variance with the agreed conditions in the contract, shall bear civil liabilities, including carrying out the contract and making compensation for damages.

In dealing with a breach of contract or disputes, the involved parties can resort to the court for arbitration and can also solve the problems through mediation.

3. *How to View the Piracy Issue?*

No one can deny that piracy exists in the Chinese mainland and it is very serious in some areas. How did such a situation arise? There are four main reasons:

First, there was no copyright law for more than 40 years between 1949 and 1991. Therefore, people have not developed a strong sense of copyright protection, especially many people in rural areas who do not regard piracy as a crime.

Second, the law on copyright protection is not completely developed. For instance, in 1991 when the copyright law was first enacted, the infringer only bore civil liabilities instead of criminal liabilities, which were added in 1994 and the penalty was imprisonment for less than 7 years. Further improvements are needed on the regulations such as guidelines to calculate compensation for damages and how to determine the liabilities that the producer and distributor of the pirated products should bear. The incompleteness of the related regulations has led to ineffectiveness in punishing those guilty of piracy.

Third, it is difficult to collect evidence of piracy in such a large country. Some copyright owners are reluctant to search for evidence, and without the copyright owner's reports, it is difficult for the law enforcement agencies to find evidence of piracy.

Fourth, new technology makes it easy to produce pirated works and make lucrative gains. This lures many people to take risks.

Piracy is a serious crime violating the interests of the copyright owner and it also undermines the market and harms the interests of law-abiding businesses. For instance, pirated products deprive the copyright owner of their income, and the pirated products take away market share with their lower prices. In recent years, the Chinese government has taken strong measures to fight piracy, such as rewarding informers with huge monetary awards. For example, informing on an illegal CD-ROM production line bring a reward of RMB300,000, or US$36,145. Over the past 10 years, the Chinese government has destroyed more than 180 illegal CD-ROM production lines. Nevertheless, compared with situations in many developed countries, piracy in the Chinese mainland is rampant and the Chinese government must continue to do more to solve this problem.

Some foreigners have little knowledge about the piracy situation and have wrong perceptions regarding the copyright issue. For instance, many people think that the Chinese mainland still has no copyright law. Some think that the Chinese government is unconcerned about copyright protection and does not want to take effective action to protect foreign copyrights. For example, one Japanese comics company heard that their cartoons were been pirated in the Chinese mainland and thought that the Chinese government was oblivious. Therefore, the company didn't authorize a Chinese publisher to publish their cartoons or sue the infringer in court.

Here are some of the author's views on the above-mentioned example. It is the foreign company that decides in which foreign country it wants to authorize publishers to publish its works. However, if pirated products emerge in other countries, the company should not stand idly by.

Copyrights are private property, and generally it is difficult for others to know that piracy has taken place if the copyright owner does not report the matter. Also, the court will have no knowledge if the copyright owner does not make a charge.

In the Chinese mainland, the situation is more serious because there are 180,000 titles published annually and 300,000 titles are circulated in a book market where copyright protection is still very poor. Without the copyright owner's appeal, the judiciary and relevant government organizations will have few chances to be aware of and then deal with piracy.

Therefore, when piracy takes place, the copyright owner should be more pro-active and use all means to stop the act and demand compensation. Although the penalty for piracy, especially the compensation for damages, is not as high as that in many developed countries, it is not very low either. (See examples in Chapter 11-D-4.) Some might say that it is also very difficult to gather evidence in a foreign country. It is true that people will encounter many difficulties when going abroad to gather evidence, especially going to a place with a different language and culture. But the law requires such actions, and it is the same in every country. If the Chinese go to other countries to appeal, they face the same difficulties.

In fact, since China joined the Berne Convention, many foreigners who appealed to Chinese courts against Chinese infringers have won their cases and received compensation, such as when the American company Disney sued Beijing Juvenile and Children's Publishing House for infringing the copyright of its artworks, and Denmark's Lego brought a charge against Tianjin Coke Toy Company. These cases can serve as references.

In addition, by Chinese law the government is also responsible for fighting piracy, thus foreign copyright owners can also bring complaints to related government organizations such as the National Copyright Administration of China and provincial copyright bureaus.

When piracy occurs, it is important to consult lawyers familiar with copyright law or copyright agents instead of casually asking around. It is word know that many Chinese, including some publishers, do not really know and understand the copyright law and the many related regulations.

Many Chinese publishing houses complain a lot when their copyrights are infringed, but not many take serious action against it. One reason is that these publishers have no strong sense on how to use the law to protect their interest and consider collecting evidence too troublesome. Another important reason is that these publishing houses are state-owned enterprises, belonging to the state instead of individuals, thus many people care much less compared to how they would towards private property. Plus, the whole environment for copyright protection in China is not very favorable, and thus they can easily find excuses to ignore the issue. After all, the losses of the publishing house have little impact on their personal lives.

In actual fact, many companies that are serious about collecting evidence and determined to protect their rights have made impressive progress in fighting piracy. Their achievement is not as great as expected, but the overall impact is very encouraging. For instance, both the Shanghai Dictionary Publishing House and a famous writer Yu Qiuyu have won their cases against piracy. The Shanghai Dictionary Publishing House resorted to all legal means and the pirates were stopped.

4. How to Handle Infringement and Piracy?

In order to prevent piracy, the foreign investor should make it contractually clear that the Chinese partner will investigate any act of infringement on behalf of the foreign investor.

Although many difficulties exist in fighting piracy, actions can be successful if hard evidence is collected, but determination is important. How to go about collecting evidence then?

Let's take a look at a recent case: in 2003 the Law Press sued both the infringer and distributor because the *Tutorial Book for the National Judicatory Examination* (three volumes) and its MP3 CDs were pirated. Then, the Law Press began to investigate the case, and even though they did not find out the producer of the pirated books, they discovered the distributor and producer of the pirated CDs.

In order to gather evidence against the distributor of the pirated books, the Law Press bought the books from the bookstore three times. The first time it bought 200 units and received a receipt; then 10 days later it bought one more unit; and one month later, it went to buy the book for the third time accompanied by a notary. With the collected evidence, the Law Press formally brought the case to court and showed the court the receipts, which indicated not only the large number of pirated copies but also that it was a long-term business. The court judged that the bookstore would pay Law Press RMB200,000 (US$24,096) in compensation and the bookstore could not sell the book within three years.

As for the producer of the pirated CDs, Beijing Polystar Digidisc Co., Ltd, Law Press had evidence of only 3,000 copies of pirated CDs, but the minimum production run is 20,000 units and the Law Press requested the court to launch further investigation. The court collected evidence for 30,000 pirated copies and ruled that the company must pay RMB300,000 (US$36,145) to the Law Press, which in total received compensation of RMB500,000 (US$60,241).

Take for example two more cases. First, American company Autodesk Inc. (legal representative Carol A. Bartz) sued Beijing Long Fa Constructional Decoration Co., Ltd. for computer software infringement. When law enforcement agents of the Beijing Municipal Bureau of Copyright carried out a survey of the copyright status of the computer software used by the defendant, it was discovered that the defendant installed and used Autodesk's software without the permission of the copyright owner. Autodesk collected evidence and then brought the case to court, demanding the defendant to stop infringement immediately and pay compensation of almost RMB1.74 million (US$209,639). The court ruled that the company had committed infringement and should pay RMB1.49 million (US$179,518) as compensation, as well as the court and legal fees. (See Appendix 2.)

The second case is the infringement of the famous *3,000 Whys of Blue Cat* ruled by the Hong Kong court. Hunan Sunchime Corporation, a well-known cartoon producer in the Chinese mainland found out that its Blue Cat cartoon was pirated, and started investigations immediately. It collected 16 different editions of pirated Blue Cat and sent the VCDs to relevant department for further identification, which indicated that the pirated producers were Hong Kong Lihong Science and Technology Co., Ltd. and Hong Kong Shenjie Science and Technology Co., Ltd. Then, Sunchime Corporation notified Hong Kong Customs which conducted raids, confiscating 10 production lines with a value of HK$80 million (US$10.26 million). Soon after the Hong Kong Customs brought the case to court, and the court ruled for imprisonment of one year for one person, imprisonment of six months for another person, confiscation of illegal gains worth HK$80 million (US$10.26 million), disbandment of the company, confiscation of properties, repeal of a immigrant card to Canada, and responsibility for the legal fee of HK$1 million (US$128,200).

The above cases show that copyrights can be protected and losses can be compensated if there is determination, and effective methods are employed.

5. How to View Provincialism?

Provincialism certainly exists in the Chinese mainland but with China's entry into the WTO, the influence of provincialism will gradually decline. This is clearly reflected by the development of many foreign businesses, such as Bertelsmann, Pearson, and RR Donnelley in publishing and Carrefour, Wal-Mart, and McDonald's in other industries. These foreign companies have branches in many regions, and they have encountered various difficulties but have rarely complained about provincialism.

The experiences of the above foreign companies show provincialism does not constitute a substantial impediment to development. Many regions are actually very keen to attract foreign investment and many foreign companies understand how to protect their interests under Chinese law.

If the interests of a foreign company are harmed by provincialism, the company can seek protection by resorting to related laws and regulations. Since provincialism is incompatible with the law and derives from parochial views, it will not last long even though it might prevail for a while. Both local Chinese companies and foreign companies should say "No" to provincialism.

6. The Language Factor

Many foreign companies are disgruntled with the lack of information from their Chinese partners. The Chinese publisher rarely informs the foreign party of relevant information and feedback on the progress of their ventures, including difficulties and problems. The Chinese party often seems indifferent to the business situation of the foreign party.

This indeed creates a problem, which will not only impact the ongoing cooperation but also has negative impact on possible future projects.

What has created this state of affairs? Are Chinese publishers indifferent by nature, or a silent group? Perhaps most of them have no interest in cooperation? The answers are all in the negative. Some people in Chinese publishing houses are less concerned about the business, but they do not usually stay long in the company and such people are few. Most Chinese publishers are hardworking people and highly concerned about their work.

There are several reasons for the phenomenon. First, most decision makers in the Chinese publishing houses such as the presidents and editors-in-chief have no foreign language skills. The fact that only a few leaders can speak foreign languages consequently leads to a lack of communication among parties.

Second, many project directors also have little knowledge of foreign languages. Many of them are excellent in project design and business promotion, and they would like to have better communication with their foreign partners, but they are impeded by the language barrier. In other words, the communication problem originates not from their awkwardness in doing business but from the lack of language skills.

Third, some people in charge of copyright exchange have no foreign language skills and rely totally on temporary translators when communicating with foreign partners. Thus, after the contract is signed, the communication comes to an end. The only thing they can remember after signing the contract is to pay royalties on time. Some even forget about this and have to be reminded by the foreign party. In such publishing houses where both the management and staff are unable to communicate with foreign partners, there is no effective communication. Nevertheless, many publishing houses have started to recruit staff with foreign language skills, who are appointed to specialize in copyright exchange and foreign cooperation. But these people often have little knowledge of the publishing business and, except for taking care of the contract negotiation are not deeply involved in the business. They are able to communicate with foreign partners but they are not the decision makers.

Many people known to the author have excellent foreign language skills and would take charge of signing copyright contracts with foreign companies every year, but have little knowledge about the book trade and the current situation of publishing in the Chinese mainland. Therefore, when they provide information to foreign companies, the information is usually fragmented and incomplete.

These are the major reasons for the lack of communication between Chinese and foreign publishers. There are, of course, some other factors such as personality differences. Generally, Chinese people are more reserved, especially those above 45 years of age—the average age of many who head the publishing houses.

The Chinese publishing houses that have the best communication with foreign companies are the ones where both the management and staff have good foreign language skills, especially the heads and even the president. Examples are the Foreign Language Teaching and Research Press, CITIC Publishing House, and the Law Press. These publishers have become the preferred partners of foreign companies seeking opportunities in the Chinese mainland.

In short, foreign companies should consider the language barrier as an important factor when choosing Chinese partners. A good choice will facilitate cooperation. The attitude of the Chinese party should also be taken into consideration. If the Chinese party is very active and sincere, it might be helpful if the foreign party has more contact and communication with them. As more people have developed excellent foreign language skills and are recruited by publishing houses, the language barrier will be overcome.

E. Potential Risks

The Chinese market is large and full of opportunities, but it also has many potential risks. In the publishing industry, foreign companies should be aware of the following issues:

    i.   The Chinese mainland is different from Taiwan and Hong Kong in both legal background and business environment. in the Chinese mainland, the legal system still needs more improvement, many laws and regulations are still in the formative process, and some enacted laws are waiting for amendments. For instance, some regulations are too general without clear details, and some laws seem blurry on important issues, which are unable to provide legal justification for business operations. Neglect over the laws can easily cause trouble and such cases have occurred many times, such as Carrefour of France once facing trouble due to its blind expansion without clear consultation with the Chinese law.

ii. The Chinese market has great potential, but disparity exists between regions. Also, it will take time for the potential to be fully exploited. The possibility of having short-term gains exists but these gains will not always happen. An expectation for rapid recovery of investment and immediate profit might lead to disappointment and even failure of the venture.

iii. It is also crucial to choose the right project. The Chinese market has its own features, and Chinese sales agents also have their preferences. Publishing is a cultural business, and cultural differences exists between the West and the East. Therefore, choosing the right joint project is very important. Take children's books as an example: American cartoon books sell well in China, while cartoon books from Germany and France do not have such good fortunes. There are various factors behind this, but cultural differences are most glaring. Chinese readers already have some understanding of American culture through media such as TV shows and movies, including many American cartoons, thus when the related books are made available, they become popular in a very short time, while the French and the German products take much longer to be accepted. The same factors helped with the lasting popularity of works by Ernest Hemingway, while it is hard for other writers to find Chinese readers so quickly.

iv. Unsuitable Chinese partners also bring risks. A majority of Chinese publishers want to cooperate with foreign companies and they are very enthusiastic in finding a foreign partner. However, some of these publishers lack the capacity to explore markets and do not have a good standing. In order to cooperate with foreign companies, many Chinese publishers will make various promises, but in reality they have no way of fulfilling these promises. Therefore, foreign companies should be careful when choosing a partner. An ideal partner emerges only after a lot of investigations, consultations, and comparisons. Without doing so, a rushed decision might bring many risks. The company that makes sufficient preparations, and is patient and prudent in making choices will have the best chance of being successful.

Appendix 1

Administrative Measures on Foreign Investment in Books, Newspapers, and Periodicals

Article 1

These measures are formulated in accordance with the "Sino-Foreign Joint Ventures Administrative Law of the People's Republic of China," "Sino-Foreign Cooperative Ventures Administrative Law of the People's Republic of China," "Foreign-owned Ventures Administrative Law of the People's Republic of China," and "Administrative Regulations of Publishing," to promote foreign exchange and cooperation, and to facilitate the administration of foreign-invested firms in book, newspaper, magazine distribution.

Article 2

These measures apply to foreign-invested firms in book, newspaper and magazine distribution that are established within the borders of the People's Republic of China.

The terms of "books," "newspapers", "magazines" in these measures refers to books, newspapers and magazines published by those with appropriate permits from the State Council administrative bureau in charge of publishing.

The term of "distribution" in these measures refers to wholesale and retail of books, newspapers and magazines.

The term of "foreign-invested firms" in book, newspaper and magazine distribution in these measures refers to joint or cooperative ventures in book, newspaper and magazine distribution established in China by foreign firms, other foreign economic entities or individuals (hereinafter referred to as foreign investors) and Chinese firms, other Chinese economic entities and individuals (hereinafter referred to as Chinese investors) under the principle of equality and mutual benefit, or wholly foreign-invested ventures in book, newspaper and magazine distribution, with the approval from appropriate departments of the Chinese government.

Foreign investors' participation in stock purchases or acquisition of a domestic-invested firm in book, newspaper, and magazine distribution is one form of establishing the foreign-invested firm in book, newspaper and magazine distribution. In cases of foreign investors' participation in stocks, or acquisition, of domestic-invested firms in book, newspaper, and magazine distribution, these firms should complete the necessary procedure of being re-categorized as foreign-invested firms according to these measures.

Article 3
The form of foreign-invested firms in book, newspaper, and magazine distribution is as a company of limited liability or corporation.

Article 4
Foreign-invested firms in book, newspaper and magazine distribution should abide by Chinese laws and regulations.

Normal commercial activities and legal rights of investment partners of foreign-invested firms in book, newspaper and magazine distribution are protected by Chinese laws.

Article 5
The selection of a commercial location of the foreign-invested firms in book, newspaper, and magazine distribution should be in accordance with municipal planning schemes.

Article 6
At the State Council, the administrative department in charge of news and publishing, and the administrative department in charge of foreign trade and economic cooperation (hereinafter referred to as State Council Administrative Department of Foreign Trade and Economic Cooperation) is responsible for the approval and supervision of foreign-invested firms in book, newspaper and magazine distribution.

Provincial and regional administrative departments in charge of news and publishing, and in charge of foreign trade and economic cooperation, according to their respective responsibilities, are responsible for supervision and administration of foreign-invested firms in book, newspaper and magazine distribution within their administrative region.

Article 7
Requirements for establishing a wholesale foreign-invested firm in book, newspaper, and magazine distribution include:

A. Both the Chinese and foreign investors are capable of assuming civil responsibilities, possess necessary experience in book, newspaper and magazine distribution, and have no record of violating laws and regulations in the last three years;

B. The legal representative or general manager should possess at least an intermediate professional designation in publishing. Distribution personnel should possess primary professional designations in publishing;

C. Fixed commercial sites related to wholesale should be of at least 50 square meters in area. Independent commercial cites should be of at least 500 square meters;

D. Registration capital should be at least RMB30 million;

E. The duration of commercial activities should not exceed 30 years.

Article 8

Requirements for establishing a retail foreign-invested firm in book, newspaper and magazine distribution include:

A. Both domestic and foreign investors are capable of assuming civil responsibilities, possess necessary experience in book, newspaper, and magazine distribution, and have no record of violating laws and regulations in the last three years;

B. The legal representative or general manager should possess at least intermediate professional designation in publishing. Distribution personnel should possess primary professional designations in publishing;

C. Fixed commercial cites should be corresponding to necessary commercial activities;

D. Registration capital should be at least RMB5 million;

E. The duration of commercial activities should not exceed 30 years.

Article 9

In cases where the Chinese investors participate in the venture in the form of state-owned properties (including serving as collateral or as cooperation condition), the state-owned properties should be evaluated according to appropriate regulations and the evaluation results shall be accompanied with appropriate certification (or filing) procedures.

Article 10

To establish a foreign-invested firm in book, newspaper and magazine distribution, an application and the following documents should be submitted to the administrative departments in charge of news and publishing of provinces, autonomous regions, or municipalities under direct jurisdiction, where the firm is to be located:

A. An application form for establishing the foreign-invested firm in book, newspaper and magazine distribution.

B. Project recommendation and feasibility study report compiled or recognized by all investing partners and signed by respective legal representatives or general managers of investing partners.

  The project recommendation should include the following items:

  1. Names and addresses of investing partners;
  2. Name, legal representative, address, commercial scope, registered capital, and total investment amount of the planned foreign-invested firm in book, newspaper and magazine distribution;
  3. Investment form and investment amount of the respective partners.

C. Commercial licenses or registration certificates, testimonials of credit and legal representatives, and certificates of professional designations of all investing partners.

D. In cases where the Chinese investors participate in Sino-foreign joint or cooperative ventures in the form of state-owned properties, the Chinese investors have to provide evaluation results and certification (or filing) documents of the concerned state-owned properties.

The administrative departments in charge of news and publishing of provinces, autonomous regions and municipalities under direct jurisdiction shall produce examination results and report to the State Council administrative department in charge of news and publishing for further examination and approval within 15 work days after receiving the application documents.

Article 11

When the administrative departments in charge of news and publishing of provinces, autonomous regions and municipalities under direct jurisdiction submit to the State Council administrative department in charge of news and publishing the application of foreign-invested firms in book, newspaper and magazine distribution, the following documents should be included:

A. Application documents as specified in Article 10 of these measures;
B. Examination results of the administrative departments in charge of news and publishing of provinces, autonomous regions and municipalities under direct jurisdiction;
C. Other documents as specified by laws and regulations.

The State Council administrative department in charge of news and publishing shall reach a decision of approval or rejection within 30 days after receiving the application and examination results and inform the applicants in writing through the administrative departments in charge of news and publishing of provinces, autonomous regions and municipalities under direct jurisdiction. A rejection shall be accompanied with justifications.

Article 12
After receiving the documents of approval from the State Council administrative department in charge of news and publishing, the applicants can apply to the administrative departments of foreign trade and economic cooperation of the provinces, autonomous regions, or municipalities under direct jurisdiction, with the following documents:

A. Application documents and approval decision of the State Council administrative department in charge of news and publishing;
B. Agreements and charter of the foreign-invested firm in book, newspaper and magazine distribution signed by legal representatives or entrusted representatives of all investing partners;
C. List and testimonial documents of members of the board of directors of the planned foreign-invested firm in book, newspaper and magazine distribution;
D. Notice of the pre-approved company name from the administrative departments of industry and commerce;
E. Other documents specified by laws and regulations.

The administrative departments of foreign trade and economic cooperation of provinces, autonomous regions, and municipalities under direct jurisdiction shall produce examination results and report to State Council administrative department of foreign trade and economics cooperation for further examination and approval within 15 work days after receiving the application and related documents.

Article 13
When administrative departments of foreign trade and economic cooperation of provinces, autonomous regions, and municipalities under direct jurisdiction submit to the State Council Administrative Department of Foreign Trade and Economic Cooperation the application of a foreign-invested firm in book, newspaper and magazine distribution, the following documents should be included:

A. Application documents specified in Article 12 of these measures;
B. Examination results of administrative departments of foreign trade and

economic cooperation of provinces, autonomous regions and municipalities under direct jurisdiction;

C.   Other documents specified by laws and regulations.

The State Council administrative department of foreign trade and economic cooperation shall reach a decision, in writing, of approval or rejection within 30 days after receiving the specified documents. With the decision of approval, the "approval certificate of foreign-invested ventures" shall be issued.

Article 14

Within 90 days after receiving the approval, the applicants of a foreign-invested firm in book, newspaper, and magazine distribution shall receive the "commercial permit of publishing" at the administrative departments in charge of news and publishing of provinces, autonomous regions, and municipalities under direct jurisdictions by presenting the approval documents and the "approval certificate of foreign-invested ventures."

Article 15

In cases where an approved foreign-invested firm in book, newspaper and magazine distribution needs to modify investors, registration capital, investment amount, commercial scope, and commercial duration, the modification and registration shall proceed according to Article 10, Article 11, Article 12, Article 13, and Article 14 of these measures;

Other modifications of the foreign-invested firm in book, newspaper, and magazine distributions shall proceed according to the regulations of foreign-invested ventures and report to the State Council Administrative Department of Foreign Trade and Economic Cooperation for approval or filing. Modification of company name, address, legal representative, key executives, and termination of ventures at the end of commercial duration of the firm in book, newspaper, and magazine distribution shall be reported for filing, within 30 days, to local administrative department in charge of news and publishing of provinces, autonomous regions, or municipalities under direct jurisdiction for filing.

Article 16

When an extension of commercial duration is needed for a foreign-invested firm in book, newspaper, and magazine distribution, an application for such extension should be submitted to the State Council Administrative Department of Foreign Trade and Economic Cooperation 180 days before the expiration of commercial duration. A decision shall be reached, in writing, of approval or rejection within 30 days after receiving the application. A decision of approval should be reported, for filing, to the administrative departments in charge of news and publishing of provinces, autonomous regions or municipalities under direct jurisdiction within 30 days.

Article 17
These measures also apply to the establishment of foreign-invested firms in book, newspaper, and magazine distribution in other provinces, autonomous regions, or municipalities under direct jurisdiction by investors from Hong Kong Special Administrative Region, Macau Special Administrative Region, and Taiwan.

Article 18
The application for establishing foreign-invested firms in book, newspaper and magazine distribution that also engage in online sales, chain shops and book clubs should proceed for approval according to the specifications in Article 7 to Article 14.

Article 19
These measures shall be in effect from May 1, 2003.

Regulations in these measures related to establishing wholesale foreign-invested firms in book, newspaper, and magazine distribution shall be in effect from December 1, 2004.

Appendix 2

Verdict on the Autodesk Case

The People's Republic of China
Beijing Second Intermediate People's Court
Civil Lawsuit Verdict
(2003) Er Zhong Min Zhu Zi #6227

Plaintiff:	Autodesk Incorporated
Address:	Enterprise Trust Center, 1209 Orange Street, Washington, New Castle County, Delaware, United States of America
Legal representative:	Carol A. Bartz, Chairman and Chief Executive Officer
Attorney:	Yinglei Jiang, lawyer, Beijing Jia Wei Law Firm.
Attorney:	Jiasheng Liu, lawyer, Beijing Jia Wei Law Firm.
Defendant:	Beijing Long Fa Constructional Decoration Co., Ltd.
Address:	Room 103, #64, 3rd Tiao (Street), Bei Xin Qiao, Dong Cheng District, Beijing, People's Republic of China
Legal Representative:	Xian Wang, Chairman
Attorney:	Shurong Tang, lawyer, Beijing Zhong Cheng Law Firm.

The civil case of computer software intellectual property rights infringement against Beijing Long Fa Construction Decoration Co., Ltd. (hereinafter referred to as Long Fa Co., Ltd.), filed by Autodesk Incorporated (hereinafter referred to as Autodesk Inc.), was accepted by this court on July 1, 2003. A collegiate bench was formed and the court proceeded with the trial sessions as of August 31, 2003. Attorneys of the plaintiff Autodesk Inc., Yinglei Jiang, Jiasheng Liu, and the attorney of the defendant Long Fan Inc., Shurong Tang, attended and participated in the sessions. The trial sessions of this case are now concluded.

The allegation of the plaintiff Autodesk Inc. claims that the plaintiff is the intellectual property rights owner of computer software applications 3ds Max 3.0, 3ds Max 4.0, 3ds Max 5.0, AutoCAD 14.0, and AutoCAD2000. 3ds Max series are solution software applications for 3D modeling, animation, and visual effects. AutoCAD 14.0 and AutoCAD 2000 are tools for 2D drawing and 3D designs. The defendant is a firm specializing in residential and public architecture decoration design and construction. On April 23, 2002 and October 11, 2003, enforcement personnel from Beijing Bureau of Copyrights inspected the computer software copyright situation at the defendant's 9 Beijing commercial sites and discovered that the defendant installed, without permission, 2 sets of 3ds Max 3.0, 10 sets of 3ds Max 4.0, 2 sets of 3dx Max 5.0, 31 sets of AutoCAD 14.0, and 16 sets of AutoCAD 2000. On June 17, 2003, the plaintiff requested pre-trial evidence protection to Beijing Second People's Court over the defendant's other four commercial sites and subsequently discovered that the defendant installed, without permission, 7 sets of 3ds Max 4.0, 6 sets of 3ds Max 5.0, 9 sets of AutoCAD 4.0 and 11 sets of AutoCAD 2000. Therefore, the plaintiff seeks this court's decision, according to the laws, to order the defendant: (1) immediately stop all acts of rights infringement; (2) issue public apologies on "Beijing Evening News" and "Beijing Youth Daily" over non-advertising newspaper spaces excluding middle folding columns; (3) compensate the plaintiff commercial losses of RMB1,737,700; (4) compensate the plaintiff litigation expenses RMB53,350; (5) assume all litigation expenses of this case.

The arguments from the defendant Long Fa Co., Ltd. claim that the defendant's computers were already installed with replacements of case-related software applications. Certain individual staff did privately install case-related software applications. The compensation demand from the plaintiff is excessive and is without reasonable base. Therefore, the defendant requests the appropriate decision of the court according to the law.

To support its claim, the plaintiff submitted to this court the following evidence and materials: (1) testimonial, notari deed and authentication certificate of 3ds Max 3.0; (2) testimonial, notarial deed and authentication certificate of 3ds Max 4.0; (3) testimonial, notarial deed and authentication certificate of 3ds Max 5.0; (4) testimonial, notarial deed and authentication certificate of AutoCAD 14.0; (5) testimonial, notarial deed and authentication certificate of AutoCAD 2000; (6) investigation record of the defendant's commercial site at Ya Yun Cun; (7) investigation record of the defendant's commercial site at Tian Tong Yuan; (8) investigation record of the defendant's commercial site at Cheng Wai Cheng; (9) investigation record of the defendant's commercial site at Wan Lia Deng Huo; (10) notarial deed, "2002" Jing Guo Zheng Min Zi #8207; (11) notarial deed, "2002" Jing Guo Zheng Min Zi #8208; (12) notarial deed, "2002" Jing Guo Zheng Min Zi #8209; (13) notarial deed, "2002" Jing Guo Zheng Min Zi #8210; (14) notarial deed, ("2002" Jing Guo Zheng Min Zi #8211; (15) notarial deed, ("2002" Jing Guo Zheng Min Zi #8212; "16" notarial deed, (2002Jing Hai Min Zheng Zi #2358; (17) notarial deed, "2002" Jing Hai Min Zheng Zi #2359; (18) notarial deed, "2002" Jing Hai Min Zheng Zi #2360; (19) cite record of the defendant's commercial site at Ju Ren Zhi Jia; (20) site record of the defendant's commercial site at Huan San Huan; (21) site record of the defendant's commercial site at Dong Fang Jia Yuan, Shop of Specialty Construction materials; (22) site record of the defendant's commercial site at Dong Fang Jia Yuan, #B1, 3rd floor; (23) site record of the defendant's commercial site at Yi He Specialty Shop; (24) site record of the defendant's commercial site at Bi Xi Furniture Mall; (25) site record of the defendant's commercial site at Rui Sai Tower; (26) site record of the defendant's commercial site at Min Guang Home Supply Mall; (27) site record of the defendant's commercial site at Jin Sheng Hua An Commercial Tower; (28) site record of the defendant's commercial site at Da Zhong Si; (29) site record of the defendant's commercial site at Ju Ran Zhi Jia; (30) site record of the defendant's commercial site at Huan San Huan; (31) site record of the defendant's commercial site at Dong Fang Jia Yuan, Shop of Specialty Construction Materials; (32) site record of the defendant's commercial site at Dong Fang jia Yuan, #B1, 3rd floor; (33) site record of the defendant's commercial site Yi He Specialty Shop; (34) site record of the defendant's commercial site at Bi Xi Furniture Mall; (35) site record of the defendant's commercial site Rui Sai Tower; (36) site record of the defendant's commercial site Min Guang Home Supply Mall; (37) site record of the defendant's commercial site Jin Sheng Hua An Commercial Tower; (38) site record of the defendant's commercial site at Da Zhong Si; (39) Two CD-ROMs with AutoCAD 2000 and 3ds Max 4.0 downloaded by Beijing Guo Xin Notary Office; (40) 53 photo pictures made Beijing Haidian Second Notary Office; (41) electrical evidence from Beijing Second Intermediate Court under pretrial evidence protection; (42) statistical report by the Beijing Municipal Bureau of Copyright on the defendant's usage of software;

(43) administrative penalty decision regarding intellectual property rights, Jing Quan Penalty "2003" #3; (44) related information on the defendant's commercial cites; (45) list of site inspection reports and records of the Beijing Municipal Bureau of Copyright; (46) specialized receipt of the purchase of 3ds Max 3.0; (47) specialized receipt of the purchase of AutoCAD 14.0; (48) specialized receipt of the purchase of 3dx Max 4.0; (49) specialized receipt of the purchase of 3ds Max 5.0; (50) specialized receipt of the purchase of AutoCAD 2000; (51) specialized receipt of the purchase of AutoCAD 2000; (52) specialized receipt of the purchase of 3ds Max 3.0; (53) article of regarding how firms should react to Microsoft's market strategy ; (54) software price list of the plaintiff; (55) receipt of translation fees; (56) receipt of commercial query and consulting fees; (57) receipt of lawyer service fees; (58) testimonial of ownership between Autodesk Far East Incorporated and the plaintiff; (59) documentation, Jing Quan Lian [2001] #16; (60) documentation, 99 Jing Kan She Guan Zi #85; (61) note from Beijing Rong Chuan Da Software Technology Incorporated (hereinafter referred to as Rong Chuan Da Inc.); (62) testimonial from Beijing Nayier Technology Incorporated (hereinafter referred to as Nayier Inc.).

The plaintiff attempts, using evidence 1–5, to demonstrate that the plaintiff is the intellectual property rights owner of case-related software applications; using evidence 6–44, to demonstrate that the defendant installed and commercially used, without permission, the types and amount of the case-related software applications; using evidence 19, 29 and 45, to demonstrate that the defendant knowingly and intentionally continued rights infringement, after multiple enforcement inspections by the Beijing Municipal Bureau of Copyright; using evidence 46-54, to demonstrate the market prices of the case-related software applications and the actual commercial losses of the plaintiff; using evidence 55–58, to demonstrate the appropriate legal expenses as a result of the lawsuit; using evidence 59, to demonstrate the market prices of the case-related software applications and that the special promotional prices only apply to specific customers during specific time period; using evidence 60, to demonstrate the prices of the case-related software applications; using evidence 61, to demonstrate the reason of special promotional prices and that the special promotional prices only apply to specific customers during specific time period; using evidence 62, to demonstrate the prices and effective time period of the case-related software applications.

The defendant has no objection to the authenticity and objective of the plaintiff's evidence 1–41 and evidence 43; points out that evidence 42 has 10 units instead of 9 and includes the defendant but has no objection to the types and amount of the case-related software applications; could not confirm the authenticity of evidence 44 but recognizes the ownership of the case-related 14 commercial cites; has no objection to the authenticity of evidence 45 but considers it not case-related; has no objection to the authenticity of evidence 46–53 but does not agree with the objective of the evidences in the sense that these evidences could not fully demonstrate the market prices of case-related software applications; has objection to the authenticity of evidence 54 in the sense that the photocopies are not a true copy of the original document; has no objection to the authenticity of evidence 55–58 but does not agree with the objective of the evidences in the sense that these evidences are not case-related; has no objection to the authenticity of evidence 59 but does not agree with the objective of the evidence in the sense that the special promotional prices are still ongoing and should apply to the defendant; has objection to the authenticity of evidence 60 since the plaintiff did not provide the original document of evidence; has objection to the authenticity of evidence 61 in the sense that the plaintiff has commercial relations with Rong Chuan Da Inc; has no objection to the authenticity of evidence 62 but does no agree with the objective of the evidence in the sense that the evidence could not demonstrate the market prices.

To support its claims, the defendant submits to this court the following evidences and materials: (1) "CAD Software Copyright Enforcement" cooperation agreement; (2) specialized receipt; (3) price list related to the project of CAD software copyright enforcement; (4) price list of software applications; (5) price list of software applications.

The defendant attempts, using evidence 1, to demonstrate that the defendant is striving to promote the copyright enforcement and installed other replacements of case-related software applications; using evidence 2, to demonstrate that the defendant did purchase authentic software applications from the plaintiff and therefore, is aware of the issue of copyrights; using evidence 3, to demonstrate that the client price of AutoCAD 14.0 is RMB4,950; using evidence 4, to demonstrate that the special promotional price of AutoCAD 2000 is RMB15,500; using evidence 5, to demonstrate that the special promotional price of 3ds Max 4.0 is RMB21,500.

The plaintiff argues that evidence 1 from the defendant is not case-related and the actual enforcement could not be proved; argues that evidence 2 from the defendant is not case-related and is not a CAD software application; has objection to the authenticity of evidence 3 from the defendant and even it's authentic, the related price only applies to regional copyrighted block purchases; has objection to the objective of evidence 4 in the sense that it is the special promotional price, not market price, of AEC and does not apply to the defendant in the cases of rights infringement; has objection to the objective of evidence 5 in the sense that the special promotional price does not apply to the cases of rights infringement.

This court decides to affirm the part of evidence with no objection from both sides. Even though the plaintiff evidence 42 states 9 units but the actual number is 10 units, this court decides to affirm it. Since evidence 45 is about the case-related software application, this court decides to affirm its authenticity and the objective of evidence. Even though the defendant has objection to the objectives of evidence 46, 47, 49–54, it could not provide any adequate counter evidence. Therefore, this court decides to affirm the above-mentioned evidence of the plaintiff. The plaintiff attempts to use evidence 48 to demonstrate that the price of 3ds Max 4.0 is RMB35,000. But this price is different from the price of RMB18,800 in plaintiff evidence 46 and price of RMB24,000 in plaintiff evidence 49, both affirmed by this court. Therefore, this court decides not to affirm the objective of plaintiff evidence 48. This court decided to affirm the authenticity and relevancy of plaintiff evidence 55. But the amount of lawyer service fees is in excess of appropriate regulations and therefore, this court decides not to affirm this objective. This court decides to affirm the authenticity, relevance and objective of plaintiff evidence 56 and 57. The photocopy of plaintiff evidence 58 is accompanied with a stamp of Nayier Inc. over paper space outside the specialized receipt for value-added tax to indicate that the source of evidence is Nayier Inc. This court decides to affirm the authenticity and objective of this evidence. Even though the defendant has objection to the time period of special promotional price of plaintiff evidence 59, it could not provide adequate counter-evidence. Therefore, this court decides to affirm the authenticity and objective of this plaintiff evidence. Since the plaintiff failed to submit the original document of evidence 60, this court decides not to affirm the authenticity of this evidence. Even though the defendant has objection to the authenticity of plaintiff evidence 61 and to the objective of plaintiff evidence 62, it could not provide adequate counter-evidence. Therefore, this court decides to affirm the authenticity and objective of these plaintiff evidences. The defendant evidence 1 is related to the software of "Zhong Wang Computer Aided Design System ZWCAD V1.0," and defendant evidence 2 is related to software "3DVIZ." Both software applications are not case-related. Therefore, this court decides not to affirm the relevance of the above-mentioned evidence. Defendant evidence 3 is a printout of downloaded web page with no notary proof or other supporting evidence. Therefore, this court decides not to affirm the authenticity of this evidence. The date on defendant evidence 4 is July 29, 2003 and the date on defendant evidence 5 is August 1, 2003. On the other hand, the time period of the defendant's software infringement from evidence affirmed by this court are different from these dates and time period. Therefore, this court decides not to affirm the relevance of the above-mentioned evidence.

The court investigation shows that the plaintiff Autodesk Incorporated is a company from the United States of America.

The United States of America joined the Berne Convention for the Protection of Literary and Artistic Works on March 1, 1989. The People's Republic of China also joined this convention on July 1, 1992.

The plaintiff registered in the United States of America the 5 case-related computer software applications, 3ds Max 3.0, 3ds Max 4.0, 3ds Max 5.0, AutoCAD 14.0, AutoCAD 2000. 3ds Max is solution software application for 3D modeling, animation and visual effects. AutoCAD 14.0 and AutoCAD 2000 are tools for 2D drawing and 3D designs.

The defendant is a design and construction firm specializing in residential and public architecture decoration. On April 23, 2002 and October 11, 2003, enforcement personnel from the Beijing Municipal Bureau of Copyright inspected the computer software copyright situation at the defendant's nine Beijing commercial sites and discovered that the defendant installed, without permission, 2 sets of 3ds Max 3.0, 10 sets of 3ds Max 4.0, 2 sets of 3dx Max 5.0, 31 sets of AutoCAD 14.0, and 16 sets of AutoCAD 2000. On June 17, 2003, the plaintiff requested pretrial evidence protection to this court over the defendant's other four commercial sites and subsequently discovered that the defendant installed, without permission, 7 sets of 3ds Max 4.0, 6 sets of 3ds Max 5.0, 9 sets of AutoCAD 4.0 and 11 sets of AutoCAD 2000. A summery of above-mentioned software applications is as follows: 2 sets of 3ds Max 3.0, 17 sets of 3ds Max 4.0, 8 sets of 3ds Max 5.0, 40 sets of AutoCAD 14.0, and 27 sets of AutoCAD 2000.

The market price of 3ds Max 3.0 is RMB18,800. The market price of 3ds Max 5.0 is RMB24,000. The market price of AutoCAD 14.0 is RMB10,000. The market price of AutoCAD 2000 is RMB18,500.

This court decides that the plaintiff is the intellectual property rights owner of software applications 3ds Max 3.0, 3ds Max 4.0, 3ds Max 5.0, AutoCAD 14.0, and AutoCAD 2000. Both the People's Republic of China and the United States of America are members of the Berne Convention for the Protection of Literary and Artistic Works. The Convention confirms the "principle of national treatment." According to laws of this nation, intellectual property rights of foreign software is protected by laws, based on the agreements signed between, or under the international treaty participated both by, China and the country to which the developer is a citizen or resident. Therefore, for the plaintiff as the owner of the intellectual property rights of the five case-related software applications, its intellectual property rights should be protected by the laws of this country.

The defendant is a design and construction firm specializing in residential and public architecture decoration. The copying and installation of the five case-related software applications in its operations for commercial benefits are commercial use of the software applications. These acts by the defendant constitute the infringement on the intellectual property rights legally owned by the plaintiff, and therefore, the defendant should assume appropriate legal responsibilities. Therefore, this court supports the plaintiff's request that the defendant immediately stop all acts of rights infringement.

Since the defendant continued its rights infringement act even after it was imposed of the administrative penalty by the Beijing Municipal Bureau of Copyright on April 23, 2002, its intention of rights infringement is apparent. Therefore, this court supports the plaintiff's request that the defendant issues public apologies on newspapers. This court will decide, based on the details of rights infringement, that the defendant will issue an apology, for its act of rights infringement, to the plaintiff using one published newspaper of this city.

Regarding the compensation amount of commercial losses, the court decides that the commercial losses to the computer software intellectual property rights owner caused by the unauthorized use, correspond to the market prices of normal sales and uses with appropriate authorization. Therefore, this court will base the compensation amount on the market prices of the five case-related software applications, also taken into consideration other factors including the commercial objective of the defendant's use of the case-related software, the direct intention of the defendant, the manner and consequences of rights infringement. Even though the plaintiff submitted evidence 48 to demonstrate that the market price of 3ds Max 4.0 is RMB35,800, this price is much higher than the prices of 3ds Max series 3.0 and 5.0, which are already affirmed by this court, and is inconsistent with other evidence submitted by the plaintiff. Therefore, this court will not affirm the objective of the plaintiff evidence 48 and will decide the market price of 3ds Max 4.0 using other evidences in this case and on basis of the general rules of software pricing.

Since the defendant is legally responsible for the appropriate expenses encountered by the plaintiff in the process of stopping the rights infringement, this court supports the plaintiff's request that the defendant compensate all the case-related translation fees and investigation fees. Since the lawyer service fee is in excess of that specified by appropriate regulations, this court will decide the amount accordingly.

To summarize, according to the "Copyright Law of the People's Republic of China," Article 47 Item 1, Article 48, and the "Regulations for the Protection of Computer Software," Article 5 Clause 4, Article 24 Clause 1 Item 1, and "Interpretations of Various Application Issues of Administration of Copyright Civil Lawsuit by the Supreme People's Court," this court reaches the following decisions:

A. Beijing Long Fa Constructional Decoration Co., Ltd. shall, from the day when this decision goes into effect, immediately stop all acts of intellectual property rights infringement of computer software applications 3ds Max 3.0, 3ds Max 4.0, 3ds Max 5.0, AutoCAD 14.0, and AutoCAD 2000 of Autodesk Inc.

B. Beijing Long Fa Constructional Decoration Co., Ltd. shall issue a public apology using Beijing Evening News, within 30 days after this decision goes into effect, to clear up any negative influence. (Content of the apology is subject to the approval of this court. In the case that the defendant fails to comply with the decision, this court will publicize the main part of this verdict on one local newspaper at the expense of Beijing Long Fa Constructional Decoration Co., Ltd.)

C. Within 10 days after this verdict goes into effect, Beijing Long Fa Constructional Decoration Co., Ltd. shall compensate Autodesk Incorporated commercial loss of amount of RMB1.49 million, and necessary legal expenses of the amount of RMB32,230;

D. This court dismisses other requests of Autodesk Inc.

The expenses of RMB18,968 from case processing shall be assumed by Beijing Long Fa Constructional Decoration Co., Ltd. (within 7 days after this verdict goes into effect).

In cases of any disagreement with this verdict, Autodesk Incorporated (within 30 days after receiving the verdict in writing) and Beijing Long Fa Constructional Decoration Co., Ltd. (within 15 days after receiving this verdict in writing) can submit their respective appeal, through this court, to Beijing Superior People's Court of the People's Republic of China, with appropriate copies based on number of privy members of the other side.

Presiding judge : Liu Wei
Deputy judge   : Song Guang
Deputy judge   : Liang Lijun
Court clerk   : Feng Gang

(Note: the defendant has appealed to the Beijing Superior People's Court.)

Appendix 3

Top Publishers in the Chinese Mainland, Taiwan, Hong Kong, and Macau

A. Chinese Mainland

21st Century Publishing House
Publication Category: Children's books.
Address　　: 75 Zian Road, Nanchang, Jiangxi 330009
Telephone : 0086-0791-8513749　　Fax: 0086-0791-6535519

Anhui Educational Publishing House
Publication Category: Education.
Address　　: 1 Yuejin Road, Hefei, Anhui 230063
Telephone : 0086-0551-2820011　　Fax: 0086-0551-2820011

Beijing Language & Culture University Press
Publication Category: Cultural education and languages.
Address　　: 15 Xueyuan Road, Haidian District, Beijing 100083
Telephone : 0086-010-82303223　　Fax: 0086-010-82303963
http://www.blcup.com

Beijing Publishing House (Group)
Publication Category: All categories.
Address　　: 6 North Third Ring Road, Beijing 100011
Telephone : 0086-010-62013122　　Fax: 0086-010-62012339
http://www.bph.com.cn

Changjiang Literature & Art Publishing House
Publication Category: Literature and art.
Address　　: 268 Xiongchu Dajie, Wuchang, Wuhan, Hubei 430070
Telephone : 0086-027-87679310　　Fax: 0086-027-87679300
http://cjlap.com

Chemical Industry Press
Publication Category: Chemistry and chemical industry.
Address   : 3 Huixinli, Chaoyang District, Beijing 100029
Telephone : 0086-010-64918054   Fax: 0086-010-64918089
http://www.cip.com.cn

Children's Fun Publishing Co., Ltd.
Publication Category: Children's books.
Address   : Yard No. 7, Ju'er Hutong Jiaodaokou,
           Dongcheng District, Beijing 100009
Telephone : 0086-010-84017788   Fax: 0086-010-84012882
http://www.egmont.com

China Architecture & Building Press
Publication Category: Architecture and horticulture.
Address   : Baiwanzhuang, Beijing 100037
Telephone : 0086-010-68394819   Fax: 0086-010-68319576
http://china-abp.com.cn

China Children Publishing House
Publication Category: Children's books.
Address   : No. 21, Lane 12 Dongsi, Beijing 100708
Telephone : 0086-010-64000585   Fax: 0086-010-64012262
http://ccppg.com.cn

China Communications Press
Publication Category: Communication, computer, and popular science.
Address   : 10 Hepingli Dongjie, Beijing 100013
Telephone : 0086-010-64224941   Fax: 0086-010-64206166

China Financial & Economic Publishing House
Publication Category: Finance, economics, and taxation.
Address   : Xinzhi Plaza, Jia No.28 Fucheng Road,
           Haidian District, Beijing 100036
Telephone : 0086-010-88191057   Fax: 0086-010-88191058
http://www.cfeph.com.cn

China Foreign Economic Relations and Trade Publishing House
Publication Category: Foreign trade and cooperation, social sciences.
Address   : 28 Donghouxiang, Andingmenwai Dajie,
           Beijing 100710
Telephone : 0086-010-64219742   Fax: 0086-010-64219392

China Intercontinental Press
Publication Category: All categories.
Address : 31 North Three Ring Road, Beijing 100088
Telephone : 0086-010-82008174   Fax: 0086-010-82008118
http://www.cicc.org.cn

China Light Industry Press
Publication Category: Light industry and lifestyle.
Address : No. 6 Dong Chang An Street, Beijing 100740
Telephone : 0086-010-65121122   Fax: 0086-010-65121371
http://www.chlip.com.cn

China Machine Press
Publication Category: Mechanical engineering, electronics, architecture,
                      management, and foreign languages.
Address : 22 Baiwanzhuang Road, Beijing 100037
Telephone : 0086-010-68326677   Fax: 0086-010-68320405
http://cmpbook.com

China Publishing Group
Main subsidiary companies: The Commercial Press, Zhong Hua Book
Company, SDX Joint Publishing Company, People's Literature Publishing
House, and China Fine Arts Publishing Group
Address : 54 Northern Lishi Lu, Beijing
Telephone : 0086-010-88376818   Fax: 0086-010-88376819

China Religion & Culture Publishing House
Publication Category: Religious books.
Address : 44 Houhaibeiyan, Xicheng District
          Beijing 100044
Telephone : 0086-010-64095201   Fax: 0086-010-64095202

China Renmin University Press
Publication Category: Higher education and social sciences.
Address : 157 Haidian Road, Beijing 100080
Telephone : 0086-010-62511242   Fax: 0086-010-62514775
http://www.cru-press.com.cn/

China Social Sciences Press
Publication Category: Social sciences.
Address : 158A Gulou Xidajie, Beijing 100720
Telephone : 0086-010-64073834   Fax: 0086-010-64074509
http://csspw.com.cn

China Travel & Tourism Press
Publication Category: Travel books.
Address : No.9 Jiannei Street, Beijing 100005
Telephone : 0086-010-65136283   Fax: 0086-010-5136282
http://www.cttp.net.cn

China Youth Press
Publication Category: Literature and art, and various youth reading
             materials.
Address : 21 Dongsishiertiao,Beijing 100708
Telephone : 0086-010-64033812   Fax: 0086-010-64001500
http://www.cyp.com.cn

Chongqing Publishing House
Publication Category: All categories.
Address : 205 Changjiang Erlu, Chongqang 400016
Telephone : 0086-023-68813727   Fax: 0086-023-68815818
http://www.cqph.com

CITIC Publishing House
Publication Category: Social Sciences.
Address : Ta Yuan Diplomatic Office Building No. 14
             Liangmahe Street, Chaoyang District, Beijing 100600
Telephone : 0086-010-85323366   Fax: 0086-010-85322508
http://www.citicpublish.com.cn

Cultural Relics Publishing House
Publication Category: Cultural relics and archeology.
Address : 29 Wusi Dajie, Dongcheng District, Beijing 100009
Telephone : 0086-010-64048057   Fax: 0086-010-64010698
http://www.publish.citic.com

Elephant Publishing House
Publication Category: Education.
Address : 66 Jingwu, Zhengzhou, Henan 450002
Telephone : 0086-0371-5722399   Fax: 0086-0371-5722399

Foreign Languages Press
Publication Category: Foreign works, politics, economics, medicine, and
             reference books.
Address : 24 Baiwanzhuang Road, Xicheng District,
             Beijing 100037
Telephone : 0086-010-68326642   Fax: 0086-010-68326642
http://www.flp.com.cn

Foreign Language Teaching and Research Press
Publication Category: Foreign languages studies.
Address   : 19 Xisanhuan N. Rd., Beijing 100089
Telephone : 0086-010-88817198   Fax: 0086-010-88817889
http://www.fltrp.com/

Fudan University Press
Publication Category: Higher education, social sciences, science and
                technology.
Address   : 579 Guoquan Road, Shanghai 200433
Telephone : 0086-021-65642840   Fax: 0086-021-65642840
http://www.fudanpress.com

Guangdong Education Publishing House
Publication Category: Education.
Address   : 11 Shuiyin Road, Huanshi E. Rd,
                Guangzhou, Guangdong 510075
Telephone : 0086-020-37607332   Fax: 0086-020-37606315

Guangxi Normal University Press
Publication Category: Higher education, social sciences, and science and
                technology.
Address   : 15 Yucai Road, Guilin, Guangxi 541004
Telephone : 0086-0773-5853688   Fax: 0086-0773-5853799
presstz@public.glptt.gx.cn

Hainan Publishing House
Publication Category: All categories.
Address   : 2 Jianshe Sanheng Road, Jinpan Development Zone,
                Haikou, Hainan 570216
Telephone : 0086-0898-66812763   Fax: 0086-0898-66812763

Hebei Arts Publishing House
Publication Category: Fine arts.
Address   : 8 Xinwenli, Heping W. Rd, Shijiazhuang,
                Hebei 050071
Telephone : 0086-0311-7827580   Fax: 0086-0311-7817582
http://wsbl.hebei.net.cn

Hebei Education Press
Publication Category: Education
Address   : 330 North Youyi Street, Shijiazhuang, Hebei 050061
Telephone : 0086-0311-8641265   Fax: 0086-0311-7755716

Higher Education Press
Publication Category: Higher Education
Address   : 4 Dewai Dajie, Xicheng District, Beijing 100011
Telephone : 0086-010-58581930   Fax: 0086-010-82085552
http://www.hep.edu.cn

Huaxia Publishing House
Publication Category: Social sciences.
Address   : 4 Xiangheyuan Beili, Dongzhimenwai,
              Beijing 100028
Telephone : 0086-010-64679811   Fax: 0086-010-64662584

Hubei People's Press
Publication Category: Social Sciences.
Address   : 33 Xinyucun, Jiefang Dadao, Wuhan,
              Hubei 430022
Telephone : 0086-027-85443840   Fax: 0086-027-85443731

Jiangsu Education Publishing House
Publication Category: Education.
Address   : 31 Majiajie, Nanjing, Jiangsu 210009
Telephone : 0086-025-6639114   Fax: 0086-025-3303457

Jiangsu Juvenile and Children's Publishing House
Publication Category: Children's books.
Address   : 14-15F Phoenix Palace Hotel,
              47 Hunan Rd, Nanjing, Jiangsu 210009
Telephone : 0086-025-3242350   Fax: 0086-025-3242350

Jiangsu People's Publishing House
Publication Category: Social Sciences.
Address   : 165 Zhongyang Road, Nanjing, Jiangsu 210009
Telephone : 0086-025-6634309   Fax: 0086-025-3304276

Jieli Publishing House
Publication Category: Children's books.
Address   : 9 Yuanhunan Road, Nanning, Guangxi 530022
Telephone : 0086-0771-5866644   Fax: 0086-0771-5866644

Jindun Publishing House
Publication Category: Science and popular science.
Address   : 5 Taiping Road, Beijing 100036
Telephone : 0086-010-66886179   Fax: 0086-010-68214032
http://www.jbcbs.com.cn

Law Press
Publication Category: Law and law-related disciplines.
Address   : Lianhuachi Xili, Beijing 100037
Telephone : 0086-010-63939799   Fax: 0086-010-63939622
http://www.lawpress.com.cn

Liaoning Publishing Group
Main subsidiary companies: Liaoning People's Publishing House, Liaoning
Education Press, Liaoning Literature and Art Publishing House, Liaoning
Fine Arts Publishing House, and Liaoning Publishing House.
Address   : 25 Shiyiwei Road, Heping District,
              Shenyang, Liaoning 110003
Telephone : 0086-024-23284000   Fax: 0086-024-23284198
http://www.lnpgc.com.cn/

Lijiang Publishing House
Publication Category: Chinese and foreign literature and art, and travel
              books.
Address   : No.159-1 South Ring Road, Guilin, Guangxi 541002
Telephone : 0086-0773-2802618   Fax: 0086-0773-2802018

Nanjing University Press
Publication Category: Higher education, social sciences, and science and
              technology.
Address   : 22 Hankou Road, Nanjing, Jiangsu 210096
Telephone : 0086-025-3302509   Fax: 0086-025-3303347

Peking University Press
Publication Category: Higher education and social sciences.
Address   : No. 205 Chengfu Road, Haidian, Beijing 100871
Telephone : 0086-010-62752036   Fax: 0086-010-62556201

People's Education Press
Publication Category: Educational books for primary and middle schools.
Address   : 55 Shatan Houjie, Dongcheng District,
              Beijing 100009
Telephone : 0086-010-64035745   Fax: 0086-010-64010370
http://www.pep.com.cn

People's Medical Publishing House
Publishing Category: Various medical books and medicine-related reference books.
Address   : 3 Bldg, 3rd Section Fangqunyuan Fangzhuang, Fengtai District, Beijing 100078
Telephone : 0086-010-67617319   Fax: 0086-010-67645143

People's Posts & Telecommunications Publishing House
Publishing Category: Communication, computer, Pilately, management.
Address   : 14A Xizhaosi Street, Chongwen District, Beijing 100061
Telephone : 0086-010-67129136   Fax: 0086-010-67132825
http://www.pptph.com.cn

Press of University of Science and Technology of China
Publication Category: Science and technology.
Address   : No. 96 Jinzhai Road, Hefei, Anhui 230063
Telephone : 0086-0551-3602909   Fax: 0086-0551-3602909

Publishing House of Electronics Industry
Publication Category: Electronic science and technology.
Address   : P.O. Box 173, Wanshou Road, Beijing 10036
Telephone : 0086-010-68159318   Fax: 0086-010-68159025
http://www.phei.com.cn

Science Press
Publication Category: Science and technology, medicine, and teaching supplements.
Address   : No.16 East Huangchenggen North Street, Beijing 100717
Telephone : 0086-010-64010681   Fax: 0086-010-64019810
http://www.sciencep.com

Shanghai Century Publishing Group
Main subsidiary companies: Shanghai People's Publishing House, Shanghai Education Publishing House, Shanghai Translation Publishing House, Shanghai Classics Publishing House, Juvenile and Children's Publishing House, and Publishing House of the Chinese Dictionary.
Address   : 193 Fujian, Zhonglu, Shanghai 200001
Telephone : 0086-021-53594508   Fax: 0086-021-63914288
http://www.ewen.cc

Shanghai Foreign Language Education Press
Publication Category: Foreign languages studies.
Address   : 558 Dalian Road West, Shanghai 200083
Telephone : 0086-021-65425300   Fax: 0086-021-65422956
http://www.sflep.com

Sichuan People's Publishing House
Publication Category: Social Sciences.
Address   : 3 Yandao St, Chengdu, Sichuan 610012
Telephone : 0086-028-6651814   Fax: 0086-028-6660984

Sichuan University Press
Publication Category: Higher education, social sciences, sciences, and
                technology.
Address   : 29 Wangjiang Road, Chengdu, Sichuan 610064
Telephone : 0086-028-5412526   Fax: 0086-028-5410311
http://www.scupress.com.cn

The Ethnic Publishing House
Publication Category: Social science and natural science books in
                languages of minorities and Han Chinese.
Address   : 14 Hepingli Beijie, Andingmenwai,
                Beijing 100013
Telephone : 0086-010-64212794   Fax: 0086-010-64211126

The Future Publishing House
Publication Category: Children's books.
Address   : 91 Fengqing Road, Xi'an, Shaanxi 710082
Telephone : 0086-029-4280368   Fax: 0086-029-4241368

The Tianjin Science & Technology Translation & Publishing Corp.
Publishing Category: Translations of foreign books on science,
                engineering, and medicine.
Address   : No. 244 Baidi Road, Nankai District
                Tianjin 300074
Telephone : 0086-022-87892076   Fax: 0086-022-87892476

The Writers Publishing House
Publication Category: Contemporary literature.
Address   : 10 Nongzhanguan Nanli, Beijing 100026
Telephone : 0086-010-65004079   Fax: 0086-010-65930761
http://www.zuojiachubanshe.com

Tibetan People's Publishing House
Publishing Category: Books in Tibetan and Chinese.
Address   : 23 Linkuo N. Road, Lhasa, Tibet 850000
Telephone : 0086-0891-6833595   Fax: 0086-0891-6826115
http://www.tibetinfo.com.cn

Tomorrow Publishing House
Publication Category: Children's books.
Address   : 39 Shengli Dajie, Jinan, Shandong 250001
Telephone : 0086-0531-2060055   Fax: 0086-0531-2902094
tomorrow@sd.cei.gov.cn

Tsinghua University Press
Publication Category: Higher education, science and technology.
Address   : 5-7F Xueyan Bldg. A, Tsinghua University,
             Haidian District, Beijing 100084
Telephone : 0086-010-62783132   Fax: 0086-010-62770278
http://www.tsinghua.edu.cn

World Affairs Press
Publication Category: International politics, diplomacy, economics,
             military affairs, and culture.
Address   : 51 Ganmianhutong, Dongcheng, Beijing 100010
Telephone : 0086-010-65232695   Fax: 0086-010-65265961
http://www.wap1934.com

World Publishing Corporation
Publication Category: Science, technology, languages, and reference
             books.
Address   : No.137 Chaonei Dajie, Beijing 100010
Telephone : 0086-010-64038365   Fax: 0086-010-64016320

Xinhua Publishing House
Publication Category: Social Sciences.
Address   : 57 Xuanwumen Xidajie, Beijing 100803
Telephone : 0086-010-63074022   Fax: 0086-010-63074022

Yilin Press
Publication Category: Translations of foreign literary works.
Address   : 47 Hunan Rd, Nanjing, Jiangsu 210009
Telephone : 0086-025-6631317   Fax: 0086-025-3242328

Yunnan People's Publishing House
Publication Category: All categories.
Address   : 10-15F, Yunnan Press & Publishing Building,
            609 Huancheng Xilu, Kunming, Yunnan 650034
Telephone : 0086-0871-4194289   Fax: 0086-0871-4193008

B. Taiwan

Cheng Chung Book Co.
Publication Category: All categories.
Address   : No. 20, Heng Yang Road, Taipei, Taiwan
Telephone : 00886-2-8667-6565   Fax: 00886-2-8667-6794
paul@ccbc.com.tw

China Times Publishing Company
Publication Category: All categories.
Address   : 2F, 240 Hoping W. Road, Section 3,
            Taipei, Taiwan
Telephone : 00886-2-23086222 #8214   Fax: 00886-2-23049302
http://www.readingtimes.com.tw

Chuan Hwa Science & Technology Books Co., Ltd.
Publication Category: Science and technology.
Address   : 2F, No. 20, Lane 76, Lung Chiag Road,
            Taipei, Taiwan
Telephone : 00886-2-2507-1300   Fax: 00886-2-2506-2993
service@msl.chwa.com.tw

Cite Publishing Ltd.
Main subsidiary companies: Rye Field Publishing Co., Owl Publishing
House Co., Grimm Press, Inc., Sharp Point Publishing Co., Business
Weekly Publications, Inc.
Address   : 2F, No. 141, Sec. 2, Minsheng E. Road,
            Jhongshan District, Taipei City 104, Taiwan
Telephone : 00886-2-25000888   Fax: 00886-2-25001938
http://www.cite.com.tw

Classic Communications Co.
Publication Category: Language studies, motivational books, and current
    trends.
Address   : 10F, No.76, Tun Hwa S. Road, Sec.1,
    Taipei, Taiwan
Telephone : 00886-2-27084410   Fax: 00886-2-27547755
http://www.ccw.com.tw

Common Wealth Magazine Co., Ltd.
Publication Category: Finance, economics, business management, aim-
    high inspiring, literature, art, and health.
Address   : 2F, No. 1, Lane 93, Sung Chiang Road,
    Taipei, Taiwan
Telephone : 00886-2-25173688 #905   Fax: 00886-2-25076735
http://www.bookzone.com.tw

Crown Culture Corporation
Publication Category: Literature and art.
Address   : No. 50, Lane 120, Tun Hwa N. Road,
    Taipei, Taiwan
Telephone : 00886-2-27168888
http://www.crown.com.tw

Eurasian Press
Publication Category: Social sciences.
Address   : 6F, No. 50, Sec. 4, Nanjing E. Road,
    Taipei, Taiwan
Telephone : 0800-212-629
http://www.eurasian.com.tw

Hsin-Yi Publications
Publication Category: Children's books and parenting books.
Address   : No. 75, Chung Ching S. Road, Sec. 2,
    Taipei, Taiwan
Telephone : 00886-2-23965303   Fax: 00886-2-23218884
http://www.hsin-yi.org.tw

Kid Castle Educational Institute
Publication Category: English education for children.
Address   : 8F, No. 98, Min-Chung Road, Hsin-Tien,
    Taipei Hsien, Taiwan
Telephone : 00886-2-22185996   Fax: 00886-2-22189984
http://www.kidcastle.com.tw

Linking Publishing Co., Ltd.
Publication Category: Social sciences.
Address   : No. 555, Sec. 4, Chung-Hsiao E. Road,
            Taipei, Taiwan
Telephone : 00886-2-8691-6619   Fax: 00886-2-2641-8660
linkingp@tpts6.seed.net.tw

Locus Publishing Company
Publication Category: Humanities.
Address   : 11F, No. 25, Sec. 4, Nanking E. Road,
            Taipei, Taiwan
Telephone : 00886-2-8712-3898   Fax: 00886-2-8712-3897
http://www.locuspublishing.com

Newton Publishing Co. Ltd.
Publication Category: Children's books.
Address   : No. 9, Lane 44, Sze-Wei Road,
            Taipei, Taiwan
Telephone : 00886-2-27060336   Fax: 00886-2-27079151
http://www.newton.com.tw

San Min Book Co., Ltd.
Publication Category: Social sciences.
Address   : No. 386, Fushing N. Road, Taipei, Taiwan
Telephone : 00886-2-25006600   Fax: 00886-2-25064000
http://www.sanmin.com.tw

Sitak Publication Group
Publication Category: Literature.
Address   : 10F, No. 15, Lane 174, Xin-ming Road,
            Nei-Hu District, Taipei, Taiwan
Telephone : 00886-2-17911197   Fax: 00886-2-27955824
http://www.sitak.com.tw

The Commercial Press Ltd.
Publication Category: Social sciences, and science and technology.
Address   : No. 37, Sec. 1, Chung King S. Road,
            Taipei, Taiwan
Telephone : 00886-2-23115538   Fax: 00886-2-23710274
http://www.cp.com.cn

Unalis Publication Corporation
Publication Category: Computer.
Address   : 5F, No. 339, Tun Hwa S. Road, Sec. 1, Taipei 10654,
            Taiwan
Telephone : 00886-2-27042762   Fax: 00886-2-27029705
http://www.unalis.com.tw

Unitas Publishing Co., Ltd.
Publication Category: Literature.
Address   : 10F, No. 180, Sec. 1, Keelung Road,
            Taipei, Taiwan
Telephone : 00886-2-27566759   Fax: 00886-2-27567914
http://unitas.udngroup.com.tw

Wu-Nan Book Inc.
Publication Category: All categories.
Address   : 4F, No. 339, Sec. 2, Hoping E. Road, 106
            Taipei, Taiwan
Telephone : 00886-2-2705-5066   Fax: 00886-2-2706-6100
http://www.wunan.com.tw

Yuan-Liou Publishing Co., Ltd.
Publishing Category: All categories.
Address   : 7F-5, No. 184, Sec. 3, Ding Chou Road,
            Taipei, Taiwan
Telephone : 00886-2-23926899   Fax: 00886-2-33223707
http://www.ylib.com

C. Hong Kong and Macau

China Alliance Press
Publication Category: Christianity.
Address   : 4/F, Winfield Building, 861 Canton Road,
            Yaumatei, Kowloon, Hong Kong
Telephone : 00852-27820055   Fax: 00852-27820180
http://www.cap.org.hk

Cosmos Books Ltd.
Publication Category: Social sciences, literature, and art.
Address   : Basement, 30 Johnston Road, Wanchai, Hong Kong
Telephone : 00852-2866-1677   Fax: 00852-2529-3220
cosmosbk@netvigator.com

Hong Kong University Press
Publication Category: All categories.
Address   : 14/F, Hing Wai Centre, 7 Tin Wan Praya Road,
                Aberdeen, Hong Kong
Telephone: 00852-2550-2703   Fax: 00852-2875-0734
http://www.hkupress.org

Macau Foundation
Publication Category: All categories.
Address   : No. 6 Avenida da Republica,
                Fortaleza de Sao Tiago da Barra, Macau
Telephone : 00853-966777   Fax: 00853-968658
http://www.cyberctm.com

Macau Publishing House (Ou Mun Chot Pan Se)
Publication Category: All categories.
Address   : No. 1 Av. do Almirante Lacerda, Macau
Telephone : 00853-259915   Fax: 00853-259915

Ming Pao Publications Limited
Publication Category: Social Sciences.
Address   : 15/F, Blk A, Ming Pao Industrial Centre,
                18 Ka Yip Street, Chai Wan, Hong Kong
Telephone : 00852-2595-3111   Fax: 00852-2898-2646
http://www.mingpao.com/mpp/

Next Publications Ltd.
Publication Category: Entertainment and travel.
Address   : 8 Xixi Junying Street, General Ao Industry Country,
                Kowloon, Hong Kong
Telephone : 00852-27442733   Fax: 00852-2781-0413
http://www.books.atnext.com

Popular Holdings Limited
Publication Category: Education.
Address   : 14/F Tsuen Wan Industrial Centre,
                220-248 Texaco Road, Tsuen Wan, New Territories,
                Hong Kong
Telephone : 00852-2942-9333   Fax: 00852-2333-5579
http://www.popularworld.com

Press of Chinese University HK
Publication Category: All categories.
Address　　: 7/F, Hui Yeung Shing Building,
　　　　　　　Chinese University of Hong Kong, Shatin, NT,
　　　　　　　Hong Kong
Telephone : 00852-26096500　　　　　Fax: 00852-26037355
http://www.cuhk.edu.hk/cupress/w1.htm

Publish Macau Daily News
Publication Category: All categories.
Address　　: No. 37 Rua Pedro Nolasco da Silva, Macau
Telephone : 00853-371688　　　　　Fax: 00853-331998/322630
publishmdn@yahoo.com.hk

Qin Jia Yuan Publishing Company
Publication Category: Literature.
Address　　: Unit A, 18/F, Aik San Factory Building,
　　　　　　　14 Westlands Road, Quarry Bay, Hong Kong
Telephone : 00852-25169022　　　　　Fax: 00852-25169304
http://www.treasurecc.com.hk

SCMP Book Publishing Limited
Publication Category: Fiction, prose, cartoon, business, management, and
　　　　　　　　　　　living guides.
Address　　: 2/F, Dai Fat Street, Morning Post Center,
　　　　　　　Tai Po Industrial Estate, NT, Hong Kong
Telephone : 00852-2836-6088　　　　　Fax: 00852-2573-0861
http://www.hkchinesebooks.com

Sino United Publishing (Holdings) Limited
Main subsidiary: Joint Publishing (Hong Kong) Co., Ltd., Chung Hwa Book
Co. (Hong Kong) Ltd., The Commercial Press (Hong Kong) Ltd.
Address　　: 26/F, SUP Tower, 75-83 King's Road,
　　　　　　　North Point, Hong Kong
Telephone : 00852-2503-2111　　　　　Fax: 00852-2570-9377
http://www.sinounitedpublishing.com

Appendix 4

Copyright Agencies in China

Anhui Copyright Agency
Address : No.1 Yuejin Road, Hefei 230063
Telephone : 0086-0551-2846082

Bardon-Chinese Media Agency
Address : 4F 230 Hsinyi Road, Sec. 2, Taipei, Taiwan
Telephone : 00886-2-2392-9577   Fax: 00886-2-2392-9786

Beijing Copyright Co., Ltd.
Address : 401 Guanghua Changan Bldg. Jianguomennei Avenue,
Beijing 100005
Telephone : 0086-010-65171427

Beijing Renyu International Copyright Co., Ltd.
Address : No.14 Huaying Bldg. 502-504 Fuxing Road Haidian District,
Beijing 100036
Telephone : 0086-010-63967852/63955457

Big Apple Tuttle-Mori Agency, Inc.
Address : 10F, No. 801 Jung-Jeng Road, Jung-He City,
Taipei, Taiwan
Telephone : 00886-2-32344155   Fax: 00886-2-32344244

**China National Publications Import & Export (Group)
Corporation (CNPIEC) Copyright Department**
Address : 16 Gongti East Road, Beijing 100020
Telephone : 0086-10-65086949   Fax: 0086-010-65866992
http://www.cnpiec.com

China International Book Trading Corporation
Copyright Department
Address : 303 West Wing, No. 35 Chegongzhuang West Road, Beijing 100044
Telephone : 0086-010-68437147   Fax: 0086-010-68412023
http://www.cibtc.com.cn

China TV Program Agency
Address : No. 1 Lane 3 South Lishi Road, Beijing 110001
Telephone : 0086-010-63957153/63958525
Fax : 0086-010-63955916
http://www.citvc.com.cn

Copyright Agency of China (CAC)
Address : 4F, Wuhua Building, No. 4 Chegongzhuang Street, Beijing 100044
Telephone : 0086-010-68003908/68003887-5100-5107
Fax : 0086-010-68003908/68003945
http://www.ccopyright.com.cn

Copyright Trading Department of Jiuzhou Audio-Video Publications Corporation
Address : No. 19 Fengsheng Bystreet Xicheng District, Beijing
Telephone : 0086-010-85285169

Guangdong Copyright Agency
Address : No.11 Shuiyin Road, Guangzhou 510030
Telephone : 0086-020-87662333

Guangxi Wanda Copyright Agency
Address : No. 68 Minzu Road, Nanning 530022
Telephone : 0086-0771-5516127

Hebei Copyright Agency
Address : No. 44 Chengxiang Street, Shijiazhuang 050061
Telephone : 0086-0311-7756500

Heilongjiang Copyright Agency
Address : No. 68 Forest Street Daoli District, Harbin 150010
Telephone : 0086-0451-8370148

Henan Copyright Agency
Address   : No. 73 Nongye Road, Zhenzhou 450002
Telephone : 0086-0371-5730604

Hubei Copyright Agency
Address   : No. 2 Dongting Road, Wuhan 430077
Telephone : 0086-027-8815557

Hunan Copyright Agency
Address   : No. 66 Zhanlanguan Road, Changsha 410005
Telephone : 0086-0731-4302557

Jia-xi Books Co., Ltd.
Address   : 14F-11, No. 153, Ming-Sheng E. Road, Sec. 5
             Taipei, Taiwan
Telephone : 00886-2-27654488   Fax: 00886-2-27607227

Jilin Copyright Administration
Address   : No. 124 Renmin Street, Changchun 130021
Telephone : 0086-0431-5644760   Fax: 0086-010-5642914

Liaoning Copyright Agency
Address   : No. 108 First North Road, Shenyang 110001
Telephone : 0086-024-86267326

Minghe Copyright Agency
Address   : 25/F, K. Wah Center, 191 Java Road, Hong Kong
Telephone : 00852-25975513   Fax: 00852-29600625

Red Ears Media Ltd.
Address   : 11F, No. 12-4, S-Yuan Street, Taipei, Taiwan
Telephone : 00886-2-33651676

Shandong Copyright Agency
Address   : No. 1 Zonghe Building Front Street Shengfu Road,
             Jinan 250011
Telephone : 0086-0531-6061784

Shanghai Copyright Agency
Address   : 5 Shao Xing Road, Shanghai 200020
Telephone : 0086-021-64370148   Fax: 0086-021-64332452

Shanxi Copyright Agency
Address : No. 131 Beida Street, Xi'an 710003
Telephone : 0086-029-7251870

Sichuan Copyright Agency
Address : No. 21 Guihua Lane, Chengdu 610015
Telephone : 0086-028-6277641

Tianjin Copyright Agency
Address : No. 82 Jianshan Road Hexi District, Tianjin 300211
Telephone : 0086-022-23280480

Appendix 5

Book Import and Export Corporations in the Chinese Mainland

Anhui Dragon Trade Import and Export Corporation
Address   : No. 1 Yue Jing Road, Hefei, P. R. China, 230063
Telephone : 0086-0551-2842465   Fax: 0086-0551-2848487

Beijing Publications Import & Export Corporation
Address   : No. 235 Wangfujing Avenue Dongcheng District,
            Beijing 100006
Telephone : 0086-010-65126937

Cathay Bookshop
Address   : No. 115 Liulichang East Street Xuanwu District, Beijing
Telephone : 0086-010-63035759

China Economic Publications Import & Export Corporation
Address   : No. 3 North Baiwanzhuang Street Xicheng District, Beijing
Telephone : 0086-010-68312915/68344221

China Educational Publications Import & Export Corporation
Address   : No. 44 North Three Ring Road Haidian District, Beijing
Telephone : 0086-010-62154079   Fax: 0086-010-62012278

China Fine Arts Publishing House
Address   : No. 32 North Zongbu Bystreet, Beijing
Telephone : 0086-010-65122370

China International Enterprises Cooperation Co., Ltd.
Address   : B Youyan Builing, No. 2 Xinwai Avenue, Beijing
Telephone : 0086-010-62041498

China International Publications Trading Corporation
Address   : 35 Chegongzhuang West Road Haidian District, Beijing
Telephone : 0086-010-68414284   Fax: 0086-010-68412023

China National Publication International Trading Corporation (CNPITC)
Address   : No. 504 Anhuali Andingmenwai Chaoyang District, Beijing
Telephone : 0086-010-64210403

China National Publications Import & Export (Group) Corporation (CNPIEC)
Address   : 16 Gongti East Road, Beijing 100020
Telephone : 0086-010-65082324, 0086-010-65086873/74-8112
Fax   : 0086-010-65086860

China National Sci-tech Information Import & Export Corp.
Address   : 16 Donghuangchenggen North Street, Beijing 100717
Telephone : 0086-010-84039971

Chinese Corporation for Promotion of Humanities (CCPH)
Address   : No. 5, Jianguomennei Avenue, Beijing 100732
Telephone : 0086-010-65137737   Fax: 0086-010-65137737

Cultural Relics Publishing House
Address   : No. 29 Wusi Street Beijing 100009
Telephone : 0086-010-64048057   Fax: 0086-10-64010698
Fujian Publishing Industry Trading Corp.
Address   : 13/F, Fujian Publishing Center Building, 76 Dongshui Road, Fuzhou, Fujian
Telephone : 0086-0591-7538964   Fax: 0086-0591-7538936

Guangdong Publications Import & Export Corporation
Address   : 8F, No. 11, Shuiyin Road East Huan City Guangzhou
Telephone : 0086-020-87662308   Fax: 0086-020-87754385

Guanxi Publications Import & Export Corporation
Address   : 68 Minzu Avenue, Nanning, Guangxi 530022
Telephone : 0086-0771-5862972   Fax: 0086-0771-5862907

Hainan Publication International Trading Corporation
Address   : Shenghuan Building, No. 153 Wenming East Road, Haikou
Telephone : 0086-0898-6226097

Heilongjiang Press and Publication Import & Export Corporation
Address   : No. 85 Jingyang Street, Daowai District, Harbin
Telephone : 0086-0451-8373175

Henan Publication Foreign Trade Company
Address   : No. 66 Jingwu Road, Zhengzhou
Telephone : 0086-0371-5740799   Fax: 0086-0371-5730604

Hubei Publishing Import and Export Company
Address   : No. 11 Zhongnan Road, Wuhan
Telephone : 0086-027-87815565   Fax: 0086-027-87815557

Hunan Publishing Import and Export Company
Address   : 10F Book City No. 338 Furong Zhong Road, Changsha
Telephone : 0086-0731-4421365

International Book Trade Department of Zhonghua Book Company
Address   : No. 38 Taiping Qiao Xi Li Fengtai District, Beijing
Telephone : 0086-010-63458221

Jiangsu New Trade Import & Export Corporation
Address   : 3F, No. 165 Zhongyang Road, Nanjing, Jiangsu
Telephone : 0086-025-3214485   Fax: 0086-025-3226475

Jiangxi Publishing Import and Export Company
Address   : 18F Publishing Building, No. 310 Yangming Road, Nanchang
Telephone : 0086-0791-6894972   Fax: 0086-0791-6894971

Jilin Cultural Publication International Trading Corporation
Address   : No. 124 Renmin Avenue, Changchun
Telephone : 0086-0431-5640377

Liaoning MultiMedia Publishing Import & Export Co.
Address   : 25 Shiyiwei Road, Heping District,
                   Shenyang 110003, Liaoning
Telephone : 0086-024-23284016   Fax: 0086-024-23284016

**National Library of China International Communication
Department of National Library of China**
Address   : No. 33 South Avenue, Zhongguancun, Beijing, 100081
Telephone : 0086-010-22545023   Fax: 0086-010-68419271

Rong Bao Zhai Publishing House
Address   : No. 19 Liulichang West Street Xuanwu District, Beijing 100052
Telephone : 0086-010-63035279   Fax: 0086-010-63035279

Shandong Publication International Trading Corporation
Address   : No. 36 Longdong Road, Lixia District, Jinan
Telephone : 0086-0531-8936654

Shanghai Book Traders
Address   : No. 390 Fuzhou Road, Shanghai
Telephone : 0086-021-63223200

Shanghai Hongkong Joint Publishing Co., Ltd.
Address   : No. 624 Huai Hai Zhong Road, Shanghai
Telephone : 0086-021-53064393   Fax: 0086-021-53060848

Shanxi Publication International Trading Corporation
Address   : No. 167 Jiefang Road, Taiyuan

Shenzhen Yiwen Publication Import & Export Corporation
Address   : 504 5F Jinshan Building No. 5033 Yuannan East Road,
             Shenzhen
Telephone : 0086-0755-82073130

Sichuan Publication International Trading Corporation
Address   : No. 9 North Taisheng Road, Chengdu, 610017
Telephone : 0086-028-6912721

Tianjin Publication International Trading Corporation
Address   : No. 130 Chifeng Dao Heping District, Tianjin
Telephone : 0086-022-27129262

Xia Men International Book Center
Address   : No. 809, South Hubin Road, Xiamen
Telephone : 0086-0592-5089343   Fax: 0086-0592-5087235

Zhejiang Publication International Trading Corporation
Address   : No. 41 North Ring City, Hangzhou
Telephone : 0086-0571-5109382

Zhonghua-Shangwu Trading Company
Address   : No. 23 Zhan Qian Heng Road, Guangzhou
Telephone : 0086-020-8666 9415   Fax: 0086-020-8667 8882

Appendix 6

Major Publication Information Consulting Services in the Chinese Mainland

Beijing Book Communication Institute
Service scope: Book sales market planning and book promotion
Address   : No. 135 North Lishi Road, Fuwai, Beijing
Telephone : 0086-010-68332529   Fax: 0086-010-68341646

Beijing Institute of Graphic Communication
Service scope: Research and information services regarding periodicals
Address   : Huangcun, Daxing County, Beijing
Telephone : 0086-010-69233981

Beijing Open Book Market Consulting Center
Service scope: Book market data and information consultant services
Address   : 11F No. 17 North Fuchengmen Avenue,
                  Xicheng District, Beijing 100037
Telephone : 0086-010-88390223-27   Fax: 0086-010-88390228

Chinese Institute of Publishing Science
Service scope: Information concerning policies and theories for government and publishing houses
Address   : No. 38 Xili Taiping Qiao, Fengtai District, Beijing, 100073
Telephone : 0086-010-63289843/63454854   Fax: 0086-010-63454854

Global China (Beijing) Media Consulting Co., Ltd.
Service scope: Media market research and annual trade reports.
Address   : F211B Yuanyang Building,
                  No. 158 Fuxingmen Nei Avenue, Beijing 100031
Telephone : 0086-010-66493690   Fax: 0086-010-66493733

HC International Information (Research Center)

Service scope: Market survey, advertising, and customized information services.

Address   : 9F B Huaxing Building. No. 42 North Xizhimen Avenue, Haidian District, Beijing

Telephone : 0086-010-80715673   Fax: 0086-010-80715696

Press and Media Research Institute of Chinese Academy of Social Sciences

Service scope: Information regarding polices and theories for government and publishing houses

Address   : No. 9 Building, Renmin Daily Press, No. 2 West Jintai Road, Chaoyang District, Beijing 100026

Xinhua Media Workshop

Service scope: Trade analyses, topic reports, and statistics for media professionals and investors

Address   : 6002 Baisheng Building, No. 37 Jinrong Avenue, Xicheng District, Beijing

Telephone : 0086-010-66060096-3085

Appendix 7

National and Provincial Administrations of Press and Publication in the Chinese Mainland

General Administration of Press and Publication (GAPP)
Address : No. 85 Nandajie Dongsi, Beijing 100703
Telephones: Books and Publications Administration Department
0086-010-65122716

Newspaper and Periodicals Publications Administration Department
0086-010-65212787

Audio-visual, Electronic and Network Publications Administration Department
0086-010-6521779

Publication Issuing Administration Department
0086-010-65212739

Foreign Exchange and Cooperation Department
0086-010-65231139

Fax : 0086-010-65127875
http://www.gapp.gov.cn

National Copyright Administration of China (NCAC)
Address : No. 85 Nandajie Dongsi, Beijing 100703
Telephone : 0086-010-65276930
Website : www.ncac.gov.cn

Anhui Provincial Bureau of Press and Publication
Address : Press and Publication Building, No.1 Yuejinglu, Hefei, 230063
Telephone : 0086-0551-2826650

Beijing Municipal Bureau of Press and Publication
Address : Jia No. 24 Heping Stree, Chaoyang District, Beijing 100013
Telephone : 0086-010-84251200   Fax: 0086-010-84251189
http://www.bjppb.gov.cn

Bureau of Press and Publication of Inner Mongolian Autonomous Region
Address : No. 18 Laogangfang Street, New District, Huhhot,
Inner Mongolian AR 010010
Telephone : 0086-0471-4913873   Fax: 0086-0471-4913873
http://www.nmgnews.com.cn

Chongqing Municipal Bureau of Press and Publication
Address : Fu No. 1, Jiangxin Donglu, No. 3
(the 17th floor of Baiyexing Building),
Jiangbei District, Chongqing 400020
Telephone : 0086-023-67708966

Fujian Provincial Bureau of Press and Publication
Address : No. 76 Dongshuilu, Fuzhou 350001
Telephone : 0086-0598-7531397   Fax: 0086-0598-7554378
http://www.fjbook.com.cn

Gansu Provincial Bureau of Press and Publication
Address : No. 292 Qingyanglu, Lanzhou, Gansu 730030
Telephone : 0086-0931-8456905   Fax: 0086-0931-8454360

Guangdong Provincial Bureau of Press and Publication
Address : No. 11 Shuiyinglu, Huangshi Donglu, Guangzhou 510075
Telephone : 0086-020-37606288   Fax: 0086-020-37607205

Guizhou Provincial Bureau of Press and Publication
Address : No. 289 Zhonghua Beilu, Guiyang 550004
Telephone : 0086-0851-6828614

Hebei Provincial Bureau of Press and Publication
Address : No. 330 Youyi Beidajie, Shijiazhang, Hebei 050061
Telephone : 0086-0311-8641007
http://www.hebeichuban.com

Helongjiang Provincial Bureau of Press and Publication
Address : No. 68 Shenlinjie, Daoli District, Harbin 150010
Telephone : 0086-0451-4614553   Fax: 0086-0451-4617379
Website : www.northeast.com.cn

Henan Provincial Bureau of Press and Publication
Address   : No. 66 Jingwulu, Zhengzhou 450002
Telephone : 0086-0371-5721344
http://www.hnxwcb.com

Hubei Provincial Bureau of Press and Publication
Address   : No. 75 Huanglilu, Wuchang District, Wuhan 430077
Telephone : 0086-027-86783629   Fax: 0086-027-86792531
Website   : www.hbnp.com.cn/

Hunan Press Publishing Bureau
Address   : No. 11 Zhanlanguanlu Changsha 410005
Telephone : 0086-0731-4302513
Website   : www.hnppa.com

Jiangsu Provincial Bureau of Press and Publication
Address   : No.56 Gaoyunling, Nanjing 210009
Telephone : 0086-025-3351289

Jiangxi Provincial Bureau of Press and Publication
Address   : No. 310Yangminglu, Nanchang, Jiangxi 330008
Telephone : 0086-0791-6895173   Fax: 0086-0791-6895385
Website   : www.jxpp.com/

Jilin Provincial Bureau of Press and Publication
Address   : No. 124 Renmin Dajie, Chuangchun, Jilin 130021
Telephone : 0086-0431-5644804

Liaoning Provincial Bureau of Press and Publication
Address   : No. 108 Hepingbei Yimalu, Shenyang, Liaoning 110001
Telephone : 0086-024-23261655   Fax: 0086-024-23254108

Qinghai Provincial Bureau of Press and Publication
Address   : No. 10 Tongrenlu, Xining, Qinghai 981001
Telephone : 0086-0971-614188

Shaanxi Provincial Bureau of Press and Publication
Address   : No. 15, Jianshe Nanlu, Taiyuan, Shanxi 030012
Telephone : 0086-0351-4922120

Shandong Provincial Bureau of Press and Publication
Address　　: No.1 Fuqianjie, Jinan 250011
Telephone : 0086-0531-6061779

Shanghai Municipal Bureau of Press and Publication
Address　　: No. 5 Shaoxinglu, Shanghai 200020
Telephone : 0086-021-64370176　Fax: 0086-021-64332452

Shanxi Provincial Bureau of Press and Publication
Address　　: No. 131 Dabeijie, Xi'an 710003
Telephone : 0086-029-7205000　Fax: 0086-029-7205001

Sichuan Provincial Bureau of Press and Publication
Address　　: No. 36 Dashi Xilu, Chengdu 610071
Telephone : 0086-028-87035928　Fax: 0086-028-87025838

The Bureau of Press and Publication of Guangxi Zhuang Autonomous Region
Address　　: No. 53 Jinhulu, Nanning 530021
Telephone : 0086-0771-5516001
Website　　: www.gxi.gov.cn/gxzw/dzjg/xwcbj.htm

The Bureau of Press and Publication of Ningxia Hui Autonomous Region
Address　　: Jiefang Xijie, Yinchuan, Ningxia 750001
Telephone : 0086-0951-5045667

The Bureau of Press and Publication of Tibetan Autonomous Region
Address　　: No. 20 Linguo Beilu, Lhasa,
　　　　　　 Tibetan Autonomous Region 850001
Telephone : 0086-0891-6827279　Fax: 0086-0891-6829430

The Bureau of Press and Publication of Xinjiang Uyghur Autonomous Region
Address　　: No. 346, Jiegang Nanlu, Urumqi 830001
Telephone : 0086-0991-2825760　Fax: 0086-0991-2847028

Tianjin Municipal Bureau of Press and Publication
Address　　: No. 82 Jianshanlu, Hexi District, Tianjin 300211
Telephone : 0086-022-28306463　Fax: 0086-022-28308463
Website　　: www.tjppa.gov.cn

Yunnan Provincial Bureau of Press and Publication
Address   : No. 609 Huangcheng Xilu, Kungming 650034
Telephone : 0086-0871-4196648   Fax: 0086-0871-4199038

Zhejiang Provincial Bureau of Press and Publication
Address   : No. 225 Qinchunlu, Hangzhou,   310006
Telephone : 0086-0571-87163108

References

China Electronic & Net Publishing 2003-2004, 2004, China Electronic & Net Publishing, Beijing.

China Periodical Yearbook (1st ed), 2003, China Periodical Association, Beijing.

China Periodical Yearbook (2002/2003), 2003, China Periodical Association, Beijing.

General Administration of Press and Publication, *China Statistical Data Collection of Press and Publication,* Beijing.

Hong Kong Trade Development Council 2003, *Prospects of Hong Kong's Participation in the Publishing Industry in the Chinese Mainland.*

Jiang, Q. 2002, *New Media in War*, CITIC Publishing House, Beijing.

Macau Handbook 2003 (2nd ed), 2003, Macau Daily, Macau.

Ou, H. 2003, 'British Publishers and China' in *China Book Business Report*, 28 November.

Owen, L. 2004, *Buying & Selling Rights in Literary Works: A Practical Guide Publishers in The People's Republic of China*, Law Press China, Beijing.

Shen, P. Y. 1998, *World Publishing Industry: Hong Kong and Macau*, World Publishing Corporation, Beijing.

Song, Y. L. et al (Eds) 1999, *Modern Chinese Publishing History*, Elephant Publishing House, Henan.

Survey of the Book Publishing Industry in Taiwan 2002, 2003, China Credit Information Service Ltd., Taipei.

Taiwan Publication Yearbook 2002, 2003, Taiwan Publication Yearbook Editorial Committee, Taipei.

Wang, J. 2003, 'The Production Scale and Structure of the Audio and Video Industry in China,' in *China Press and Publishing Journal*, 20 February.

Yearbook of Global Chinese Language Media 2003, 2003, Global Chinese Language Media Publishing House, Beijing.

Yu, M. et al (Eds) 2003, *Survey of the Private Publishing in China*, China Book Publishing House, Beijing.

List of Figures

Chapter Eight

Chapter Nine

Chapter Ten

Chapter Eleven